PICTURE

OF

SLAVERY

IN THE

UNITED STATES OF AMERICA.

George Bourne

Is there not some chosen curse
Some hidden thunder in the stores of heaven,
Red with uncommon wrath, to blast the man
Who gains his fortune from the blood of souls?
COWPER.

Middletown, Con.

EDWIN HUNT

1834.

Republished 1972
Negro History Press, P. O. Box 5129
Detroit, Michigan 48236

Library of Congress Catalog Card Number: 74-92420
ISBN 0-403-00179-X

ENTERED according to the Act of Congress, in the year
1834, in the Clerk's office of the District Court of the Southern
District of New-York

Reproduced from Original in the
Duke University Library.

THIS

PICTURE

OF

AMERICAN SLAVERY

IS INSCRIBED

TO EVERY

MEMBER OF THE

Anti-Slavery Societies,

AND TO

ALL OTHER PHILANTHROPISTS

WHO ARE OPPOSED TO

MAN-STEALING,

BY THEIR

Faithful Coadjutor,

GEORGE BOURNE.

THE ENGRAVINGS.

5

EXORDIUM.

WHERE is the charter found to sanctify
Despotic, base, unqualified control,
O'er *strength and will*, by man enthroned o'er man?
In Revelation's code you find it not,
Nor in Creation's multifarious laws.
The will of Heaven, when unrevealed by Christ,
Or by the sacred organs of his word,
Is sought and found in the primeval light,
Which Nature sheds through her expanded spheres.
But when with Gospel-day this light combines,
The FOOL who doubts, who asks for clearer proof
Must hood-wink'd be indeed, and darkness love.
That such resistless evidence obtains,
To evince Demoniac Slavery's turpitude,
With all the powers of brightest Truth appears,
To the impartial mind that views each source,
Whence the full streams of testimony flow.
Each text of Sacred Writ enjoining love,
Affection, justice, mercy, meekness, peace,
And piety, establishes this truth,
That *Slavery contravenes the law of God!*
         Point to me the man
Who will not lift his voice against the trade
In human souls and blood, and I pronounce,
That he nor loves his country nor his God.
Is he a *Christian*, then, who holds in bonds
His brethren; cramps the vigour of their minds;
Usurps entire dominion o'er their wills,
Bars from their souls the light of moral day,
The image of the great Eternal Spirit
Obliterating thence? Before your God,
Whose holy eye pervades the secret depths
Of every heart, do you who hold inthrall'd
Your fellow-being's liberty believe
That you are guiltless of a DAMNING CRIME?
1*

Be undeceived—and cleanse from guilt and blood
Your crimson'd conscience and polluted hands.
   Ye Gospel-Promulgators! why so dumb
Upon this solemn theme, to which each ray
Of Revelation points? And has the world
Such fascination, such corrupting power,
And vile intimidation's force, as thus
To paralyze the energies divine
Of Satan's combatants, that they will yield
To his blood-feasting hosts without one blow?
   —But hark! whence rolls that thundering peal,
Which shakes astonish'd Mammon's glittering mounds,
And rouses all the fierce and clamorous ire
Of his tyrannic votaries? Lo! begirt
With the impervious mail of martyr'd zeal,
And golden truth, a little phalanx stands,
Upon the heaven defended batteries
Of Gospel-Law, and aims the artillery
Of holy eloquence, against the dark,
The massy battlements of tyranny.
Thence tis, that those convulsing thunders break,
Which fire the sons of Avarice with rage.
Persist, ye reverend Veterans! for the cause
In which your hallow'd banner is unfurl'd,
Embraces all that makes existence dear.
Undaunted band of Christian Patriots, hail!
May Victory's bays your honour'd temples crown,
And your reward be those delights supreme
Which store the magazines of heavenly bliss—
Whose melodies divine, no human ear
Has known; whose charms unmatch'd no earthly eye
Has seen; and whose exhaustless excellence,
The mind and heart of man have ne'er conceived.

NOTICE

THE first essay in this compend, is an amended reprint of a work formerly published under the title of "*the Book and Slavery irreconcilable.*" It has not only been altered, but part of it has been written, since the contest with the kidnappers has assumed its existing, definite and tangible form. The engravings illustrate slavery as it may *now* be seen in its various degrees of turpitude, among all classes of American man-stealers, whether they are avowed infidels, or nominal Christians. If, however, any southern preaching slave driver, or his northern clerical accessory, " who when he sees the thief consents with him" should exhibit sufficient effrontery to deny the graphical accuracy of the picture; they can have the names of *their* brethren, and all the other circumstances more minutely detailed. In that case, as some of the parties are yet living, they may hear in reply, the direct application of the truth, equally appropriate as that which Nathan enforced upon David, when the king having condemned the audacious criminal whose case was presented to his consideration, with prophetic authority the servant of Jehovah sternly said, " Thou art the man."

These pages emanate not from unchristian sensibilities. Gospel charity requires not that we should believe a *lie* to be *truth*, or *injustice* to be *probity*, or that *he who stealeth his brother, makes merchandise of him, sells him, or if he be found in his hand*, whom the word of God proclaims to be a thief, is an honest man and a *Christian.* Slavery is condemned; the uprightness of those pretences which oppressors offer, why they should be considered Christians, is the subject of investigation; and the melioration of the church and of our country is the motive which produced, and the object which is desired by this publication. The contest is for the sacred cause of truth: and however severe it may be when individualised in its application, the sentiments are in full unison with the holy scriptures, and with every honest man's unsophisticated convictions; therefore, to temporize would be criminal. "A rough truth is better than a smooth falsehood." That delinquent is peculiarly guilty, *who calls evil good, bitter sweet, darkness light;* or who endeavours so to commingle them, that no difference is discernible between the requisitions of religion and the solicitations of vice.

No desire is felt to propitiate professing Christians, while they steal "souls and hands." Their guilt against God and man who hold slaves in Columbia, is equal to his criminality, who sails to Congo and kidnaps a cargo of Africans; and it is altogether a burlesque upon every thing sacred for a *man-robber* to pretend to Christianity; and far more dishonourable and injurious to the church, to permit him to preach, and rule in the spiritual affairs of immortals.

Many persons to whom the severest censures apply as slave-holders, possess other estimable qualities; but can that man be *a Christian* who enslaves his coloured neighbour, who unmercifully whips her, although far advanced in pregnancy, who gives her no comfort of any species for her services, and then sells her with her offspring for an increased price, on account of the children whom he had kidnapped? Such men would immure their white *fellow-citizens* in bondage, and ingulph them in similar misery.

No argument is requisite to justify a work which honestly defends the rights of man, and opposes "a licensed system of wholesale robbery and murder," and maintains the eternally paramount claims of equity and mercy; which develops the absurdity of all pretensions to *pure and undefiled religion* in him whose whole life is a ceaseless rotation of stealing and cruelty; points the path of duty to the upright inquirer; and which expostulates with those whose diurnal practice is a continual violation of the spirit and letter of the moral law, a flagrant departure from the steps of the Redeemer and his primitive servants, and an open disgrace to republicanism and Christianity.

INTRODUCTORY.

THE corruption of the human heart and the deceitfulness which accompanies it are inconceivable. Among the various modes by which they are displayed, *the detention of men in bondage indefinite*, should receive unmitigated execration: and the principles upon which *slave-holding* is defended, with the characters of those who engage in its support, are most melancholy demonstrations of duplicity, and of that promptitude with which men can be deluded *to change the truth of God into a lie.* Is it not a fact too alarming to be recorded without the utmost dread, and will it not in futurity be deemed almost incredible, that a system which includes horrors tenfold more than Egyptian servitude is incorporated with most of the *religious!* and civil institutions, which are established in this land of boasted freedom? Will subsequent ages credit so monstrous a statement: that preachers of the gospel, eighteen hundred years after angels had sung, *on earth, peace, good will to men*, were characterized as proverbially devoted participants in all the enormities and iniquity of man-stealing? and nearly sixty years after the promulgation of the Columbian Declaration of Independence, practicably reprobated its *self-evident truths*, as unsound propositions, because their covetousness, and their barbarous robbery of the rights of man would have been restrained.

That any persons should have imbibed effrontery sufficient to commence and persist in an infernal trade with the bodies and souls of men, where the illumination of the Gospel determines our duties, responsibility, and destiny, is proof more than ample, of the innate tendency of the human race to every moral obliquity. What apology shall be patiently heard, at the present era, for upholding a traffic which necessarily includes every species of iniquity, and which is the offspring of an unhallowed avarice that conducts to hell?

The cunning and pertinacity with which men, who
have not the plea of ignorance to excuse their aberrations, maintain and justify their ungodly practices, is a
most lamentable and irrefragable testimony of the vitiated
propensities of the soul.   But although, it is scarcely possible to discover an individual who will calmly palliate
the evil nature of those more flagrant transgressions of
the moral law, those plebeian violations of decency which
are equally debasing and disgusting; yet, they who denounce these crimes and the perpetrators of them in terms
of unqualified reprobation, with equal zeal will excuse
more fashionable sins, especially if they are menaced with
the consequences of their guilt.

The conduct of religious professors and rulers loudly
demands the severest castigation.   It requires more than
Christian charity to allow many persons the characteristic
of *sincerity;* for the contradiction is so vast, that if the
highest interests of the human family were not connected,
their discrepancy would excite ridicule.   But as man's
eternal doom is indissolubly combined with the rectitude
of his present practice; the heart is filled with the keenest
compassion for that obduracy which rejects truth, for that
blindness which transmutes its individualising qualities,
and for that hypocrisy, which, to evade scriptural censures,
distorts *the book* into a sanction of the vices that it unequivocally condemns.

Human inconsistency and corruption cannot be developed in a stronger light, than by a dispassionate review of
the multifarious artifices which are adopted to veil the
horrors of slavery, and the evasions by which the charge
that they are the most enormous sinners against God and
man, is repelled.   Had this compound of all ungodliness
no connexion with the church of Christ, however delete-
rious are the effects of it in political society, however necessary is its immediate and total abolition, and however
pregnant with danger to the *Union* is the promulgation of
the system, to legislators the redress of the evil would
have been committed.   But *slavery* is the *golden calf*
which has been elevated among the tribes, and before it
the priests, and the elders, and the *nominal* sons of Israel,

eat, drink, rise up to play, worship, and sacrifice—there are *Balaams* among us, who prophesy in the name of the Lord, but covet the presents of Balak—we have an *Achan* in the camp, whose unsanctified love of money troubles us—this is *Delilah*, whose fascinations have bewitched Christians, until they are involved in impurity and murder—this is *the idol which the children of Israel have set up in their hearts: the stumbling-block of iniquity which the house of Judah have placed before their faces*—this covetousness recoins the thirty pieces of silver for which Judas betrayed his Lord—and this is that *love of the present world*, for which Demas forsook the Apostles' doctrine and fellowship.

The Mosaic law declares every slaveholder a THIEF; Paul the Apostle classes them among the vilest criminals; the Presbyterian confession of faith asserts, that he is the most guilty of all thieves; the Methodist book of discipline avows, that no man can have a sincere desire to *"flee from the wrath to come,"* unless he refuses to enslave, buy, and sell human flesh; "the supreme law of the land" formally pronounces that his practice is totally irreconcilable with the principles of justice and humanity;" and the bills of rights promulge, that the immunities of man, which are indispensable to the possession of life, the acquisition of property, and the enjoyment of happiness, are natural, inherent, and inalienable. Therefore, every man who holds slaves, and who pretends to be a Christian or a Republican, is either an incurable idiot, who cannot distinguish good from evil, or an obdurate sinner, who resolutely defies every social, moral, and divine requisition.

The denunciations of the sacred volume must not be mitigated. The predominance of vicious tempers, and the consequent exhibition of unholy conduct, are totally incompatible with the instructions and the example of Jesus of Nazareth and his Apostles. A direct and incessant violation of the eighth commandment, cannot be compounded with the rectitude which Christianity enjoins. The worst of all thieves, is not the most devout believer. That internal chemistry, which extracts the essential qualities of genuine religion, and then combines the *caput mortuum*

with constant crime, that it may be palatable to an ignorant
or careless conscience, must be opposed.   The complicated
enormity of kidnapping, and the hypocrisy which he displays, who while he is a perpetual thief, wishes to be
honoured as a Christian ; who, while he preaches and rules
in the church, steals his neighbour, and dooms his brother
to wretched and endless servitude, must be, in plain scriptural language, reprobated.

The most obdurate adherents of slavery, are preachers
of the gospel, and officers and members of the church.
A son of Belial is easy convinced.   He offers no palliative.
He denounces, although he perpetuates the evil ; but con-
ceiving himself absolved from all moral obligation, he
is desirous to participate in the gain, as long as it can be
grasped.   Christians defend *man-stealing*.   They marshal
the examples of men, who lived not under the moral code
dispensed by Moses.   They misinterpret varied regulations
of his law, and thereby transform truth into error, and the
dictates of justice into the vilest improbity.   They claim
the silence of our Lord and his apostles and evangelists, as
a proof that slave holders then were *innocent ;* and they
affirm, that no New Testament command or denunciation
is directed against involuntary servitude.   These *wrest the
scriptures unto their own destruction ; being led away with the
error of the wicked.*   To tolerate slavery, or to join in its
practice is an insufferable crime, which tarnishes every
other good quality.   For *whosoever shall keep the law,
and yet offend in one point, he is guilty of all.*   It is duplicate
malignity.   The word of God, is transmuted into indulgence for sin.   Infidels and worldlings are encouraged to
believe that Christianity is a mere deception, when its
expositors and disciples contend for "injustice and inhumanity" by the gospel ; what blasphemy ! and slavery,
with its abettors, is "a mill-stone hanged about the neck"
of the church, from which she must be loosened, or she
will "be drowned in the depth of the sea."

The flagitious acts, concerning slaves, which Christians
daily and publicly perpetrate without remorse, are a just
subject of animadversion.   Repentance, reformation, and
restitution, are much more suitable for a *slave-driver*, than

the palliation of his guilt, or excuses for his enormous crime; and it is the height of delusion, to suppose him an " acceptable" believer, who detains his fellow-man in the most dreadful vassalage. But the most guilty and daring transgressor is a gospel minister, who steals, buys, sells, and keeps his brethren in slavery, or supports by his taciturnity, or his smooth prophesying, or his direct defence, the Christian professor who unites in the kidnapping trade. Truth forces the declaration, that every church officer or member, who is a slave-holder, records himself, by his own creed, a hypocrite.

What shall an expositor of the truth do ? dare he connive at evils which obstruct the prosperity of the church ? Though convinced of the absolute impossibility to reconcile the bondage and traffic of men with evangelical philanthrophy ; shall *he hold his peace*, and refuse to combat the injustice, and to expunge the inconsistency of professing Christians, who are participants in " a system of incurable injustice, the complication of every species of iniquity, the greatest practical evil that has ever afflicted the human race, and the severest and most extensive calamity recorded in the history of the world."

But how shall an earnest contender for *the Faith, which was once delivered to the saints*, act ? dare he cry PEACE, when God declares there is no peace ? dare he deliver smooth things, when God urges penitence and reform ? can he scrutinize this mass of corruption, and not warn his fellow Christians to touch not, taste not, handle not ? dare he, from dread of offending, disobey the books of which he professed his belief, and to which he promised a conscientious practical conformity ? And will he burden his shoulders with the curse of handling the word of God deceitfully ? will he load his conscience with the conviction, that, while men are deceiving themselves, he uses no means to remove their destructive delusions ? will he conceal the truth, which unfolds the endless evasions and artifices of sin and Satan, to insnare the soul in perdition everlasting ? and dare he deny the evident, undeniably correct interpretation of the word of God, to teach the per-

2

verse disputings of men of corrupt minds, and destitute of
the truth, that gain is godliness.

The Bible, the unbiassed convictions of every man's
conscience, and the natural sensibilities of the heart, establish this doctrine : but officers and members of the church
endeavour to intimidate and silence the promulgers of
truth : while the shameless attempts which have latterly
been made, to sustain a system of merciless horrors upon
evangelical principles, and by men whose authority will
be adduced, and whose example will be imitated by the
thoughtless and the covetous, imperiously require the exertions of those who would preserve the character of sincere Christians.

That so monstrous an anomaly as American man-stealing should ever have existed, almost surpasses credibility :
but that Messiah's disciples should be guilty of this highest
transgression against human nature, and defend its abominations, never could have been believed, were not the awful fact indisputably verified.

The uniform conduct of slave-holders who profess Christianity, is denied as " misrepresentation." Notorious
facts are contradicted, upon the plea of " exaggeration."
An aversion to detaining men in the basest, irretrievable
degradation, is reprobated as " the offspring of a turbulent
and factious spirit." Attempts to extirpate black slavery
are denounced as the " fanaticism of reckless maniacs,"
and the " firebrands of enthusiastical incendiaries." A
solicitude to terminate the agonies of violated females, and
the tortures of two millions of American citizens is lampooned as " the poetry of philanthropy." And even Christian efforts to meliorate the mental, moral, and religious
condition of our coloured people, are not only reviled, but
authoritatively attempted to be nullified by legislators and
judges, who, like their prototype characterized by Christ
the Lord of all, neither fear God nor regard man. All this
shameless complication of iniquity is boastfully perpetrated by men who have the impudence to assume the stations of gospel ministers, and officers in the Christian
church.

Yes ! It is the *misrepresentation* with which they charged

Elijah, when, on Mount Carmel, he denounced the priests of Baal as the soul-destroyers of the Israelites. It is the *exaggeration* with which the Jews calumniated Jeremiah, when he delivered the tremendous information, that, for enslaving their brethren, the Lord *proclaimed liberty to the sword, the pestilence, and the famine.* It is the *turbulence* which characterized Peter, when he avowed before the Sanhedrin, that *he would obey God rather than man.* It is the *factious spirit* which was imputed to Stephen, when he declared the truth to the Jewish council; *Ye stiff-necked and uncircumcised in heart and ears, who do always resist the* Holy Ghost, *as your Fathers did, so do ye.* It is the *world-upside-down-turning* disposition, which emboldened Paul to preach *repentance* and the *resurrection of the dead* to the Areopagites. It is the *turbulence* for which they reviled Martin Luther, when he dared to defend the *truth,* though Rome and her imps had determined to destroy him. It is the *factious spirit,* by the influence of which, John Knox silenced Mary of Scotland, when he assured her, that her judgment, being unenlightened, conducted her into the paths of error and irreligion. And it is that *misrepresenting, exaggerating, turbulent and factious spirit,* which peopled the Columbian wilds, rather than surrender to any tyranny, the rights of man, and the illumination of the Book.

O for more "*misrepresenters,*" who have the boldness to display the abominations of *American citizen tanners!* O for more "*exaggerators*" who will heap confusion upon *pretended* Christians, by lucidly developing their constant violations of the eighth commandment! O for more *turbulent* and *factious souls,* who will not connive at officers and members of the church, *stealing men,* with impunity, and without censure!

O God, grant us all the exuberance of that spirit which impelled the reformers, the martyrs, the prophets, and the apostles of Jesus Christ! Amen.

Therefore, being decided against any compromise between justice and injustice, gospel sincerity and human dissimulation, and to combat this Goliah of iniquity, *the sling and the stone* are taken. " *Who is this uncircumcised Philistine, that he should defy the armies of the living God?*"

SLAVERY OPPOSED TO THE LAW OF GOD
AND MAN.

So abhorrent from our natural sensations is the system of stealing, buying, selling, and enslaving immortal creatures, that it is difficult accurately to delineate this wretched degradation of man. *A slave is a rational, responsible being, with an abject mind and broken heart; without any will: all whose rights are robbed; whose liberty is despoiled, and whose life is prolonged at the caprice of a* tyrant. No difference is perceptible between the traffic in human flesh on the coast of Africa or in the interior of America. Every slave in these states is as notoriously *kidnapped*, as if they had been purloined from Guinea: and he who claims a coloured child as his property, and nurtures and detains it in slavery, is equally a *man-thief* with the *negro-stealer* on the Gold Coast.

Those persons who denounce the African *flesh-merchant*, and who *seem* to admit, that the imported souls could not have been justifiably captivated, deny that they unrighteously grasp their brethren, and denominate themselves " *innocent slave holders:*" but this is *self-confutation.* Can that be *innocence* in the temperate zone, which is the *acme of all guilt* near the equator? can that be *honesty* in one meridian of longitude, which at one hundred degrees east, is the climax of injustice? and would not he who appropriates to himself all the children born around him, immediately as they enter the world, upon the same principles, make a descent upon Congo, and kidnap a ship load? No real distinction exists between him, who steals the woman from her husband, the child from its parent, or the whole family, on the eastern or the western shores of the Atlantic, whether for exportation or domestic vassalage.

These identical individuals would rage, if it were attempted thus to exculpate any other felon. Innocent horse-thief is more consistent language than innocent slave-holder; for the crime of the latter exceeds that of the former, as much as the limited and temporary powers of the animal are surpassed by the extensive capacities and never-ending existence of man. " We know men to whom the truth is become unintelligible, in consequence of the disguise in which they have taken the pains to clothe it; and who have accustomed themselves to palliate vice, till they are incapable of perceiving its turpitude."

He that stealeth a man, and selleth him, or if he be found in his hand, he shall surely be put to death. Exodus, xxi. 16. By this law, every man-stealer, and every receiver of the stolen person, lost his life : whether the latter stole the man himself, or gave money to a slave-captain or negro-dealer to steal for him. All kidnapping and slave dealing are prohibited, whether practised by individuals or the state.—*Adam Clarke.*

If a man be found stealing any of his brethren of the children of Israel, and maketh merchandise of him, or selleth him, then that thief shall die. Deuteronomy xxiv. 7.

Christianity has annihilated that distinction of nations which was once established ; every man is now our brother, whatever be his nation, complexion, or creed. How then can the merchandise of men and women be carried on, without transgressing this commandment, or abetting those who do ? If a man steal a horse or sheep, he is condemned ; but if he steal, or purchase of those who steal, hundreds of men and women, he not only escapes with impunity, but grows great by this unnatural commerce ! According to the law of God, whoever stole cattle restored four or five fold ; whoever stole one human being though an idiot or an infant, must die. He who stole any one of the human species, in order to make a slave of him, or to sell him for a slave, whether the thief had actually sold him, or whether he continued in his possession, was punished with death: but if we are true Christians, we shall have no occasion for penal statutes to restrain us from stealing or enslaving our brethren of the human species, and trading the bodies of men.—*Scott.*

Thou shalt not deliver unto his master, the servant who is escaped from his master unto thee : He shall dwell with thee, even among you, in that place which he shall choose, in one of thy gates where it liketh him best; thou shalt not oppress him.—David said to the Egyptian, canst thou

2*

bring me down to this company ? and he said, swear unto
me by God, that thou wilt neither kill me, nor deliver me
into the hands of my master, and I will bring thee down
to this company.—Take counsel, execute judgment; make
thy shadow as the night in the midst of the noon-day :
hide the outcasts, bewray not him who wandereth.—Thou
shouldst not have stood in the cross-way, to cut off those
who did escape; neither shouldst thou have delivered
up those who did remain in the day of distress. As thou
hast done, it shall be done unto thee : thy reward shall return upon thine own head.

These scriptures proclaim that slave-holding is an abomination in the sight of God: for it justifies the slave in
absconding from his tyrant, and enjoins upon every man
to facilitate his escape, and to secure his freedom. Does
this injunction comport with a Christian's advertising as a
fugitive criminal, a man who has merely fled from his cruel
captivity, or with his aiding to trace and seize him who
had thus burst from " durance vile ?" It is a reiteration of
the theft : yet he professes to be influenced by the Gospel !

But the man-stealer states, that this is injustice, as it
destroys his property ; and that it is base to aid a slave to
fly from his chains, or not to assist in recapturing him.
Were the master placed in similar misery with the victim
of his cruel avarice, and he should escape, rather than be
seized, he would slay the assailant. His heroism would
be honoured, and his contest for freedom being righteous,
he would be exonerated : but if a coloured person wounds
a kidnapper, he is ignominiously executed, and almost
without form : for the trial of negroes is the highest burlesque upon the administration of justice, that despotism
ever devised.

> " For 'tis establish'd by your partial laws,
> No slave bears witness in a white man's cause.
> Beings you deem them of inferior kind,
> Denied a human or a thinking mind.
> Happy for your slaves, were this doctrine true,
> Were feelings lost to them, or given to you !"

A man cannot assist in seizing a slave, and robbing him
again of his liberty or life, when he is inculpable before

society, without violating the law of love, and the command of God.

"Slavery! virtue dreads it as her grave
Patience itself is meanness in a slave.
Yet if the will and sov'reignty of God,
Bid suffer it awhile, and kiss the rod,
Wait for the dawning of a brighter day,
And snap the chain the moment when you may!"

The prophecies are filled with divine denunciations against Judah and Israel, for their oppression, fraud, rapine, cruelty, and the varied enormities which originated in their covetousness; and Tyre was destroyed for having traded the persons of men.

The gospel censures these sinners with celestial authority. Paul characterises the Romans who were slave-holders, as inventors of evil things without natural affection, implacable, and unmerciful.

Among the most corrupt transgressors, he classes *man-stealers*. This crime among the Jews exposed the perpetrators of it to capital punishment; and the apostle classes them with sinners of the first rank. The word he uses, in its original import, comprehends all who are concerned in bringing any of the human race into slavery, or in detaining them in it. Stealers of men are all those who bring off slaves or freemen, and keep, sell, or buy them. To steal a freeman is the highest kind of theft. In other instances we only steal human property, but when we steal or retain men in slavery, we seize those who in common with ourselves, are constituted by the original grant, lords of the earth.—*Presbyterian Confession of Faith*.

Man-stealers!—The worst of all thieves; in comparison of whom, highway robbers and house-breakers are innocent! What then are traders in negroes, and procurers of servants for America.—*Wesley*.

Men-stealers are inserted among these daring criminals, against whom the law of God directed its awful curses. These kidnapped men to sell them for slaves; and this practice seems inseparable from the other iniquities and oppressions of slavery; nor can a *slave-dealer* keep free from this criminality, if 'the receiver be as bad as the thief.'—*Scott.*

They who make war, for the inhuman purpose of selling the vanquished as slaves, are really men-stealers. And they who encourage that *unchristian* traffic by purchasing the slaves which they know to be thus unjustly acquired are partakers in their crime.—*Macknight.*

The Lord God who judgeth her, will effuse his wrath upon Babylon, because she makes merchandise of slaves, the bodies and souls of men.

To number the persons of men with beasts, sheep, and horses, as the stock of a farm, or with bales of goods, as the cargo of a ship, is a most detestable and antichristian practice.—*Scott.*

Shall Protestants renounce that merchandise of Rome, which consists of odours, and ointments, and chariots, and purple, and silk, and scarlet, and continue that more scandalous traffic in slaves and souls of men?—*Robinson.*

In ages to come, it will scarcely meet with credit, that we who boast ourselves of being a free nation, should have been capable of buying and selling souls. If there were no other cause, this is enough to bring down the severest of the divine judgments! No political motives whatever can justify this diabolical traffic. Such has been the general practice of mankind in every age preceding the introduction of the gospel: and it is the introduction and profession of that gospel, which render the dealing in slaves so enormously wicked! A Christian buying and selling slaves! A man, who professes that the leading law of his life, is to do as he would be done by, spending his time and amassing a fortune in buying and selling his fellow-men!—*Simpson.*

The Methodist discipline asserts, that there is "one only condition previously required of those who wish admission into these societies, a desire to flee from the wrath to come, and to be saved from their sins." But how shall they evidence that their desire is real and genuine? "By avoiding evil of every kind, especially that which is most generally practised: the buying or selling of men, women, or children, with an intention to enslave them."

The ancient Jews understood the words in the decalogue, Thou shalt not steal, of man-stealing; and thought
that the other sorts of theft were implied in the last precept, Thou shalt not covet.   Under the Mosaic law, man-
stealing was the only capital robbery; for the theft of property was expiated by ample restitution.   But to enslave
a Jew, was deemed an equal crime with murder; and as
it virtually involves the same consequences, it insured the
same punishment: and it was no subject of inquiry,
whether the slave was actually kidnapped by the claimant,
or purchased from another; but if it could be manifested,
that such a person was detained by him contrary to the
law of God, no alternative existed, death was his immediate portion.

The principles of moral right and wrong are invariable.
They are not circumscribed by geographical boundaries,
or particular periods of time; but apply to every individual,
of all communities, and in every age.   Practices condemned among the Israelites, upon the basis of eternal rectitude, never can be justified : and Jewish aberrations from
the requisitions of their own heaven-promulged law, instead of furnishing us an example to copy, provide a bea-
con for alarm and instruction.

The public formularies of the United States, exhibit the
vast contradiction between our doctrine and practice, with
oracular authority.

" We hold these truths to be self evident, that all men
are created equal; that they are endowed by the Creator,
with certain unalienable rights; that among these are life,
liberty, and the pursuit of happiness."—*Declaration of Independence.*

" All men are born equally free and independent; all
men have certain natural, essential, and inherent rights;
among which are, the enjoying and defending life and
liberty, acquiring, possessing, and protecting property;
and, in a word, of seeking and obtaining happiness.
Among the natural rights, some are in their very nature
unalienable, because no equivalent can be given or received for them.   Of this kind, are the rights of conscience."—*New-Hampshire.*

"All men are born free and equal, and have certain natural, essential and unalienable rights: among which may be reckoned the right of enjoying and defending their lives and liberties; and that of acquiring, possessing, and protecting property; in fine, that of seeking and obtaining their safety and happiness."—*Massachusetts.*

"All men are born equally free and independent, and have certain inherent and indefeasible rights, among which are those of enjoying and defending life and liberty, of acquiring, possessing, and protecting property and reputation, and of pursuing their own happiness."—*Pennsylvania.*

"Through divine goodness, all men have by nature, the rights of worshipping and serving their Creator, according to the dictates of their consciences, of enjoying and defending life and liberty, and acquiring and protecting reputation and property, and, in general, of obtaining objects suitable to their condition, without injury by one to another; and these rights are essential to their welfare."—*Delaware.*

"All men are by nature equally free and independent, and have certain inherent rights; of which, when they enter into a state of society, they cannot, by any compact, deprive or divest their posterity; namely, the enjoyment of life and liberty, with the means of acquiring and possessing property, and pursuing and obtaining happiness and safety."—*Virginia.*

"All men are born equally free and independent, and have certain natural, inherent, and unalienable rights, among which are the enjoying and defending life and liberty, acquiring, possessing, and protecting property, and pursuing and obtaining happiness and safety."—*Vermont.*

"There shall be neither slavery nor involuntary servitude in the said territory, otherwise than in punishment of crimes, whereof the party shall have been duly convicted."—*North-Western Territory.*

"All men are born equally free and independent, and have certain natural, unalienable rights, among which are the enjoying and defending life and liberty, acquiring, possessing, and protecting property, and pursuing and obtaining happiness and safety. There shall be neither slavery, nor involuntary servitude in this state."—*Ohio.*

How callous must that heart be to all shame, which, notwithstanding these self-evident truths, can gravely maintain the necessity of protracting slavery, and uphold its horrors by his actual participation : for every liberal mind is thoroughly convinced of the unrighteousness and inexpediency of this, the most cruel, detestable, and consummately wicked measure, that has been ever devised by mercantile avarice, or sanctioned by a sordid, narrow and misguided policy.

" What hypocrisy and villany, to profess that we are votaries of liberty, while we encourage or countenance the most ignoble slavery. We cannot form to ourselves an idea of an object more ridiculous, than an American patriot signing declarations of independence with one hand, and with the other brandishing his whip over his affrighted slave."

How awfully deluded must he be, who, wilfully closing his eyes to the splendour of divine illumination, and shielding his soul from all the arrows of conviction, will consider himself Messiah's disciple, though by the bible, his conscience, his own theological and republican creed, and the supreme law of the land, he stands condemned for injustice and inhumanity before the church and the world—*A cruel man-stealing Christian!*

The wholesale man-stealer, like Cain, bears the mark in his forehead ; he is a *fugitive and a vagabond upon the earth :* and the " Christian broker in the trade of blood," whose wealth is increased by alienating all social affections, by severing all relative ties, by dissolving all domestic relations, and by transplanting from one state to another these wretched creatures, because they have a different tinge from himself, is the primeval murderer's own offspring.

" These same slaveholders would wade through seas of the blood of white men, as well as black men, to gratify their despotic propensities, if they were not restrained : it is the *fear*, not the *love* of either God or man, that restrains them."

These are the unadulterated truths of the gospel. Can a follower of the meek and lowly Jesus be connected with a system which essentially generates such malevolent principles, and such barbarous conduct? Yet church-officers display a predominant insensibility to this complicated turpitude. The quintessence of all wicked absurdity is to hear an oppressor, in the name of him " who touched Isaiah's hallowed lips with fire," expatiate upon the BOOK delivered to Jesus in Nazareth.

As equity and injustice, philanthrophy and barbarism, vice and religion, cannot coalesce ; every officer and member of the church who steals slaves, although he professes to believe and inculcate the evangelical charity which he does not exemplify, is equally culpable with the Ishmaelite, who kidnapped their African ancestors.

SLAVERY IMPIOUS, UNJUST, AND CRUEL.

THE Slavery of our species combines every base characteristic. When that august period shall have arrived, that the total extinction of this monster shall be celebrated with the triumphs of Christianity—the inscription which will narrate its existence will simply record—here lies the enemy of man, whose principles were irreligion, whose dispositions were cruelty, whose language was falsehood, whose conduct was injustice, and whose pretensions were hypocrisy. An impious, barbarous, and deceitful thief! Yet this idol has usurped a prominent station in the temple of God, and silences the voice of those who minister and serve in the sanctuary—until the *blind are leading the blind into the ditch of perdition.*

Slavery is *impious*, for it directly subverts the divine authority. The supremacy of the great Jehovah is denied, and his government of the human family entirely wrested from him by this vile usurpation. Every principle which dignifies, every affection which refines, and every action which adorns, are inseparable from a permanently operative and deeply impressed conviction of our responsibility before God, for the correct improvement of the privileges with which he has enriched us: but all these are extinguished as soon as man is degraded to a brute.   No alternative exists; inferiors in wealth and civil stations must be considered as moral agents, or must be classed with the flocks and herds of the field.   Hence, slavery involves the most awful consequences, and wretchedness irremediable.   It is a wilful disobedience to the commandments of God ; and not only exposes the criminal to the wrath of the judge, but is a most artful and diabolical invention to exclude even the sufferer by this ungodly machination from the celestial regions of bliss.

He who has scrutinized the uniform tendency of involuntary servitude; who examines the unvarying practice of those who ingulph the bodies and souls of men in the net of their selfishness and insensibility ; and who, with the eye of Christian philanthropy, has investigated the moral character of the servants, knows, that a slaveholder is an unfeeling despot, who would overthrow God's jurisdiction.

Very few men-stealers comparatively, are even nominal Christian believers.   How can a person pretend to be a disciple of the crucified Jesus, who hinders his worship and contravenes his commands; in whom all evangelical charity is extinct; and who will neither enter the kingdom of heaven, nor permit those to approach who would crave admission at the gate ?   The spirit of Christianity and the practice of men-thieves are at total oppugnation ; and consequently they exert their energies to counteract the progress of " pure and undefiled religion."   By their example and influence, they endeavour to diminish all regard for sacred institutions, to impede the acquisition of all necessary knowledge, and to obstruct their slaves from listening to the admonitions of divine truth.

Christianity promulges liberty to the captive ; it depicts all the misery which must necessarily follow an equitable remuneration, if God requites the slave-holder, as he has abused his fellow-man ; it inculcates the doctrines of justice, which the man-stealer ever violates ; of mercy, which never regulate his intercourse with others ; of love, which are swallowed up by an avaricious, dissipated extinction of feeling ; and of religious fear, which has been exterminated from his heart, by his deliberate rejection of the light

2

to life, and by his obduracy in opposing " the truth as it is in Jesus," because it condemns his theft and barbarity.

Hence the Sabbath is disregarded, the means of grace are neglected, and the gospel ceases at all to interest, until the candlestick is removed from its place, and both the tyrant and the slave, realizing a marble-hearted indifference, mingle the same profane execrations, exhibit an identical dishonour of God, and manifest an equal insensibility to worlds everlasting. But if the slave, convinced of the value of his soul, and solicitous to be rescued from the wrath to come, is desirous to receive gospel instruction, it is altogether denied him, or his attendance at the house of prayer is so restricted, that it includes all the qualities of a total prohibition.

" All those masters who neglect the religious and moral instruction of their slaves, add a heavy load of guilt to that already incurred, by their share in this unjust and inhuman traffic."

The laws of the slaveholding states denominate a variety of meetings by the coloured people unlawful ; but the clause was so indeterminate, that it empowered the magistrate to decide what assemblies subjected the attendant to fine and punishment. By an act of the year 1804, all night meetings, upon whatever pretext, insured the parties, if convicted, a *whipping :* but this act being a direct violation of religious freedom, it was subsequently amended and explained : and a higher stigma upon legislation, if the clause is viewed in connexion with the relation which man sustains to the Supreme Creator, can scarcely be traced upon record ; except that every law connected with slavery is equally insulting, wicked, and absurd. " Nothing in the said act shall prevent the masters or owners of slaves from carrying or permitting his, her, or their slave or slaves to go with him, her, or them, or with any part of his, her, or their white family, to any place whatever, for the purpose of religious worship; provided, that such worship be conducted by a regularly ordained or licensed white minister."— *Virginia.*

The total obstruction is not one jot more hostile to the progress of the gospel, more subversive of every natural right, or more daring in its defiance of Jehovah's supremacy. How men, who swear by the Book to perform their official duties, could enact such regulations for the government of immortal souls, cannot be explained upon any principle, which does not overwhelm them with the utmost disgrace.

Some years ago, a comical old formalist, all whose religion consisted in a long demure countenance for two hours upon the Lord's day, at the meeting house, and a sleepy parrot-like form of words for half an hour, which he called a prayer, used severely to whip those of his slaves, either before or after his hypocritical mummery, who were too shrewd to be imposed upon by this impiety, and who therefore endeavoured to evade being present at his shocking ceremonial, by which he so glaringly insulted the God of Love and the Saviour of Mercy.

Men-stealers prevent their slaves "from being instructed in a religion which proclaims the equality of all men; all proceeding from a common stock, all participating the benefits of creation, and among whom, with the Father of men, there is no acceptation of persons. Slavery therefore is an outrage upon Christianity." For the above old man-thief, who used to go through his rounds with his bible in one hand and his cowskin or whip in the other, was a subject of astonishment to his (*Christian!*) accomplices, because he even wished the slaves to be near him when he was praying. They knew well that no slave could be found, who was so great a dolt as not to discern the impassable gulf between evangelical devotion and the highest kind of theft.

Even those who have a small portion of conscience remaining, display their depravity; for their pride revolts if the descendants of Africa are seen within the walls of the temple; generally no convenient stations are provided for slaves, that they may hear the truth; and where a man contrives to preserve the forms of domestic worship with the *stealing* and *trafficking in human flesh;* the victims of his merciless robbery are excluded—and is it a subject of surprise? How a man *can pray* in his habitation, with a

horde of slaves around him, is inexplicable upon any principle of feeling, affection, or Christianity !   The unconcern
which slaveholding produces in the tyrants, with respect
to the eternal peace of their own children, and the salvation of the wretched objects of their compound avarice and
cruelty, evince that slavery is impious, since it tends to exterminate the authority of Jehovah.

This subversion of the divine government necessarily
follows from the adoption of the LIE, that one man can justifiably be so reduced to the command of another, as to
have no will but that of his director.

Man owes to his Creator and Judge duties, from the
performance of which no terrestrial power can possibly
absolve him.   Among these are the cultivation of devotional tempers and the fulfilment of Christ's requisitions.
The existing relation between the slave-driver and his
vassal, proclaims the impracticability of a compliance with
his obligations, and consequently, that he who steals a
man or keeps him in his hand, is a bold usurper of celestial
jurisdiction, and a merciless violator of human right, freedom, and responsibility.   Does not the absolute uncontrolled dominion which the master possesses over his slave,
render even the existence of spiritual mindedness almost
impossible ; by opposing to a regular use of the means necessary to strengthen a pious disposition, vast obstructions
which counterbalance if not destroy the force of the Saviour's
claim, and make his commands nugatory ?   When the injunction of God and the order of the slave tyrant are directly
at variance, when the law of heaven and the mandate of
the citizen-thief are both compulsory at the same period,
to the earthly authority the slave must primarily submit ;
and when the everlasting welfare of the servant's soul,
and to facilitate the sensual gratifications of his barbarous
despot, are placed in competition, both parties may be
condemned by the Most High, but the doubly cruel volup-
tuary must not be disappointed.

" Negroes are in all respects, except in regard to life
and death, *cattle*.   They are bought and sold, fed, or kept
hungry, clothed, or reduced to nakedness, beaten, turned

out to the fury of the elements, and torn from their dearest connexions, with as little remorse as if they were beasts of the field.

Their situation is rendered far more miserable than 'if they were brutes. Their food is so coarse and bad, that nothing but necessity could compel them to eat it; while their labour and their punishments are severe and cruel.— *Rowland Hill.*

" This torturing system has been pursued so far as to prevent the development of the mental faculties. In Virginia they are not allowed to learn to read. To have been able to read cost a black man his life. He demanded that the Africans should share the benefits which American liberty promised, and he supported this demand by the BILL OF RIGHTS. The argument was without reply. In such cases, where *refutation is impossible*, ALL TYRANNIES having *features* which *resemble* each other, the NEGRO *suffered on the gallows.*"—*Gregoire.*

Are slaves taught to read, so that they can peruse the divine records? If one of ten thousand has attained sufficient learning to spell the plainest passage of Christian instruction, is not the labour which attends it an obstacle to the acquisition of necessary knowledge almost insuperable? But so few of the whole body of the coloured race have arrived even at this stage of illumination, that they are in a great measure incapacitated to comprehend the force of the most homely and common illustrations of the BOOK.

In an act concerning these heirs of misery, a clause was inserted particularly relating to free coloured children, which demonstrates an unwavering resolution in the civil authorities to impede every possible melioration of the degraded state of these *rational cattle*. " It shall not be lawful for the overseers of the poor who may hereafter bind out any black or mulatto orphan, to require the master or mistress to teach such orphan, reading, writing, or arithmetic."—*Virginia*. What must be the unavoidable result of this impenetrable ignorance! How highly must the wrath of heaven be provoked against us, for such flagrant dishonour to his name, and such cruel injustice to the objects of his paternal care.

The plea of slavery is not offered; these are *free* children, bereft of all parental affections, the management and control of whose tender years are assumed by the public; and that authority which proffers them its guardian protection and solicitudes, grasps them for no other purpose, than to nurture them in remediless degradation. What vile hypocrisy! what unfeeling despotism! what daring impiety! what tremendous national guilt does this corruption involve! We steal the parents; Providence liberates them from servitude: God calls them to his dread bar; their children survive them. We deny them the noblest privilege of man, we refuse them all intellectual expansion, we doom them to disgrace during their mortal pilgrimage, and for their degraded condition alone, seize them by some infernal machination, at a subsequent period, as public nuisances: and sell the youth to domestic task-masters, who chain them in interminable vassalage.

With a fatigued body and a dispirited mind, broken with incessant labour, tamed by a constant privation of every comfort, and often lacerated with severity unmingled with mercy, the slave can feel little anxiety to devote any part of that time which is indispensable to rest his wearied and tortured frame, to the care of his soul. How can he be solicitous to mingle with the worship of God in the family where he resides, if devotional forms are maintained!

If he can ascertain the meaning of the bible, or the hymn, or the petitions to the throne of grace, he must perceive that every portion of the exercises condemns the nefarious temper and the barbarous heart which reduced him to bondage; that all which Christianity includes and commands is a contradiction to all that he suffers and that his master practises; and convinced, therefore, that such a profession of religion is delusion or hypocrisy, he begins to consider Christianity itself as nothing more than a form devised by corrupt men, to conceal their cruel insidious designs, and to cloak their malignant actions.

The Lord's day is generally devoted to pursuits, occupations, and pleasures so dissonant from the sacred injunction, that the debased servant cannot even enjoy it as relaxation from labour.   He has no choice : the filth of the week must be his companion, or the hours must be devoted to necessary ablutions ; and thus the opportunities of evangelical instruction are inevitably lost : and can he be ready to attend public worship in due season, the haughty looks and the contemptuous aversion of the Christian *manstealers* (!) who are assembled, are of equal validity with a formal vote of exclusion from the synagogue.   Hence the slave absents himself altogether from a fruitless attendance upon the house of prayer ; and thus is banished from the enjoyment of that illumination which is indispensable to the soul's peace, temporal and everlasting.   If the Son of Man by his spirit graciously maintains the sense and life of godliness in the slave's heart, every thing connected with him constantly counteracts the very exterior appearance, as well as the internal predominance of religion. The ignorant and profane creatures who are his associates ; their bestial mode of life by promiscuous cohabitation ; the want of requisite privacy for meditation and prayer; the constant loss of all those means of grace which are necessary and favourable to religious melioration, and the endless disquietude which he must feel, when he endeavours to join a sincere profession of the Christian religion, meekness and philanthropy, with the turbulent despotism and the unmerciful exhibitions of his master, all must either totally eradicate the love of that which is good, or so diminish its influence, that God is robbed of his glory, the Saviour of the affection due to him, religion of its ornament, the church of the services of her members, the world of its salt and light, and the soul of the peace which Christianity was revealed to bestow.   Hence, as slavery unavoidably extinguishes all religion in those who are made wretched by its sway over them, the jurisdiction which is claimed and exercised, is an impious usurpation of the divine supremacy.

" Slavery is made up of every crime that treachery, cruelty, and murder can invent ; and *men-stealers* are the very worst of thieves. What a universal uproar it would make in this land if but one poor child were kidnapped from his parents! and yet this kidnapping is a regular practice among professing Christians! "These are the people whom the scripture describes as being past feeling. The most knavish tricks are practised by these *dealers in human flesh;* and if the slaves think of our general character, they must suppose that Christians are Devils, and that Christianity was forged in Hell. These slave purchasers talk of a damaged slave, as of a damaged horse; some want *working-slaves,* and others *breeding-slaves;* for the children of slaves are not, according to the law of nature, the property of their parents, but of their owners; and when the planters and their overseers have children by these negroes, instead of regarding the offspring of their vicious passions, they breed up and sell their own children in slavery like others. What a dishonour in us to carry on such an abominable traffic, and to attempt to vindicate or even to palliate it, when every principle belonging to it is founded upon incurable injustice! Shall we call ourselves Christians or Devils? can a race of Devils act against us worse than we do against them? In art and wickedness, as it relates to our principle and practice, we abundantly exceed. The horrid business of slavery in the whole of its establishment is founded on the "mammon of unrighteousness," on a selfish love of the world; and the result of this infernal traffic is, a regular system of *wholesale licensed thievery and murder.*

> " We blush with holy shame, that men
> Who bear thy sacred name, O God!
> Should dare one single man enslave,
> Or shed one drop of human blood."
> *Rowland Hill.*

All those who devise or execute any iniquitous measures, by which men are impeded from honouring God, and from performing the duties which they owe to him and their own souls, in their moral relation to their Creator, are the most contemptuous rebels against his authority: and if they superadd a claim in competition with the command of Jehovah, they exemplify the audacity of Sa-

tan, who was hurled to everlasting despair for attempting
to dethrone the Sovereign of the Universe. This charge
applies to every slaveholder; for services totally incompatible with the devotional exercises of the believer are invariably, at the most unseasonable hours, and during the
day of rest, required of these unfortunate victims of that
savageness, which, by a most diabolical infatuation, has
been combined with Christianity; and which has long
exposed the truths of religion to reproach, the sacred cause
to ridicule, the solemnities of the house of prayer to con-
tumely, and the very character of a believer to suspicion.
While, therefore, a power is usurped and legalized which
enables its possessor to defy the law of God and to obstruct
the duties of men; and unqualified submission to every
arbitrary, unjust, and irreligious mandate cannot be evaded, without the sacrifice of mortal existence; slavery must
be the *acme of all impiety;* consequently, it is *impossible*
that a slaveholder can be a *sincere Christian.*
    Slavery is the climax of cruelty. By it every affection
of the soul is exterminated. It severs all natural ties, and
separates all social relations. Matrimonial engagements,
when it commands, are dissolved; the chain which links
parents and children, by its touch, is shivered to atoms;
and at its approach, every domestic duty dies. Hearts,
animated by the most delicate love, indulge their mutual
affection, not for a father's and mother's gratulations, but
for a *tyrant's* gain. Brothers and sisters mingle their fraternal sensibilities, not in futurity to bless each other by
reciprocal aid, but to increase their unmitigated torments.
Seldom do they reside many years in the same habitation;
a transfer is necessary; and it is made not according to
family or moral connexions, but by the proportionate value
in different markets.
    What are the pungent feelings and exacerbations of the
slave in every part of his existence! Doomed from the
earliest period of youth to toil, with no necessary relaxa-
tion, for the gratification of another's inordinate desires;
pinched by hunger, bereft of raiment, denied requisite ac-
commodations at night to repose his enervated and emaciated frame; and for the most trifling inadvertency or the
most innocent indulgence, scourged by a cruel and merce-

nary taskmaster, until his stripes incapacitate him from
active duties; impeded from all religious instruction; tortured with every agonizing anticipation; and terrified by
the prospect of pain, labour and bereavement, the miseries
of which are diminished by no hope of melioration, he
travels the pilgrimage of life, forgetful of God, himself,
and eternity; until the lacerations of his heart urge him
to the crime, for which, by the sacrifice of his mortal existence, he atones; or, combined with a diseased body, he
drags out his temporal probation amid the unfeeling complaints of his *kidnapper*, that he can no longer force him to
fulfil the daily task; the neglect of all around him; and
the want of every consolation both internal and external,
which might enable him with patience to bear his complicated affliction.

Persons called Christians, and officers of the church,
buy and sell the *stolen* coloured people, with little or no
regard to their wishes or affections. They are deprived of
needful sustenance, are supplied with little and very in-
sufficient raiment, and possess no suitable conveniences
for refreshing rest. They are unmercifully, and in general,
undeservedly chastised; their health, intellects, religion,
morals, peace, and comfort are all disregarded, except the
despot's interest would be affected by neglecting them:
and this diabolical machination cannot exist without the
perpetual exhibition of this malignity by the *slave tyrant*.
Does this degradation include no cruelty? Do these privations result from the *pure and undefiled religion* which
Jesus taught his disciples on the mount? Is this that lucid
proof of condescending love to the brethren which your
Master demands? Is this the justice that the two commandments on which hang all the law and the prophets
inculcate? Is this the mercy which the book enjoins us to
display to the wretched, the indigent, and the oppressed?
And can that man, whose heart with perennial uniformity
evinces the predominance of those principles that produce
such consequences, momentarily believe, upon scriptural
authority, that he is transformed into the similitude of
HIM who was *meek and lowly in heart :* or can he unfeign-
edly affirm, I know that I am passed from death unto life,
because I love the brethren?

For this thing which it cannot bear, the earth is disquieted. The Gospel of peace and mercy preached by him
who *steals*, *buys*, and *sells* the purchase of Messiah's blood!
Rulers of the church *making merchandise* of their brethren's
souls!—and Christians trading the persons of men!—Lovers of their own selves: covetous, proud, fierce; men of
corrupt minds, who resist the truth; having a form of godliness, but denying the power thereof—from such turn
away. 2 Timothy 3. 2, 5.

The slaveholder's claim is founded on falsehood. So
completely have the varied vicious dispositions which attend man-stealing blinded the eyes and indurated the
hearts of flesh-merchants, that they converse respecting
slaves as their property, with as much gravity as if they
were honestly acquired, and as if no law had been violated.
This infatuation has infected not the open reprobate only,
who neither fears God nor regards man, but the professed
believer in Christianity, thereby demonstrating the evil nature, the hardening, blinding tendency, and the consummate
deceitfulness of sin.

He who steals his brethren, and sells them, and makes
merchandise of them, pleads, that the victim of wrong is
legalized property; that the slave is equally a transferable
possession with any other acquisition; that he is chargeable
with no crime for having invested some of his money in
souls and hands; that all the progeny of the creatures
whom he originally purchased, of right belong to him; and
that he violates no rule of equity, no moral principle, and
no Christian affection, by accumulating wealth through this
medium.

On the contrary, we asseverate; that no rational being,
by any transmutation possible, can ever become property;
that no terrestrial legislators, without the most diabolical
impiety, can legalize this claim upon the human family;
that to traffic in flesh and blood animated by the reason-
ing capacities is the greatest practical indignity which can
be offered to men as immortals; that he purchased an article, which he knew at the time of the pretended transfer
was stolen; that every coloured child born in his house,
which he claims and holds as his property, is shamelessly
kidnapped; and that every principle of justice, decency,

order, rectitude and religion, is annulled by this most unrighteous claim and its effects. Notwithstanding, he demands to be recognised as a sincere, consistent Christian.

These principles result from our situation as rational creatures. Human life is altogether placed out of the control of any terrestrial power, except in those extreme cases, where for the welfare of the body politic, it is indispensable to extirpate a pest. But the means necessary to preserve that existence, and to execute the varied duties for which it was originally imparted, are equally requisite to its possessor. Slavery annihilates all. Man is justly subjected to moral law; but property, a slave who has no will, cannot be the proper object of rewards and punishments.

"A young woman in the state of servitude is not able to maintain her virtue against the solicitations of a master who promises her liberty, or a remission of toil, upon her yielding to his desires;" and for such refusal, many chaste females are most barbarously lacerated, until agony forces a reluctant compliance with the debauched tyrant's lust. A slave will not strenuously object to the perpetration of any wickedness to obtain his freedom, or even a diminution of his daily task: indeed those temptations might be thrown in his way, which human nature cannot resist, but by means of the most gracious principles; even he might be scourged into compliance; or his labour might be so increased as to make him for a little respite eagerly embrace the most nefarious proposal which his master could offer; for being absolute property, there is no earthly tribunal to which he could appeal for justice; and very few slaves support themselves under their trials by the recollection of a future judgment."

Slaves after having thus perpetrated the crimes projected by their despots, have been arraigned upon the charge and evidence of their merciless tyrants; have been feloniously condemned and ignominiously deprived of life, to screen the master from disgrace, and for the sake of the value which is allowed to every individual, for the criminal whom he had previously seduced to violate the law, and then contrived, under the sanction of its forms, to murder. The legislative act which allows the master an adjudged price

for his guilty slave, is the very compound of all unrighteousness.

"Lives there a savage ruder than the slave?
Cruel as death, insatiate as the grave,
Is he who toils upon the waiting flood,
A Christian broker in the trade of blood;
Boisterous in speech, in action prompt and bold;
He buys, he sells, he steals, he kills for gold.
  "Lives there a reptile baser than the slave?
Loathsome as death, corrupted as the grave,
See the dull man-thief at his pompous board,
Attendant vassals cringing round their Lord;
He stalks abroad; through all his wonted rounds,
The Negro trembles, and the lash resounds.
This is the veriest wretch on nature's face,
Own'd by no country; spurn'd by every race.
His soul? has he a soul whose sensual breast
Of selfish passions is a serpent's nest?
Whose heart mid scenes of suffering senseless grown,
E'en in his mother's lap was chill'd to stone;
Whose torpid soul no social feelings move;
A stranger to the tenderness of love.
His motley haram charms his gloating eye,
Where ebon, brown, and olive beauties vie.
His children, sprung alike from sloth and vice,
Are born his slaves, and loved at market price:
Has he a soul?—With his departing breath,
A form shall hail him at the gates of death,
The spectre conscience,—shrieking through the gloom,
Man, we shall meet again beyond the tomb."
                                        Montgomery.

  A human creature is not an article of traffic, for the law of
God gives not the absolute disposal of one man's life and
freedom to another.   What he has not made an object of
donation, can never be bestowed by a creature; and as no
person can possibly offer any equivalent for a human soul,
no purchase could ever be honestly made of a rational being; and of course, he never could be even claimed, much
less stolen and transferred, without the highest degree of
4

iniquity : for no terrestrial power can possibly legalize that which God has peremptorily prohibited.

Many persons propagate the notion, that the acts of earthly lawgivers can make any practice legal, however base and corrupt its tendency : upon the validity of this sentiment, the superstructure of " detaining men in slavery" is founded.

Our civil institutions are professedly established upon their conformity with the word of God : and the fundamental principles of the social compact, as they are declared in the Bills of Rights adopted by the several states, are generally in unison with the decisions of the sacred volume. But all these standard declarations of liberty and justice directly condemn the terrestrial authority which infringes the rights of man, and presuppose, if they do not openly avow, our dependence upon God, and the obligation to obey his law, to be paramount to any other claim or relation. The leaders of the last generation are chargeable with the most consummate hypocrisy. Before the world, they boldly denounced the king of Great Britain, that he would force the introduction of Africans into these states, as slaves. Having thus solemnly challenged mankind to the contemplation of this unrighteous conduct ; they authorized the importation of kidnapped Africans during a period of thirty years. The whole union is included in the stigma of having licensed the enormities of this complicated system of moral turpitude, and national infamy, this most iniquitous traffic of " incurable injustice" and barbarity ; and a system which afforded ample subject for the display of eloquent invective, when applied to a foreign potentate, is still sanctioned by the law of the land, and the avaricious, dissipated propensities of the citizens, although it is directly opposed to truth, decency, virtue, conscience, and God.

In no aspect, whether political or moral, can the Government of the United States, after the final settlement of the Revolutionary conflict, be more deeply condemned than for their acts in reference to slavery. The signers of the Declaration of Independence, with daring boldness recorded their indignant denunciation against the British superior authorities, as having coerced the Colonies against their will, to receive

African slaves among the population. It should, therefore, have been a natural result of the 4th of July, 1776, that the foreign traffic should instantly have been terminated, and the municipal thraldom also destroyed. Instead of which, slavery and its horrors have attained a castle and a power, the contemplation of which appals every patriot and Christian.

In the year 1776, the United States stood, in fact, seven free to six slave colonies, for the slaves then north of Maryland, are unworthy of notice. Since that period, six additional slave states have been added to the Union, and only three free states. For Vermont and Maine being then settled as now, are not numbered in this relation. Now the states instead of reckoning seven to six on behalf of freedom, are truly thirteen to eleven in favour of Slavery.

This has given to the slave states in the Senate of Congress, the power of coercing all the legislation of the United States ; so that all hope of deliverance from that source is a mere idle dream. This is our love of reciprocal justice and universal freedom.

From the termination of the revolutionary conflict in 1783, until the commencement of the year 1808, it has been proved, that far more slaves were kidnapped from abroad, and landed in this country, than during the whole anterior one hundred and fifty years ; and this fact very comically is alleged to prove, what dignified, wise, and sincere assertors of the rights of man, were the southern members of the Congress of 1776, and of the Convention of 1787, who avowed that they would scatter the federal compact to atoms, rather than build the edifice of Freedom upon the abolition of slavery, and their abandonment of man-stealing.

When, in the year 1776, all men were proclaimed free and equal, the coloured citizens were comparatively so few, and the exultation of the period so overpowering, that they would instantly have fallen into their own station in society ; and it is scarcely questionable, that at this era, they would not have numbered one more than on the day of their liberation.

Now under the existing system, every circumstance is changed. Their physical force has multiplied to a

frightful extent; their exasperation daily augments; their
knowledge and capacities to break their yoke, continually
become more evident; and their determination to be free,
has assumed the character of that unyielding fortitude,
which falters not until the shout of triumph.

With all these facts before our eyes, and this criminality
attached unto us, we still annually revile the British
administrations of 1765 and 1775; apparently forgetful,
that the little finger of one American Government is
thicker than the loins of all the combined Grenvilles and
Norths; and, that if the old British Bashaws formerly
chastised our white citizens with whips, the Virginians,
Carolinians and Georgians, with their confederated man-
stealing pirates, chastise our coloured citizens with scorpions!

Every ramification of the doctrine, that one rational creature can become the property of another, is totally repugnant
to the rule of equity, the rights of nature, and the existence
of civil society: and every attempt to palliate this enormity is nugatory. Of all his natural and inalienable privileges, the slave is virtually, if not actually divested; his
life is of no value to him for he cannot devote it to any
useful purposes; his liberty has altogether flown, for he is
incarcerated only in an enlarged prison; and he is defraud-
ed of all ability or capacity or opportunity to pursue the innocent and laudable enjoyments, which Providence may
place within his attainment. Whatever may be the legislative decision or permission, with whatever impious
usurpations those who assented to it may be chargeable,
the claim to a fellow-creature as property originated in the
vilest depravity of man, is perpetuated by the hard-heartedness and self-delusion of sinners, and cannot be justified
by the acts, however formal and numerous, of any terrestrial government.

The exhibition of our brethren and sisters in a public
market for sale and hire; the examination to which they
must submit that their condition may be ascertained, and
the remarks which they must hear upon their varied capacities, are the greatest insult to decorum, the highest
violation of rectitude, and the vilest outrage which can be

offerĕd to humanity. Justice frowns upon the obdurate transgressor, who has so far obliterated his senses as to be unable to distinguish rational creatures from horses and cows; yet these displays, transfers of human flesh animated by an immortal spirit, professed Christians behold without any pungency of soul; until the beneficence of the gospel has vanished, and sordid gold becomes the centre of every affection and desire.

Reciprocity is a principle acknowledged by all mankind, incorporated with all our feelings, and adopted in all our intercourse, and when it is equitably and impartially ad ministered, it furnishes a safe ground of conduct in all our relative acts. As thou hast done, it shall be done unto thee; thy reward shall return upon thine own head. This retaliatory doctrine demonstrates, that the bondage of the human species must be contradictory to truth and right; because they who are guilty of the highest oppression, would not admit the validity of the claim, were an attempt made to enforce it upon themselves.

What an intolerable evil! How incredible! How disgraceful! that men in the land of liberty and filling official stations under the authority of the bible, require to be instructed, that to steal, buy and sell men, women and children is contrary to the gospel; that to defraud the labourer of his hire, to rob the mind of necessary light and the heart of indispensable melioration, and to doom the human race to labour lasting as their existence, without food, raiment, a habitation, and other necessaries to support life and recruit nature exhausted by endless fatigue; are totally incompatible with the precept, do justly, love mercy, and walk humbly with God; and that all who engage in this odious and most criminal violation of the eighth commandment, should cease from every pretension to Christianity.

Should Providence ever permit the same misery and wrong, in one instance only, to assail us which we have inflicted, the nation would as one man rise to arms. Could a single vessel from the Gold-coast arrive on our shores, with impunity escape, and carry away a hundred families of our white population; the injustice, the enormity, the cruelty and the abomination of the act would be dilated

4*

upon, until language had lost the practicability of illustrating the subject, and eloquence itself had ceased to interest.
But nearly two hundred years was this disgraceful procedure tolerated and legalized, by successive generations of
Columbians ;—for a long time they declared that it was
against their consent, the practice being enforced by
foreign arbitrary power: but their insincerity is apparent;
for as soon as Providence enabled them to discard all external jurisdiction, they voluntarily imbued their hands in
negro blood, and voraciously grasped the price of African
souls.

Retaliation ! How complete would be the petrifaction
of a feeling heart, to see his wife and daughter in the rude
hands of an unfeeling, mercenary debauchee, maintained,
as long as convenient, for impure indulgences, and then
transferred by the wretch, with the offspring of his illicit
intercourse, his own children, to another unprincipled tyrant, from him to receive similar insults, with him to realize the same degradation. You cannot contemplate
without horror, the involuntary transportation of your family to Guinea ; there to be debased in multiform wretchedness without hope, each member of the family severed
from you at an impassable distance, and you obliged to
form an unwilling connexion with another, that you may
generate rational cattle like to yourself, for the increase of
your tyrant's wealth.

From this view, you with abhorrence avert your eyes ;
you shudder at the mention of such detestable atrocity ;
you declare that every claim upon you, marked by such
characteristics, is totally null, because it is founded upon a
lie; you aver that all the constituted authorities, even all
the people of every nation in Africa combined, could never
transform this fiction into verity, and this vilest of all thefts
into justice ; and you would resentfully complain, that
" this mischievous kidnapping, purchase, sale and transfer
of me, as if I were a horse or an ox merely for labour,
while I am not treated with as much care and kindness as
that to which those beasts are accustomed, is the very quintessence of all infernal brutality." Your doctrine is irre-

futable; it is self-evident; it is so true, that it can neither be denied nor proved.

Can you, therefore, hold a slave?   A sincere Christian cannot engage in this malevolent commerce; this compound of all turpitude.   A preacher of the gospel ought not to be patiently listened to, even, who eloquently depicts the blessing of that liberty with which Christ hath made us free, while he holds his fellow disciple, him to whom he administers the symbols of a Saviour's redeeming love, in a most dreadful and lacerating bondage.   An officer of the church cannot, without the most deplorable ignorance of himself, pretend to believe and solemnly engage to inculcate the doctrines of the Presbyterian Confession of Faith, and the Methodist Discipline, who enslaves, purchases, transfers, whips, neglects, starves, and by these accumulated wrongs, probably kills, the purchase of Messiah's blood? The pulpit is dumb and the Lord's table is polluted; because preachers and lay officers need to be taught that the greatest possible violation of the eighth commandment cannot without the most awful delusion be reconciled with a credible profession of Christianity.

" Let us look to the words of our Saviour; let us deeply weigh one of the most splendid doctrines of the Christian dispensation, a doctrine, which served more than any other to illustrate the unparalleled beauty and grandeur of that most amiable of all religions; a doctrine, before which slavery was forced to fly; and to which doctrine, I attribute the memorable and glorious fact, that soon after the establishment of Christianity in Europe, human slavery was abolished.   This doctrine is, high and low, rich and poor, are equal in the sight of God!   This is a doctrine which requires only to be daily impressed on the heart of man to extinguish the term of slave; and accordingly, what all the ancient systems failed to do, Christianity accomplished. To the pure light which this great doctrine of our Saviour diffused over the heart of man, the abolition of slavery must be ascribed."—*Fox.*

" If we determine to surrender ourselves without reserve to the domination of hard, unfeeling avarice; to sell ourselves for gain; let us achieve some clearly profitable villany, some masterstroke of wickedness ; we shall then be justified on our own principles; but slavery incurs the utmost guilt in pursuit of the smallest and most questionable profit, and discredits not your hearts only, but your understandings.

As slavery ought indisputably to be considered a most enormous crime ; it is our duty to prohibit and punish, if we cannot effectually annihilate the perpetration of it. I can admit of no compromise when the commands of equity and philanthropy are so imperious. I wash my hands of the blood that will be spilled. I protest against it, as the most flagrant violation of every principle of justice and humanity. I never will desert the cause. In my task it is impossible to tire ; it fills my mind with complacency and peace. At night I lie down with composure, and rise to it in the morning with alacrity. I never will desist from this blessed work."— *Wilberforce.*

Theft is the acquisition of another's goods, without returning him a satisfactory equivalent : but the worst of all robbers is he who steals not the bodies only, but the life and the souls of men ; and for this felony, no restitution or remuneration can be made.

Every African introduced into this country was kidnapped. They never voluntarily entered a slave ship ; and had they even contracted to sell their personal freedom, and that of their posterity for ever, the contract was void ; for by no compact, could they alienate their inherent rights. But the theft of the father and mother, in a slave-holder's system of morals, authorizes him to steal the son and the daughter, through all generations.

Our horror at the robbery of the negroes in Congo, is mitigated by the distance at which the villany is performed ; but how can men, who have been kidnapping coloured people, from their infancy, in America, be so miserably self-deluded, so awfully blinded, as not to know that the highest sin on the Gold Coast, when perpetrated in Columbia, is vastly aggravated, by the splendid illumination which we enjoy on all religious subjects ?— how can Christian professors expose themselves to derision, by gravely declaring that Hawkins and his gang were negro thieves, three hundred years ago on the coast of Africa, but they who have practised his abominations, through all succeeding ages here, are innocent slave holders ? How dare expositors of the book attempt to persuade persons who hold slaves, that the proceeds of man-stealing are now transformed into honest acquisitions; that incurable injustice on the Windward shore, by a voyage over the ocean, is transmuted into Christian integrity ; and that a man who kidnaps a parent is a monster of hell; but if he steals children, he is an heir of heaven ?

Every slave in the union, has been barbarously stolen ; all the traffic in slaves is irreconcileable with the principles of justice and humanity; and every negro-dealer, as Moses and the supreme law of the land pronounce, is a cruel thief.

A man who would buy a stolen horse, when he was privy to the robbery, is innocent, compared with a slave-purchaser ; for the former, if convicted, will acknowledge his guilt; but the latter, with his accumulated iniquity, pleads that he is not guilty, while he kidnaps his neighbour; and that he abets not theft, by receiving goods knowing them to be stolen, though he beheld the trader rob the property.

From the womb, the child is doomed to all the horrors of bondage, and its birth excites joy, only because it aggrandizes wealth; for a tyrant grasps it, notwithstanding a father's claim, a mother's affection, and in opposition to the command of God, the law of nature, the dictates of equity, and the thunder of conscience. Thus professors act, and seduce their progeny into the ungodly practice. A sinner redeemed by grace divine ! A chimera ! His portion in Jesus delivered him not from man-stealing, and if there were no penitentiary, he would purloin a horse or an estate: and to steal a beast, or to defraud a man of a section of land, is a vastly inferior crime, in the balance of the sanctuary, than to kidnap, buy, sell, or hold a slave.

It is of no importance by what means the slave was acquired; whether by our own robbery, purchase from the thief, donation from the primary kidnapper, or from him to whom he was transferred, or by bequest; the guilt is identical : if the rational creature, a slave be found in our hand; we are involved in all the criminality of man-stealing, and shall not escape the retribution of God, when in righteousness the Son of Man shall judge the world.

" You are a professor of religion ; you believe that all mankind are brethren; that God is their father; that Jesus Christ died for men ; that men ought to glorify him in body and spirit; that it is just and merciful to keep the purchase of the blood of Christ in slavery! You are a professor of religion ; you believe that every man is accountable to God, and that all mankind must stand before the judgment seat of Christ, to give an account for the deeds done in the body : can you answer for the consequences of slavery ? Alas ! is there no contradiction in this profession? Can reason and conscience reconcile such a scheme ? You are a professor of religion ; you believe that love to God and all mankind is the true spirit of Christianity ; that this commandment have we from him; that he who loveth God, loveth his brother also ; and that to detain your fellow-creatures in slavery, is the most excellent way to show your love to them ? Is it love to little children to keep them in ignorance and nakedness, to grow up like the wild ass' colt, while you are forcing their parents to labour for you and your's? Is it kindness to women that induces you to trample upon virgin modesty, and all the maternal affections? Is it your love to the American black man which gives rise to those institutions which consign him to eternal servitude?

You are a minister of the gospel ; you preach deliverance to the captives; peace and salvation to a fallen world through Jesus Christ ; you denounce the wrath of God which is revealed from heaven against all ungodliness and unrighteousness of men who hold the truth in unrighteousness; and yet you hold your fellow-creatures in slavery ? Thou that condemnest others and dost the same thing thyself, thinkest thou that thou shalt escape the judgment of God ? You are a minister of the Gospel! you are engaged to recommend the religion of the meek and lowly Jesus, both by precept and example—does slavery give mankind the highest idea of the excellency of religion ?

Ah ! where is glorying now ? what advantage hath the Christian slave-holder over the sceptic philosopher, the Jew, the Turk, or the Pagan? what reward have ye? what do ye more than others? do not even the publicans, all the nations, the same ?

Slavery is the source of all kinds of injustice; for it is incompatible with equity and civil rights, and is the greatest of all tyrannies. The monarchies and aristocracies which have been so often decried by politicians, as oppressive and violent, are independence, in comparison of that bondage in which the American black man is kept. It exterminates the rights of women and children; for it is a mere state of barbarism, in which neither the delicacy and chastity of sex, nor the debility and ignorance of children, are regarded. All the physical and commercial distinctions of labour and property are destroyed by it; for slavery is a monopoly, which takes from another what one has no right to claim, and withholds that which belongs to him."—*Smithin.*

What conformity with the moral code, does a flesh-dealer exhibit? Thou shalt not kill: slavery in its most benign form, is slow-paced murder. Thou shalt not steal: this law, in the comprehension of the Israelites, solely prohibits man-theft, detaining persons in perpetual bondage. Thou shalt not bear false witness against thy neighbour: no man can possess a slave, until he has virtually sworn, that men, women, and children are brutes. Thou shalt not covet thy neighbour's house, thou shalt not covet thy neighbour's wife, nor his man-servant, nor his maid-servant, nor his ox, nor his ass, nor any thing which is thy neighbour's; the slave-holder not only sinfully desires, but actually steals them, with his neighbour also; thus consummating his guilt by the most daring rebellion and transcendent depravity.

Every dictate of God's word is flagrantly disobeyed; for reciprocal equity is banished, as soon as slavery appears. Thou shalt not defraud thy neighbour, nor rob him: this unceasing cheating and robbery commence when the child first breathes, and ends only at his death. Thou shalt not oppress him who is poor and needy, lest he cry against thee unto the Lord, and it be a sin unto thee : is stealing a man and giving him no necessaries, oppression? Thou shalt neither vex a stranger, nor oppress him : they kidnap the stranger, to chain him in endless vexations and calamities. Behold, the hire of the labourers who have reaped down your fields, which is of you kept back of fraud, crieth : and the cries of them who have reaped, are entered into the ears of the Lord of Sabaoth : the slave-tyrant's reapers are never paid. Ye shall not afflict any widow or fatherless : the incessantly afflictive experience of coloured females and orphans, neither eloquence can display, nor imagination comprehend. I will come near to you to judgment; and I will be a swift witness against false-swearers, and against those who oppress the hireling in his wages, the widow, and the fatherless, and who turn aside the stranger from his right, and fear not me, saith the Lord of Hosts : with this menace, the slave-holder, according to his morality, has no connexion ; for a slave is not a hireling, and being a brute, can neither be a widow nor fatherless, and he cannot be a stranger turned aside from his rights—he never possess- ed one—and he was born on the plantation: but the man-thief may recollect, that his false swearing affords him the only basis for these excuses. In the midst of thee, have they dealt by oppression with the stranger : is it oppression or Christianity, to kidnap men, and ceaselessly torment them, until they die? Rob not the poor, because he is poor ; nor oppress the afflicted in the gate ; for the Lord will plead their cause, and spoil the soul of those who spoiled them : are slaves rich? is not oppression daily added to their dis- tresses? has the slave-holder the fear of God before his eyes? does he anticipate remuneration, with the measure that he meted misery? Loose the bands of wickedness, undo the heavy burdens, let the oppressed go free, take away the yoke : if the Lord had commanded flesh-merchants to act precisely contrary, how exactly would they have complied! They bind the bands of wickedness, they aggravate the heavy burdens, they incarcerate the oppressed, they increase every yoke, they starve the hungry, they banish the poor, they pillage the naked, they despise their brethren, they contemn the African, they converse in lies, and they mul- tiply the afflictions of the wretched. Yet they have the impudent hypocrisy to pretend that they are Messias disciples!

But the hiring of slaves equally involves the sin of stealing them, as it is an encouragement for the kidnapper to repeat his crime: and the payment of the labourer, as well as the master, will not exonerate any man from a participation in the guilt. He aids the man-thief; for he supports another who defrauds his neighbour, who robs him of his wages, and who thereby perpetuates his oppressions. The renter of slaves is generally more rigid and severe even than the kidnapper himself: for the latter shows them the kindness which is indispensable to promote his interest, and thus in some measure and at certain intervals admits one cheering ray into the gloom; but the hirer's sole study is to ascertain by what process he can drive the poor creatures so as to procure from them, during the period of possession, for their death he is not responsible, the utmost quantum of labour, at the least practicable expense. Although he retains no slaves as the produce of his own theft, he unites with a man-merchant, pays him for his iniquity, and joins to defraud the poor of his recompense, and to augment the agonies of the miserable. Some other cause, and not religion or conscience, hinders him from citizen-stealing; and he who rents a slave, is partaker of his crime who stole him, and can make no juster pretensions to the character of a Christian than the kidnapper himself: for he hates instruction, and casts the words of God behind him; when he sees a thief, then he consents with him; he gives his mouth to evil, and his tongue frames deceit. Therefore he is a wicked sinner.

From the dawning of life until aged decrepitude, barbarity and injustice, are the slave's uniform portion; his existence is abbreviated, and dissolution is his only comfort. His terrestrial pilgrimage is toil and pain; his corse is interred without sympathy; no Christian recollections mingle around the grave which entombs the sleeping dust: he lived in scorn, his death excites no regret but the loss of gain, and he is deposited in oblivion, until the morning of the resurrection.

Notwithstanding all the political evils in our country

combined, are trifling when contrasted with the social mischief which slavery diffuses; and although its compound
iniquity far exceeds any other sin against God and our
neighbour that we can possibly practise: for it is a most
audacious rebellion and falsehood against Jehovah; it is
impious disobedience to the Saviour, and it is cruelty, pollution and improbity towards man; yet preachers, church-
officers and Christian professors, either participate in these
enormities, or palliate them to disguise their horrors, or by
their silence connive at the perpetrators, and by acknowledging them as Messias' disciples, sanction their ungodly
transactions.

Many transgressions incompatible with the bible, may be
upbraided with all apostolic fervour : but if a preacher, desirous that he may be pure from the blood of all men, shuns
not to declare the whole counsel of God; introduces man-
stealing, within the walls of the temple ; the reproaches, the
contempt, the hatred, the persecution and the menaces which
overwhelm him, evince that slavery is a legion of devils.

It is impossible to amalgamate a system which boldly
aims to overthrow the jurisdiction of heaven, with due
submission to Jehovah's authority, or to prove him who
joins in such audacity, the humble docile follower of the
Lamb ;—much less can the quintessence of cruelty be combined with the beneficence of the book, or a man void of all
sensibility be animated with apostolic love; equally inefficient would be every attempt to connect the perennial
impudent falsehoods of slavery, with the unimpeachable
uniform veracity of divine Revelation, or to demonstrate
that an unvarying falsifier is an acceptable disciple of the
heart-searching God, who desires truth in the inward parts;
and not less preposterous would be the endeavour to cement
the continual unrighteous impositions of man-stealing with
the constant unbounded rectitude of heart, lip, and life, of
body, soul, and spirit, which the gospel demands, or to
evince that the same mind is in him which was also in
Christ Jesus, and that Paul's integrity directed the malign
proceedings of an impenitent, ceaseless, cruel thief!

That man-stealers can possibly venture to preach concerning justice, mercy, and pardon upon evangelical prin-

ciples; that they can unblushingly presume to serve at the table of the Lord; or that they can calmly seat themselves around the sacred board—is a manifest demonstration of that obduracy of heart, which sin naturally engenders, and of that blindness of vision, which nothing but the Holy Spirit's energy can possibly remove.

Our life past may suffice us to have wrought the will of the Gentiles: now it is high time to awake out of sleep, to discard this iniquity, to repent, and to reform this atrocity; or we may fearfully anticipate that he who holdeth the seven stars in his right hand, who walketh in the midst of the seven golden candlesticks, will come unto us quickly, and will remove our candlestick out of his place, except we repent; that he will lay his axe unto the root of the tree, hew it down, and cast it into the fire: and that he whose fan is in his hand, will thoroughly purge his floor and gather his wheat into the garner; but he will burn up the chaff with unquenchable fire.

Ye shall know them by their fruits. Do men gather grapes of thorns, or figs of thistles? Even so every good tree bringeth forth good fruit; but a corrupt tree bringeth forth evil fruit. A good tree cannot bring forth evil fruit, neither can a corrupt tree bring forth good fruit. Every tree that bringeth not forth good fruit is hewn down, and cast into the fire. Wherefore by their fruits ye shall know them. The fruit is a destruction of every devotional temper, the tree is daring impiety: the tree is incessant cruelty, the fruit is unparalleled insensibility to human wo; the tree is invariable deception, the fruit is unintermitted falsehood; and the fruits are every diversified unrighteousness, the tree is uninterrupted injustice: therefore, as all the fruits are atrociously and detestably corrupt, the tree itself must be incorrigibly rotten.

As no participant in this complicated enormity can possibly be innocent of the guilt which it comprises; every slave-holding professor, is either so wretchedly besotted by the influence of sin as to be wilfully ignorant of the true nature and requisitions of the gospel, or he has assumed a profession of Christianity as a cloak for his malignant and ungodly conduct; hence, whether he be perversely deluded, or a contumacious deceiver, unless he manifest a sincere contrition, by immediately desisting from all concern with a combination of impiety, barbarism, falsehood and dishonesty, he ought to be excommunicated from the church of God.

———

SLAVERY

INCOMPATIBLE WITH THE GOSPEL.

SLAVERY is adverse to all the principles and requisitions which the scriptures reveal. The purchase, or sale, or vassalage, or involuntary hire of men or women, destroys the rights which are granted to the human family by the God of nature ; extinguishes all capacity for the fulfilment of terrestrial duties and a compliance with divine injunctions ; nullifies the evangelic law of love and equity ; and is unequivocally denounced by the Holy Bible, as the highest degree of criminality connected with this temporal state of probation.

"Slavery naturally tends to destroy all sense of justice and equity. It puffs up the mind with pride ; teaches youth a habit of looking down upon their fellow creatures with contempt, esteeming them as dogs or devils, and imagining themselves beings of superior dignity and importance, to whom all are indebted. This banishes the idea, and unqualifies the mind for the practice of common justice. If I have all my days, been accustomed to live at the expense of a coloured man, without making him any compensation, or considering myself at all in his debt, I cannot think it any great crime to live at the expense of a white man. If I rob a coloured man without guilt, I shall contract no great guilt by robbing a white man. If I have been accustomed to think a coloured man was made for me, I may easily take it into my head to think so of a white man. If I have no sense of obligation to do justice to a black man, I can have little to do justice to a white man. In this case, the tinge of our skins, or the place of our nativity, can make but little difference. If I am in principle a friend to slavery, I cannot, to be consistent, think it any crime to rob my country of its property and freedom, whenever my interest calls, and I find it in my power. If I make any difference here, it must be owing to a vicious education, the force of prejudice, or pride of heart. If in principle a friend to slavery, I cannot feel myself obliged to pay the debt due to my neighbour. If I can wrong him of all his possessions, and avoid the law, all is well."—*Rice.*

" The holding of our fellow creatures in perpetual slavery is inconsistent with the honour and brotherly love, which Christians acknowledge to be due to all men. Honour all men. The Lord make you to increase and abound in love to one another and to all men. We are to love and honour all men as the partakers of the same human nature, as descended from the same original parent. God hath made of one blood all nations, and hath determined the bounds of their habitations : also as having immortal souls capable of saving grace, capable of being members of Christ and temples of the Holy Ghost. But the slavery, in which American citizens are now detained, indicates hatred and contempt, instead of honour and love. It is invidiously restricted to those of a certain complexion ; deprives them of the common rights of man ; and exhibits them to be bought and sold like beasts.

" The evil consequences which have constantly attended slavery, are sufficient to make every Christian abhor it. It is shocking to relate the many instances, disgraceful to human nature, of the dreadful punishment inflicted on these miserable captives for slight offences, of the excessive labour to which they are compelled, of the scanty and unwholesome allotment that is given them of the necessaries of life, and of other sorts of cruel treatment. The education of slaves in the principles of our holy religion, is universally neglected. Hence, they are grossly ignorant of religion and openly immoral in their practice. Thus a race of heathens or infidels is propagated ; whose example and conversation must be an infectious and destructive plague to the rest of the inhabitants of the land. Nor is there any reasonable prospect of the reformation of persons while in

5*

a state of slavery; for the masters are generally possessed
with a notion, that slaves are unteachable, and that knowledge would render them more intractable. Besides, slaves
are naturally and justly prejudiced against the instructions
of their oppressors."—*Brown.*

"Liberty conducts to every thing that is sublime in genius
and virtue, while slavery extinguishes all. What sentiments of dignity or of respect, can those mortals have for
themselves, who are considered as cattle, and who are often
staked, by their masters, at cards or billiards, against bar-
rels of rice or other merchandise. What can individuals
perform when degraded below the condition of brutes, over-
wrought, covered with rags, famished by hunger, and for
the slightest fault torn by the bloody whip of an overseer ?
Slavery supposes all the crimes of tyranny, and engenders
all its vices. Virtue can hardly thrive among men who
have no consideration, who are soured by misfortune,
dragged into corruption by the example of crimes, driven
from all honourable or supportable ranks in society, deprived
of religious and moral instruction, placed in a situation
where it is impossible to acquire knowledge, and struggling
against obstacles which oppose the development of their
faculties. In their place, perhaps, we should have been
less virtuous, than the virtuous among them, and more
vicious than their worst characters ; for their vices are the
work of the nations called Christian."—*Gregoire.*

Revealed religion is predicated upon the natural equality,
the individual responsibility, the reciprocal duties of the
human family, and the paramount claims of the most high
God to the services, and the obedience of all his creatures.
Slavery does not merely diminish the energy, and mitigate
the obligation of the sacred scriptures, but it totally nullifies
all the fundamental principles of Christianity.

Paul assured the Areopagites, that God made of one flesh
all nations of men. The dissimilarity of the rational species, upon the pretext of colour, is consequently a chimera ;
and if the members of the various countries of the globe are
derived from a different origin, they cannot be bound by the
same laws as ourselves. This aggravates the iniquity of
slave-holding to an inconceivable degree because it pre-

supposes the right to grasp every reasonable creature who bears not our own external conformation, or whose features differ; but the same principles in reaction would justify every country in enslaving its neighbours, and every individual for stealing defenceless men.

Slavery is the legitimate offspring, and the frequent cause of a rejection of the bible.   Christian instructors may justly be alarmed; they cannot be silent upon man-stealing, much less excuse, defend, or engage in it, without a virtual admission that divine revelation is not our sole infallible directory.

Men calumniate the coloured people, that they may claim a right to enslave them; and for justification of their culpable conduct.   The accusers are both judges and executioners.

Slavery extinguishes all the rights of man : from his equal rank in creation, the slave is ignominiously debased to a brute; and the immunities which naturally inhere to him, are all stolen.   The thief becomes a despot, and the kidnapped immortal is buried in terrestrial vassalage, without hope and without end.   His life is at the disposal of a barbarian, who may render it as wretched as he will uncontrolled, or shorten its duration by every refinement of torture : of his freedom he is altogether divested : and his labour, his comforts, his children, and his all, are the property of the most guilty violator of the eighth commandment.   What peculiarly daring effrontery do men display, when they assume the garb of religion, and deny its most obvious principles, its most luminous prescriptions, and its most tremendous denunciations!

"The principles of conjugal love and fidelity in the breast of a virtuous pair, of natural affection in parents, and a sense of duty in children, are inscribed there by the finger of God; they are the laws of heaven; but an enslaving law directly opposes them, and virtually forbids obedience.   The relations of husband and wife, of parent and child, are formed by divine authority and founded on the laws of nature.   But it is in the power of a cruel master, and of a needy creditor, to break those tender connexions, and for ever to separate those dearest rela-

tives. This is ever done at the call of interest or humour.
The poor sufferers may expostulate; they may plead with
tears; their hearts may break; but all in vain. The laws
of nature are violated, the tender ties are dissolved, a final
separation takes place, and the duties of these relations
can no longer be performed, nor their comforts enjoyed.
Would slaves perform the duties of husbands, wives, parents and children; the law puts it out of their power.
Hence, it is evident that the law of nature or the laws of
men are wrong."—*Rice*.

If holy resentment is excited at the support given to
such criminality by national regulations, what Christian
commiserates not those, who defend this villany, and who
consent with a man-stealer, by acknowledging him an
acceptable believer; thus transforming the eternal reprobation which God has affixed upon slavery, into a ratifica-
tion of their ungodliness. Are not these ecclesiastical
officers, blind watchmen, shepherds who cannot understand, looking to their own way, every one for his gain,
from his own SLAVE quarter? Isaiah 56: 10, 11. Did
all the preachers faithfully delineate this iniquity, and
the curse which attends it, slavery would immediately
expire.

As individuals, we are accountable to God, for all our
actions; but by denying to our fellow creatures, the use
of their reason, the acquisition of knowledge, and the exercise of their powers, we interpose a claim between the
Creator and man, equally insulting to Jehovah, disgraceful to the church, and injurious to our neighbour. By refusing him requisite-instruction, we extinguish his capacity, and by chaining his will, we preclude his obedience
to the divine commands.

Ere long eternity will open to our incredulous eyes;
the Lord of the servants will come, and reckon with them.
The kidnapper and his slave, the legislator and the
preacher stand before the righteous Judge. The man-
stealer pleads interest as his apology. The property excuses himself upon the impracticability of fulfilling his
duties. The legislator urges the exigency of the case,
and the bad policy of emancipation. The minister is ad-

dressed; didst thou inculcate, that the slave merchant was the greatest criminal in society? didst thou enjoin the exhibition of love, and justice, and mercy? didst thou preach deliverance to the captive? didst thou warn the lawgiver of his usurpation, in enacting laws subversive of my supremacy, contradictory to my word, derogatory to thy nature, and condemned by thy conscience? "No, Lord," must the wretched Judas acknowledge: "I was afraid, and went and hid thy talent in the earth." Thou a Christian and a slave-holder! thy portion is with thieves. Thou a man and not obey my commands! but thou didst not know thy Lord's will, thou shalt be beaten with few stripes. Thou a legislator, and overturn the law of God! Thou didst love and make a lie: drown him and his policy in everlasting fire. Thou a watchman, and not admonish them: "cast ye the unprofitable servant into outer darkness!" GOD BE MERCIFUL TO YOU SINNERS!

Slave-holders plead that they are Christians. In what principles does Christianity consist? Buying souls, kidnapping children, tormenting women, brutalizing men, robbing the labourer, and oppressing the innocent captive? then are they indeed saints!

But the Gospel unequivocally declares, that to enslave a man is the highest kind of theft; to purloin children is the compound of all robbery, as it steals a father's joy, a mother's tenderness, a brother's delight, and a sister's affection; to excruciate a female by stripes or by violation, is the height of barbarity; to divest man of his rational characteristics is the most diabolical impiety; to defraud the friendless and overpowered dependant of his just recompense, is the very mass of all injustice; to destroy feminine modesty is the source of all other crimes personal and relative; to profane the sabbath absolutely disavows the authority of God, and salvation by Jesus Christ; and to prolong human existence in agony, the mind bereft of consolation and the body of needful support, is a concatenation of crime indescribable. Can the perpetrators, the defenders, the compromisers, the participators, and the connivers, who by any mode protract such inexpressi-

ble flagitiousness be Christians? One of the most eulogised preachers in Virginia sometime ago remarked: "to
call this a Christian state is absurd. It is a community
of profligate infidels, with a few scattered Christians
among them." The fact is undeniable, and why? Scep-
tics, Deists and Worldlings ridicule with scorn all endeavours to combine slavery and Christianity; and candidly
acknowledge that it is utterly impracticable to compound
gospel morality, Columbian republicanism, reciprocal justice and natural humanity, with American slave-holding,
and the common traffic in the flesh, blood, and souls of our
fellow citizens.

The word of God condemns this turpitude as the most
atrocious criminality: and no man can momentarily admit, that unerring rectitude sanctions this system of iniquity. Whether we advert to the motives, the objects,
or the results of slavery, it is totally incompatible with
Christianity.

Slave-holding is a substitution of Mammon for God.
Avarice originated and perpetuates man-stealing. Wealth
is the grand desire of every flesh-merchant; and all traders in the persons of men exhibit conduct, which is as
essentially different from the devotional, philanthropic,
and equitable demands of the gospel, as the purity of
Paradise is dissimilar to the depravation of Pandemonium.

Are any persons so lamentably blind, that they cannot
discern the anti-christianity of robbing the rights of man,
the impiety of turning the blind from the way, disobedience in rendering all sacred ordinances a nullity, cruelty
in the diversified pain with which they burden their fellow
citizens, and dishonesty in falsehood, fraud, and stealing;
who should expose their delusions, and rouse them from
their stupor? The *Ministers of the Sanctuary.* "By their vo-
cation," says Cugaono, "the clergy are the messengers of
truth. They ought to watch society, to expose its errors,
and bring the wicked back to virtue. If their conduct be
otherwise, the public sins will fall on their head. Either
they know not the truth, or they *dare not reveal it,* and are
therefore *partners in national crimes.*"

Persons through satanic delusion, will hear the most

PICTURE OF SLAVERY. 59

solemn verities, unaffected. An expositor of the scriptures may enforce justice and mercy ; but the kidnapper avows, that he is a righteous man, for he only bought his slaves and stole their children ; he did not sail to Africa and transport them. He alleges, that he is merciful, for he bestows upon his slaves meat once weekly, his neighbours give them none. A preacher should demonstrate, that his pretended justice is a cheat ; that his mercy is savageness ; and that he who turns away his ear from hearing the law, even his prayers are an abomination to the Lord. He regards iniquity in his heart, the Lord will not hear him. But if the PULPIT, the trumpet gives an uncertain sound, none can prepare himself for the battle.

To pray and kidnap ! to commune and rob men's all ! to preach justice, and steal the labourer with his recompence ! to recommend mercy to others, and exhibit cruelty in our own conduct ! to explain religious duties, and ever impede the performance of them ! to propound the example of Christ and his apostles, and declare that a slaveholder imitates them ! to enjoin an observance of the Lord's day, and drive the slaves from the temple of God ! to inculcate every social affection, and instantly exterminate them ! to expatiate upon bliss eternal, and preclude sinners from obtaining it ! to unfold the woes of Tophet, and not drag men from its fire ! are the most preposterous delusion, and consummate mockery.

Slavery is a flagrant violation of every law of God, nature, and society ; it cannot be reconciled with the gospel ; and he who ever acts in direct opposition to the Messias' government, and who indurates his soul against the impressions of that LIGHT, which would convict and regenerate him, cannot be a genuine disciple of HIM, who when the hour was come, invoked his Father, " Sanctify them through thy truth ; thy word is truth !"

EXCUSES FOR SLAVERY.

THE whole defence of slavery is comprised in a plea of right or apology. Every argument upon these principles is nugatory; and may be effectually retorted. They all may be reduced to these allegations.

The antiquity and extensiveness of man-stealing; the design of God that the descendants of Ham should be servants of servants; Jewish example; the silence of the New Testament upon slavery; the title acquired by purchase; the injustice of depriving men of property without an equivalent; the legal impediments to emancipation; the dangers attending a general liberation; and the impracticability of safely effecting the manumission of the slaves.

Ancient and universal practice justifies no transgression. Prophecy is neither the rule of duty nor a vindication of crime. Christ is our exemplar. The scriptures condemn involuntary servitude. No claim to man as property is valid. Men should resign their thefts and make restitution. All civil laws which annul the ordinances of God, are a nonentity. The path of duty is safety. Tyranny with avarice predominates; therefore no method is devised, by which, Columbian slaves! may enjoy the rights of man.

"No formal reproof of slavery occurs in the New Testament. Other vices prevailed at that period, which are not expressly reproved: but they were certainly condemned by the Redeemer and his disciples, as evidently contrary to their doctrine. Polygamy and divorce were allowed and practised, yet no express prohibition of them is recorded; but in many passages of the gospel it is necessarily implied. To detain our fellow men in perpetual slavery is unjust, from many scriptures, particularly from the apostle's exhortation: "Masters, give unto your servants that which is just and equal: knowing that ye also have a Master in heaven: neither is there respect of persons with him."—Colossians 4 : 1. This command alone is sufficient to confute and denounce every man-thief. A slave-holder's justice defrauds his neighbour of his wife, his children, and their labour, deprives them of all religious instruction, and robs them of every terrestrial comfort. His equalizing beneficence destroys all civil and moral relations, amid his stolen dependants. Notwithstanding he simulates that he is the follower of those, " who continued in the apostles' doctrine and fellowship, and in breaking of bread and in prayers, and who parted their possessions and goods to all men, as every man had need." Can it be believed, that he who thus displays his non-conformity to Paul's injunction, is an acceptable member of the same "church of Christ which daily improved not in numbers only, but in the zeal and fervour, holiness and charity of its members; beginning a kind of heavenly life upon earth, and being even in their worldly goods, as well as in their hearts and affections, so perfectly united, that they became the wonder of their very enemies." Neither of the twelve apostles, nor of the seventy disciples, nor of the one hundred and twenty, nor of the three thousand Pentecost converts, nor of the five thousand believers, who saw the miracle performed upon the lame man, nor of the multitudes who were of one heart and one soul, nor of the priests who were obedient to the faith, were man-stealers. Peter and John were not kidnappers; they avowed ; " silver and gold have I none." Joses Barnabas, though a Cyprusian, and all those upon whom was great grace, were not slave pedlars; they sold and gave away lands and houses, but no souls. Paul was no slave driver ; " these hands have ministered unto my necessities, and to them who were with me : we wrought with labour and travail night and day." A slave-holder has no juster claim to the Christian character, than Demas, who forsook the apostle, for the love of the present world ; or Alexander the copper-smith, who did him much evil : " Of whom be thou ware also; for he hath greatly withstood our words."

> " The Fool who doubts, who asks for clearer proof,
> Must hood-wink'd be indeed, and darkness love."

This is the condemnation, that light is come into the

world, and men love darkness rather than light, because their deeds are evil.

The apologists for tyranny state, that Paul advised servants to be contented with their servitude, and obedient to their masters; whom, though he charges to use their slaves well, he commands not to set them free; and that the apostle exhorts bond-servants or slaves to abide with God in that condition: whereas if slavery be sinful, they should not remain in vassalage.—1 Corinthians 7: 20—24.

"Christians were at that period under the government of the heathen; who were watching every opportunity to charge them with designs against the government, to justify their bloody persecutions. In such circumstances had the apostle proclaimed liberty to the slaves, many of them would have been exposed to certain destruction, and the Christian cause might have been ruined, without freeing a single man: this would have been the height of madness and cruelty. It was wise and humane merely to hint, If thou mayest be free, use it rather."—*Rice.*

"This clearly intimates that the persons in slavery whom he addressed might use the means to obtain their freedom. But although a man, from the impossibility of procuring his liberty, may continue with patience and holy contentment in bondage; yet he who detains him in that state, is chargeable with injustice and oppression."—*Brown.*

No man-stealer could have belonged to the church of Christ at Corinth: for this admonition, which is triumphantly adduced as an unanswerable defence of slaveholders, is equivalent to the law of Moses, which prohibits any person from attempting to obstruct a slave in his escape, and enjoins upon all to aid his flight from bondage. Paul knew that the exactions and degradation of captivity were totally incompatible with his preaching: he therefore advised slaves, to procure their freedom without delay, in subordination to the dictates of the Gospel. Wealthy primitive Christians bought the liberty of converted slaves; but though they were thus purchased, Paul instructs the buyers that they were not property; for he commands the manumitted brethren to be no longer unconditional servants, as

they were the Lord's freemen.   He who attempts to arrest
a runaway slave, is a cruel and base citizen-thief; and not
less culpable than the tyrant, who scourges his returned
slave to an inanimate corpse ; for he is an accessory.

The bondage of Onesimus and the high character of
Philemon are often cited to sanction the abominations of
slavery.   Onesimus was a servant for debt, who absconded
previous to its discharge ; yet evangelical philanthropy
exonerated him from all obligation.   When a Christian
kidnapper ! can prove that his slaves owe him any
thing, the plea derived from the servitude of Onesimus
shall be heard.   But while he has done all possible wrong
to his brother, and has stolen his life, his liberty, and his
happiness; and as long as his whole conduct is " incurable injustice ;" we shall affirm, that man-stealers and
their coadjutors are the unlearned and unstable, who wrest
this, as they do also the other scriptures to their own destruction.   Like Simon Magus, slave holders and their
abettors have neither part nor lot in the matter.   They
are in the gall of bitterness and the bond of iniquity ; for
" their hearts are not right in the sight of God."

" It is asserted, that our fellow citizens are made slaves
by law.   They are converted into property by an act of
the legislature ; and under the sanction of that law they
are purchased ; therefore I have a legal claim to them.   To
repeal this law, to annihilate slavery, would be violently
to destroy what I legally purchased with my money, or
inherit from my Father.   It would be equally unjust with
dispossessing me of my horses, cattle, or any other species
of property.   To dispossess me of their offspring would be
injustice equal to dispossessing me of the annual profits of
my estate.

" Many years ago, men, being deprived of their natural
rights were made slaves, and by law converted into property.
That law established iniquity.   It was against the law of
humanity, of common sense, of reason, and of conscience.
However, under the sanction of it, a number of men, regard-
less of its iniquity, made their fellow men their property.
The question is concerning the liberty of a man.   He himself claims it as his own property.   He pleads that it was

originally his own; that he has never forfeited, and he could not alienate it; and therefore by the common laws of justice and humanity, it is still his own. The purchaser of the slave claims the same property. He pleads, that he purchased it under the sanction of a law, enacted by the legislature; and therefore it became his. Who has the best claim? Did this property belong to the legislature? Was it vested in them? If legislatures are possessed of such property as this, may another never exist!" Amen and Amen.

"No individual of their constituents could claim it as their inherent right; it was not in them collectively; and therefore, they could not convey it to their representatives. The legislature could not be possessed of it, and therefore, could not transfer it to another; for they could not give what they themselves had not. Does the property belong to him, who received it from a legislature that had it not to give, and by a law which they had no right to enact; or to the original owner, who could never forfeit his right? If a law should pass to sell an innocent man's head, and I should purchase it, have I in consequence of this law and this purchase, a better claim to the man's head than he has himself? To call our fellow men our property, is a gross absurdity, a contradiction to common sense, and an indignity to human nature. The owners of slaves, then are licensed robbers, and not the just proprietors of what they claim: freeing them is not depriving them of property, but restoring it to the right owner; it is suffering the unlawful captive to escape. It is not wronging the master, but doing justice to the slave, restoring him to himself.

"You say, that emancipation would be unjust, because it would deprive men of their property: but is there no injustice on the other side? Here is a man deprived of all property, of all capacity to possess property, of his own free agency, of the means of instruction, of his wife, of his children, and every thing dear to him; and a man deprived of four or five hundred dollars, which he had stolen. Who is the greatest sufferer, and which is treated with the greatest injustice; Emancipation only takes away property that is its own property, and not ours; property that has the same right to possess us, that we have to possess it; property that has the same right to convert our children into dogs, and calves, and colts, as we have to convert theirs into those beasts: property that may transfer our children to strangers, by the same right that we transfer theirs.

"In America, a slave is a standing monument of the tyranny and inconsistency of human governments. He is declared by the united voice of America, to be by nature free, and entitled to the privilege of acquiring and enjoying property; and yet by laws passed and enforced in these states, he is retained in slavery, and dispossessed of all property and capacity of acquiring any. They have furnished a striking instance of a people carrying on a war in defence of principles, which they are actually and avowedly destroying by legal force; thus using one measure for themselves, and another for their neighbours. All men are by nature free, and entitled to freedom, until they forfeit it. Now to enact that men are slaves, contradicts ourselves; proclaims before the world our inconsistency, and warns men to repose no confidence in us? What credit can we ever expect? What confidence can we repose in each other? NONE.*

"Are we rulers? How can the people confide in us, after we have thus openly declared that we are void of truth and sincerity; and that we are capable of enslaving mankind in direct contradiction to our own principles? What confidence in legislators, who are capable of declaring their constituents all free men in one breath; and in the next, enacting them all slaves? In one breath, declaring that they have a right to acquire and possess property; and, in the next, that they shall neither acquire nor possess it during their existence here? Can I trust my life, my liberty, my property in such hands as these?† Will the colour of my skin prove a sufficient defence against their injustice and cruelty? ‡ Will the particular circumstance of my ances-

---

* The legislatures of the slave holding states have not the confidence of Christians, because they *nullify* the scriptures.

† You are an *idiot*, if you trust men who swear that American citizens are property.

‡ They would *tan* you, or paint you *black*, or steal you *white*, if they dared.

6*

tors being born in Europe, and not in Africa, defend me?*
Will straight hair defend me from the blow that falls so
heavy on the woolly head?†

"If gain is my God, and this may be acquired by unrighteous laws, I may rejoice to find them enacted; but I never
can believe that the legislature were honest men; or repose
the least confidence in them, when interest leads them to
betray it. I never can trust the integrity of that Judge,
who can sit upon the seat of justice, and pass an unrighteous judgment, because it is agreeable to law, when that
law itself is contrary to the light and law of nature."—
Rice.

There is the Connecticut Legislature of 1833, with their
sapient governor, and the honest Judges who expounded
their black law, and all their mischievous accessaries, drawn
by *Rice*, a Presbyterian Minister, in the Kentucky Convention nearly forty years ago, with as much graphical accuracy, as if he had been a resident of Canterbury green,
and had been employed only in watching and depicting
Connecticut barbarism and ungodliness: occasionally
calming his perturbed Christian sensibilities, by the survey
of *Prudence Crandall*, engaged in her "work of faith, and
labour of love, and patience of hope in our Lord Jesus
Christ."

"A legislative contract for the continuance of slavery
must have been void, even from the beginning; for it is
an outrage upon justice, and only another name for fraud,
robbery and murder; as well might an individual think
himself bound by a promise to commit an assassination.
Our proceeding on such grounds, would infringe all the
principles of law, and subvert the very foundation of
morality. Slavery is a mass, a system of enormities,
which incontrovertibly bid defiance to every regulation
which ingenuity can devise, or power effect, but a total
extinction."—*Pitt.*

---

* They would as willingly *kidnap* you as an African; as is
proved by the legislature of Georgia, and the magistrates of George-
town, S. C.

† Yes, until they are not afraid to strike. Witness the Christian Cherokees, and the legislative blood hounds of the South.

" Man-stealers excuse themselves upon the plea, that if the slaves were emancipated, they could hardly be restrained from disorders, which might endanger the public peace. No apprehension of this kind can excuse our continuing in an unjust and inhuman practice. The fear of man bringeth a snare. When the path of duty is plain, Christians should resolutely adhere to it, leaving the event to the Providence of God."—*Brown.*

" Why ought slavery to be abolished? Because it is incurable injustice. Why is injustice to remain for a single hour?"—*Pitt.*

" If the situation of slaves were as happy as servitude could make them, I must not commit the enormous crime of selling man to man; for which not one reason can be given, that is consistent with POLICY, HUMANITY, or JUSTICE."—*Fox.*

" Never was a system so big with wickedness or cruelty; in whatever part of it you direct your view, the eye finds no comfort, no satisfaction, no relief. It is the prerogative of slavery to separate from evil its concomitant good, and to reconcile discordant mischiefs; it robs war of its generosity, it deprives peace of its security. You have the vices of polished society without its knowledge or its comforts; and the evils of barbarism without its simplicity. Its ravages are constant and unintermitted in the extent; in the continuance, universal and indiscriminate. No age, no sex, no rank, no condition is exempt from the fatal influence of this wide-wasting calamity! Thus it is the full measure of pure, unmixed, unsophisticated wickedness; and scorning all competition or comparison, it stands without a rival in the secure, undisputed possession of its detestable pre-eminence."— *Wilberforce.*

Yet in Columbia! Gospel ministers and professing Christians not defend only, but engage in this unparalleled villany! " My bowels, my bowels! I am pained at my very heart; my heart maketh a noise in me: I cannot hold my peace."

Constantine, in the year 313, published an edict which declared all those free who had been condemned to slavery by Maxentius; commanding, under the severest penalties, all who held them in captivity to restore them to their liberty. In the year 316, he enacted another law, and addressed it to Protogenes of Smyrna; by which he permitted all masters to enfranchise their slaves in the presence of Christians, assembled with their pastors in the church, without recurring to the prætors and consuls. "Thus the manumission of slaves which before was attended with great difficulties and expense, became easy, and not chargeable." Christianity will always abolish slavery. No danger attaches to immediate and universal emancipation. The only effectual mode to eradicate the evil, is to destroy thieving by law; to follow Constantine's example; to break every yoke, to let the oppressed go free; and to fulfil Paul's direction, let him that stole steal no more.

The ancient and universal extension of slavery is an effectual argument against the system. Its origin in days of moral darkness affords a powerful plea against its equity and continuance; and the support which modern men-stealers derive from this example is visionary. Servitude in Abraham's family was very different from the degradation of our coloured population. Eliezer of Damascus was the patriarch's steward; and his servants, had he died childless, would have been his heirs. But as they worshipped Abraham's God, and were included in the covenant made with him, they were governed with paternal benevolence. The heads of families when they lived a wandering life, were civil governors of all who served them.

The original Hebrew states not that the domestics whom Abraham bought with his money, or who were descended from them, were involuntary servants; for the word includes no such idea, as modern slavery. Our laws, opinions, practice, and management of these degraded sons of wretchedness, all declare, that in our judgment, they are merely cattle in human shape.

From the conduct of Isaac and Jacob, no principle can be deduced in defence of slavery. Modern slave-holders shall have all the consolation which they can extract from

their long-protracted man-stealing, when they can evidence
their title to the approbation which the Lord expressed of
those patriarchs.

By almost universal antiquity, an incessant violation of
every law of decency, virtue, and religion might be established as the highest duty of man.

How astonishing the fact! Professing Christians transform the bible into a minister of unrighteousness; and
when impelled from one subterfuge resort to another. If
Nimrod's oppressions are urged against their impiety, they
take refuge in Abraham's faith; and if the patriarch's justice and judgment, which they never exemplify, inculcate
their condemnation, they shelter themselves under the prediction of Noah, which denounced servitude as the inheritance of Canaan's posterity; thus perverting the word of
God into a sanction of their abominations.

The declaration that Canaan's descendants shall be servants is thrice repeated; but Ham's other posterity are
not included; for Ham's name is not even introduced.
The denunciation of Noah has been remarkably verified
in the history of the Canaanites, who from the period
when the iniquity of the Amorites was full, have seldom
been released from the exactions of foreign tyrants. But
if the prophecy be referred to the descendants of Ham
generally, the curse has not been experienced by these
people. The partial slavery of the modern Africans will
not invalidate the truth; because no ancient and accessi-
ble part of the inhabited globe is so completely unknown,
as the interior of Africa.

Would the passage even bear the construction which
slave-dealers assert, their criminality would not be diminished. The mercy of God has not revealed to us the
knowledge of future occurrences, if the actions which
shall produce the events detailed include guilt in the perpetrator, that we may unite in the completion of them; but
that the truth of the scriptures may be indubitably established.

This transmutation of the word of God, by claiming a
prophetic curse, or a controverted doctrine, or a dubious
scripture, as a rule for our actions, and a defence for our

sins; thereby authorizing any man to distort the sacred oracles into a prediction of crimes which he had resolved to commit, is a most dangerous and reprehensible delusion. God has most emphatically attested, that his wrath shall be effused upon Babylon; but the persons who shall execute the judgment will doubtless perform the grand design, from selfish and ambitious views. Christians will mark the progress of the vengeance, and rejoice in the destruction, but they will not actively participate in the horrors of the tremendous overthrow.

Martin Luther and Henry VIII. were employed in diminishing the Papal supremacy. The reformer engaged the antichristian domination with the armour of God; his was a bloodless contest, waged from celestial motives, conducted with evangelic ardour, productive of the most glorious triumphs, and rewarded with honour and immortality. A tyrant's acts, through the dispensations of an all-benevolent God, involved a partially similar result; but his arms were terrestrial power, his war was a combat for superiority, his impulse was lasciviousness, his fervour was the offspring of ambition and sensuality, and his memory is consigned to unmitigable execration.

American citizen-dealers adduce the Mosaic law and Jewish example as an excuse for their avarice; but this originates in ignorance of the ancient economy, or misinterpretation of the Book, or a falsification of the facts, or corrupt deductions from the scriptural narrative.

Every practice which requires a sophistical interpretation of the sacred volume to countenance it, must be sin. The path of duty is illumination: and in morals and religion, any action which obliges us to search after arguments to pacify us in the perpetration of it, is a transgression of the divine command.

The theocratical establishment was appointed by God, to preserve the children of Israel a distinct nation. To them were committed the divine oracles, that the fundamental principles of all religion and morality might not be totally banished from the earth. The severest regulations respecting their intercourse with idolaters were consequently indispensable. All the inhibitions of their lawgiver, which referred to the Gentiles, were promulged to preserve the Israelites pure from the surrounding contagion; and it was necessary that the worshippers of false gods who might reside among them, or who might be subdued in war, should be considered as people inferior to themselves, on account of their ignorance of Jehovah, the only true God. They were therefore authorized to retain such persons as bond-servants. But the Jewish writers attest, that Heathens who had been thus held, if they continued idolaters at the close of the first year, were remanded to the country whence they were procured. If they remained in the land, having acknowledged the Lord God of Israel, unless they voluntarily consented to stay with their masters, and the recognition of this fact was most solemn and public, they were manumitted at the return of the Sabbatical year. Even if they had thus devoted themselves to the service of others, at the sound of the Jubilee trumpet, every man throughout the land of Canaan, was instantaneously free. Had not this been Jewish practice, it would not have displayed the events which it was destined to prefigure.

The Mosaic law has been most grossly distorted for avaricious purposes. By it the Jews were authorized to retain the neighbouring idolaters for bondmen, but their offspring could not have been thus held in bondage; because every child born in the family was circumcised at eight days old, became a member of the covenant, and was heir to all the blessings of Palestine, as much as a real descendant of the Father of the faithful: a Jew could not steal, sell, or make merchandise of one of these, more than he could have violently transported one of his brethren for sale to the land of the Ishmaelites.—Levit. 25 : 44—46.

Jewish history affords an insurmountable objection to slavery. Joshua and the elders, to punish their deception, doomed the Gibeonites to perpetual attendance at the temple; but Saul's oppression of their descendants was the cause of a three years' dearth in the land.—2 Samuel 21 : 1—14. The sword, pestilence, and famine, were denounced against Judah, in consequence of their unrighteous exactions from the widow, the orphan, the impo-

verished, the stranger, and those whom they had enslaved.—Jeremiah 34 : 8—22.

How seductive is avarice! Notwithstanding the Jews
had not long been released from Chaldean vassalage, yet
speedily after their return to Canaan, they began to oppress
the poor, and to defraud the wretched; contrary to the law
of Moses, and in direct defiance of their own sensibilities,
agitated still with the remembrance of the miseries which
in banishment they had endured. Nehemiah 5 : 1—12
If involuntary servitude be defensible upon moral principles,
high example would sanction it; but it would not be
known that slavery existed among the Jews, if the prophets
had not menaced them for this atrocious criminality.   So
far is the Mosaic code from legalizing the cruelty which
slave-dealers constantly exhibit, that a considerable proportion of the Jewish legislator's mandates are solely directed
to the inculcation of merciful tempers, and the exhibition
of generous affections towards inferiors.

To impress the children of Israel with a permanent sense
of all the horrors of captivity, to imbue them with the most
active sympathy for human wo, and to nurture the most
ardent desires and zeal to mitigate the distresses of their
fellow-men; they were continually reminded of the degradation, wretchedness, and oppressions, under which their
ancestors in Egypt so long groaned, and whence they were
delivered solely by the arm of Jehovah Nissi.   The recollection of their former national servitude, and the miracles
which were requisite to deliver them from their task-
masters, must have inspired in every pious Jew, a holy
and insuperable aversion to the principles and practice of
slavery, and every iniquitous approach to the infliction of
that wo.   Soul-merchants can designate no heaven delega-
ted prophet, no exemplary priest, no Christian apostle, no
martyred disciple of the Lamb that was slain, no triumphant
reformer, and no immortal stern confessor of the rights of
man and liberty of conscience, who was a slave-driver! nor
can they name one of them upon whom was great grace,
of " whom the world was not worthy, strangers and pilgrims on earth," who was a man-stealer's coadjutor.
From the exalted abodes of perennial felicity, in which the

spirits of just men " made perfect" dwell, if they know what
passes upon earth, they must feel all holy indignation,
" that men of corrupt minds, destitute of the truth, who
suppose that gain is godliness," should pervert their characters, opinions, and example, into a mass of hard-heartedness, worldly equivocations, and the "highest kind of
theft ;" with the direct view of procuring a sanction from
the pious dead, for the iniquitous practices of the ungodly
living.

Columbians plead justification for stealing and enslaving
Africans.   They are of a different colour, and not Christians; therefore, we are authorized to kidnap them for our
avarice and luxury.   Such was an old Algerine's defence
for selling every "infidel dog" whom he could grasp.   " He is
not a Mussulman," said the Corsair ; " his white skin shows
that he is not of our prophet's family ; seize, work, and torment him."

Thus men depart from the ways of righteousness ! Their
principles are deceptive.   Their desires are replete with
covetousness.   Their solicitudes are earthly, sensual,
devilish ! And to them the gospel is hid, because the god
of this world hath blinded their minds !

Christ and the apostles are our sole infallible pattern.
The admission of varied temporary indulgences among the
Israelites, as a basis for our conduct, would totally destroy
society.   If the examples of David, Solomon and others,
are valid, in cases where they acted without or against the
directions of the Mosaic code, the gospel is nugatory, and
Christ has died in vain.

At the promulgation of the law from mount Sinai, to render its prescriptions more authoritative, the Lord enforced
its requisitions by reminding them of *his* mercy and power,
and of *their* misery ; claiming obedience for his character,
his loving-kindness, and their deliverance.   " I am the
Lord thy God, who brought thee out of the land of Egypt,
out of the house of bondage."

A company of Ishmaelites, with a horde of stolen captives,
approach the habitation of a man who conscientiously desires to fulfil the law of God.   They offer to sell him an
Egyptian. A Levite accosts him, and asks ; Can you recon-
7

cile the purchase of that man, with all the horrors which
are included in the declaration of Jehovah, as the exordium
of the law, and with the mercy which the code invariably requires? With this recollection could he buy a
bondman?

An Arab with a number of kidnapped Africans traffics
slaves at a Columbian's door. Say to him, were not you
oppressed by a foreign power, you rebelled and obtained
your freedom, how can you enthral these outcasts? dare
you purchase these heirs of wo, who were stolen at their
birth, and can you enslave them forever? You swear, that
all men are born free; you believe, that man-stealing is
the greatest criminality; you know, that slave-holding is contrary to equity, humanity, and reciprocal benevolence;
you feel, that you would most ardently reprobate and resist
such conduct if it were attempted respecting you; and
your conscience assures you, that God will requite you, as
you injure your fellow-men. But he buys, and enslaves
these wretched victims of avarice! A Christian republican! No charity can induce the belief that a man who
acknowledges the excellence of pure and undefiled religion,
can be so incurably blinded; or that the moral sense can
be so completely extinguished. that he is incapable to perceive the difference between evangelical righteousness, and
incessant cruelty, rapine, and oppression.

No disciple of Messias can plead Jewish example.
" Call no man master upon earth." Slave-dealers must
demonstrate, either that the Lord and his primitive disciples were slave-holders, or that their doctrines and precepts
countenance the system.

As he who had not where to lay his head and his apostles were not human flesh weighers, oppressors plead,
that the New Testament is altogether silent upon slavery;
and if it were so condemnable, it would have been pointedly
reprobated. Our Lord did not admonish man-stealers, by
their own appellation, to desist from their ungodliness; but
he who can reconcile the Redeemer's doctrines and apostolic injunctions with American bondage, can join heaven
and hell. To him, vice and virtue, equity and injustice,
kindness and cruelty, oppression and benevolence, thieving

and probity, infidelity and religion, all are identical. All defence of slavery, upon the silence of the New Testament respecting this crime, is baseless.

" All things whatsoever ye would that men should do unto you, do ye even so unto them ; for this is the law and the prophets." If any man can deduce the injustice, the barbarity, and the oppressions of man-stealing, from this fundamental rule of social reciprocity, his moral alembic must combine properties vastly different from any extractor yet discovered.

The holy scriptures either immediately reprobate covetousness, extortion, and tyranny, or they inculcate justice, philanthropy, and mercy ; and it is absolutely impossible to conjoin their directions and examples with the bondage of men ; or even to explain them in any manner, by which slave-holders are not most indignantly and awfully censured.

American citizen stealers aver, that they have a just title to their slaves. How can a claim to the human race as property be valid? All our terrestrial possessions were included in the original grant made to Adam in Paradise ; and to Noah and his sons after the deluge. But human life, with all the concomitants which are necessary to a fulfilment of its objects, was excepted. Therefore, no title, by any lapse of time, or any distance of transfer, or any terrestrial authority, ever could be made to the persons of men.

" They innocently and honestly obtained possession of their slaves, they say, and if the State liberate them, they ought to be remunerated." What obduracy ! Men require to be paid for ceasing from the highest kind of theft ; and demand to be requited for delivering up that which they have stolen. How can a slave-driver be innocent or honest, in his connexion with his dependants ? No domestic tyrant believes his own assertion, he feels, that he is a cruel oppressor ! and instead of rewarding men for stealing no more, the whole that they have *filched* from their kidnapped and tortured fellow citizens, with ample additional damages for all the misery and cruelty which they have endured, should be righteously exacted.

Among all the proofs of matchless impudence in practical villany, slavery and slavites furnish that example which defies any comparable similitude. The Americans who have been constantly kidnapping, and robbing, and torturing their defenceless fellow citizens, for sixty years past, demand compensation for abandoning that traffic which, by the supreme law of the United States is piracy, when perpetrated in another form, and in a different climate.

In all the annals of crime, where the iniquity has been perpetrated by only one or a few felons, no obdurate effrontery equal to that of American slave-holders has once been recorded. Who ever heard of a robber, or a forger, or a plundering assassin standing up in a Courthouse, and boldly admitting and justifying his theft and bloodshed. Not only denying the propriety of his arrest, and denouncing all his pretended trial as irrelevant ; but also defending the legality of his claim to the property which he had purloined, and demanding compensation for the value which had been taken from him, with a full guaranty against all future interruption in his *honest* employ. The Court in compassion might pronounce such a man a fit resident for the Lunatic Asylum, but they could not accept his defence of the robbery and murder. This, however, is childlike innocence when contrasted with the audacious turpitude of American men-stealers.

On the face of the globe, American slavites have now no counterparts except in two distinct bodies of men. the gangs of banditti who watch the passes of the Alps, the Appenines, &c., to pilfer all they can seize, and to obtain which booty, they will shoot or stab one or twenty opponents without concern or remorse. But when the *gentlemen* have terminated the affray ; those humane and merciful people will restore your wife and children and your baggage which to them may be useless, for a sufficient compensation—and will also give you a token to preserve you from all further alarm and plunder ; only provided that you agree to pay a certain sum to any of their honourable professional brethren, who in future may meet you within their domains. We are always reviling this system, because it places in jeopardy every stranger who visits Italy, or Spain, or France. Our denunciations may be spared; for our own civilized land-pirates kidnap a thousand where those *more honourable* mountain bandits grasp but one. Our felons are always stealing without excuse; whereas those half starving outcasts of the European world only plunder and kill when sensuality, or hunger, or opposition, or their satanic religion, Popery, enforces them.

The other allies of the American "brokers in the trade of blood" are those proverbially amiable and self-denying philanthropists, the exemplary hordes of wandering Arabs. In them the family likeness is complete; for they feel no puling reserves; they profess no canting scruples; but fearlessly maintain their simple code of laws in all their authority. Whatever promotes their interest or enjoyment is *expedient*, and that which is expedient is *right,* provided power can obtain it; and then as one of their American confederates adjudges, "*the majority are justly entitled to divide the spoil.*" These Ishmaelites in two respects are exactly like the western caitiffs. They will release from captivity, their "*worn out, damaged, diseased and aged slaves,*" and let them "return to their own country," if they can be paid their claim in sequins or dollars. Thus their American accomplices will liberate and transport to their Botany Bay in Africa, the creatures whom they have previously starved and tortured to death's door. This is their republican and Christian benevolence! The Arabs also declare, that their mode of life has been prolonged through a hundred generations, and custom is law. Just such is the defence of the man-stealers in Virginia, Carolina, and Georgia. "Our fathers stole Africans, and we will kidnap Americans. Blessed be the Lord God!" say these impious servants of the devil, "our ancestors could only procure a few score thousands; but since the declaration of Independence, we have caught about ten times as many in proportion; and we will never abandon our glorious trade and employment." Yet these are the men, who are always boasting of their Christianity and their republicanism. Not only Mohammed, but even Satan himself can advance just as good a claim, and exhibit equally honest pretensions to be either one or the other.

7*

" I would rather be a dog, and bay the moon,
Than such a Democratic Christian!"

Legislatures have obstructed the emancipation of slaves.
Thus slave-holders elect men to enact iniquitous laws, and
exonerate themselves by the legislative proceedings. Every
voter for a public officer, who will not destroy the system,
is as culpable as if he participated in the evil, and is responsible for the protraction of the crime. If a slave cannot
be liberated in one state, he may in another, and it is an
individual's duty to exonerate himself. No human law
should be obeyed when it contravenes the divine command ;
but slavery is the combination of all iniquity, and therefore
every man is obligated not to participate in its corruption.
In all cases obedience to the divine will combines the
most certain safety. God will protect those who act in
conformity with his commands : and as no plea can avail
for the continuance of slavery one moment; the most secure mode to be absolved from danger, is to " cease to do
evil and learn to do well." The national difficulty is not
from emancipation, but from servitude. Slave pedlars say
that if the coloured people were free, the property and lives
of the white inhabitants would be jeoparded. They know
that this excuse for their sin is impudent mendacity. Some
slaves probably are so vitiated, that at first they might
commit a few petty depredations, but they would soon be
corrected by the restraints of the civil law. Besides, as
the southern coloured citizens have never witnessed any
practices in their tyrants but oppression and robbery, it
would be preposterous not to anticipate, that the unin-
structed inferior would act like them, whom he has seen
honoured and beloved in proportion to the quantum of his
theft. A white person in the southern states, who is not
a man-thief, is despised. If he has kidnapped twenty, he
is a gentleman ; but if he has stolen a hundred, he is a
nabob.
How shall we expel the evil ? Colonization is not only
totally impracticable ; but it is merely a *swindling scheme
to obtain money upon fraudulent pretexts ! Eject slave-holders
from all public offices ; and exclude all men-stealers from the*

church of Christ! All other measures are futile. Every plea and excuse in support of slavery being therefore invalid, originating in depravity, sustained by corruption, and productive of all diversified ungodliness, no Christian consistently can allege them, to extenuate or justify that "mystery of iniquity."

SLAVERY AND SLAVEHOLDERS.

The ensuing essay was written originally for the prize which was offered by the late President of the N. E. Anti-Slavery Society, for the best concise discussion upon that subject. The convention to whom was confided the examination of the comparative merits of the pieces which might be submitted to their inspection, never assembled, and consequently no award was made. In an abridged form modified for the purpose, it has been delivered as an oration, both in Boston and Providence, and not without effect, in aid of the cause of truth and freedom.

To no part of this picture of slavery will there probably be more objections. It is anticipated that every base epithet which slavites and their accessaries so well know how to employ, will be applied to this faithful exhibition of the natural effects of slavery upon the slave-holders; but no reply will be made to any caviller, unless he is a preacher, and signs his own name; and unless omitting all irrelevant topics, he confines himself to the pages which he may venture to condemn.

Time and labour now are too precious to be wasted in boyish fencing with a blunt lath, and shooting, children like, with pop guns. *The present contest is a war for the extermination of slavery.* We have drawn " the two-edged sword of the spirit," and have cast away that vile scabbard, " the fear of man that bringeth a snare," in which, alas! it has been too long buried to the hilt; and we defy all preachers of every denomination to point out any essential inaccuracy in the ensuing delineations.

The manuscript of this essay, was submitted to a most competent judge in the southern states, who expressed unqualified approbation of the fidelity with which the effects of slavery herein are described. When it was announced in Boston, after the meeting was dissolved, a minister of that city remarked to me,—" Although your delineations are doubtless correct, as I have witnessed them during several years in Carolina ; yet I doubt, that they will mislead. They are not introduced as isolated cases, but as generally descriptive of slavery." I replied, " Certainly. I have given you a picture of slavery, as I saw it for nearly seven years in Virginia. There are doubtless some exceptions ; but they are so ' few and far between,' that the number of them is altogether unimportant. Oblige me by running your mental survey for a moment over the field which you know." He paused as if in deep thought, and presently added, " It is best to say nothing about it."

There was present at the same meeting in Boston, an old penitent slave-trader, who had commanded a ship for kidnapping Africans, and who had sailed from Charleston in that piratical traffic, I think, not less than twenty years. He not only declared aloud that the descriptions were correct, but that the only fault was in their deficiency ; and also publicly stated frightful circumstances, which he affirmed at that period were notorious in Carolina as the day. One only of those public facts that he narrated, could it possibly be placed before our northern ladies, would make every female ear tingle ; and would raise a storm of Christian enthusiasm, which all the Neros and Domitians in Columbia and Milledgeville, in vain would attempt to appease.

THE NATURAL EFFECTS OF SLAVERY ON THE SLAVEHOLDERS.

All our principles respecting slavery, are comprised in the following fundamental axioms of reciprocal justice and philanthropy.

" Thou shalt love thy neighbour as thyself.

Jesus Christ, Lord of all.

" He that stealeth a man, and selleth him, or if he be found in his hand, he shall surely be put to death." Exodus 21 : 16. " Thou shalt not deliver unto his master the servant, who is escaped from his master unto thee : he shall dwell with thee ; thou shalt not oppress him." Deuteronomy 23 : 15, 16. " If a man be found stealing one of his brethren of the children of Israel, and maketh merchandise of him, then that *Thief* shall die." Deuteronomy 24 : 7.

Moses, the Lawgiver to Israel.

" As thou hast done, it shall be done unto thee, thy reward shall return upon thine own head." Verse 15.

Obadiah, a Jewish Prophet.

" Give unto your servants that which is just and equal." Colossians 4 : 1. " The law is not made for a righteous man ; but for men-stealers." 1 Timothy 1 : 10.

Paul, a Christian Apostle.

" All men are by nature equally free and independent, and have certain inherent rights ; of which, when they enter into a state of society they cannot, by any compact deprive or divest their posterity ; namely the enjoyment of life and liberty, with the means of acquiring and possessing property, and pursuing and obtaining happiness and safety."

Virginia Bill of Rights.

" If there be, within the extent of our knowledge and influence, any participation in this traffic in slaves let us pledge ourselves, upon the *Rock of Plymouth*, to extirpate and destroy it. It is not fit that the land of the pilgrims should bear the shame longer. Let that spot be purified, or let it be set aside from the Christian world ; let it be put out of the circle of human sympathies and human regards ; and let civilized men henceforth have no communion with it.

I invoke those who fill the seats of justice, and all who minister at her altar, that they exercise the wholesome and necessary severity of the law. I invoke the ministers of our religion, that they proclaim its denunciation of those crimes, and add its solemn sanction to the authority of human laws. If the pulpit be silent, whenever or wherever there may be a sinner bloody with this guilt, within the hearing of its voice, the pulpit is false to its trust."

Daniel Webster.

"There is a law above all the enactments of human codes; the same throughout the world; the same in all times; such as it was before the daring genius of Columbus pierced the night of ages, and opened to one world the sources of power, wealth and knowledge; and to another, all unutterable woes; and such as it is this day. It is the law written by the finger of God on the heart of man ; and by that law, unchangeable and eternal, while men despise fraud, and loath rapine, and abhor blood, they shall reject with indignation the wild and guilty fantasy, that man can hold property in man."

Henry Brougham.

The natural effects of slavery, as it now exists in the United States, upon the slaveholders, comprise a pungent and shocking topic for consideration, replete equally with sorrow and alarm.   Slavery is contrary to justice, the rights of man, common benevolence, the dictates of reason, mercy, natural conscience, and the spirit and practice which are inculcated by the religion of Christ Jesus.   Hence all the laws that have ever been enacted, or which are now in force, that admit the right, or the operation of slavery before God, are utterly null and void; being an audacious usurpation of the divine prerogative; a daring infringement of the law of nature; a base overthrow of the very foundations of the social compact; a complete extinction of all the relations, endearments, and obligations of mankind; and a presumptuous transgression of all the Lord's commandments.

Consequently, to expect any thing but evil, and evil continually, as the result of slavery, is equally absurd, as to anticipate, that we can "gather grapes from thorns, and figs from thistles." Causes and effects are inseparable. Moral corruption invariably engenders iniquity; and in no circumstances, has the proverbial truth, "like begets like," been more infallibly and awfully verified, than in the history of slavery and slaveholders.

Slavery originated in avarice, indolence, treachery, evil concupiscence, and barbarity; and its constant fruits have been robbery, disease, faithlessness, profligacy of every species, and murder. Crimes of every degree, and blood-stained with all hues of atrocity and cruelty, have incessantly marked its course, until, after three hundred years of infernal desolations, the long-suffering of God, and the patience of man are almost exhausted. An exhibition of the unavoidable "effects of slavery on the slaveholders," as they have been proved by the experience of successive generations, may excite the zealous efforts of Christian philanthropy for the extinction of that appalling abomination; and may also induce the superior grade of the present race of oppressors to pause, reflect, "cease to do evil, and learn to do well;" and thus to escape from the gulf of destruction and despair, which is yawning to receive them.

1. The first effect of slavery on the slaveholders, is this: *it inflames them with haughty self conceit.*

It is the primary and most permanent notion which an infant in a slaveholder's family imbibes; that a slaveholder, is a being of a superior nature, character, quality, and rank. By that vile system, which transforms one class of mankind into a species of brutes, he is unceasingly influenced, and in every variety of form. As soon as the child can make a sign or may be transferred to another's care, some other child of the same, or of the different sex, is constituted the young despot's tool and property. To it he holds an admitted title; and the coloured boy or girl is considered as nothing more than a machine, which may be coerced to perform every act that the caprices of a froward child may dictate; or to submit to any mischievous tricks, which the youthful domestic tyrant may devise for his amusement.

As the child grows in capacity to observe the state of society around him he perceives, that there is a broad palpable distinction existing between those who are of a white appearance, and human beings with a coloured skin. He beholds differences which are too obvious and influential, not to make a decisive and lasting impression upon his moral character. A white man and woman, as they pass under his cognizance, are comfortably housed, sumptuously clothed, luxuriously fed, instructed, and without employment; all whose days revolve in one perennial round of sensual ease, thoughtless indulgence, and dissipating amusements. On the contrary, he views the coloured people excluded from all comfort, and immured in a hut far inferior in proportionate warmth, cleanliness, and conveniences to the stable, or the chicken-coop, or the doghouse, or even the hog-pen. Men and women, with scarcely covering enough to conceal their bodies, and of a quality so coarse, or in such a tattered condition, that it is little security against the weather, and which defies all ingenuity to render it whole and decent, he daily witnesses, subject to every possible privation. In vain for the American coloured citizen, are cows milked, swine fattened, poultry fed, the calf killed, and exuberant harvests gathered into the garner! Of the products obtained by his own labour, the wretched slave partakes not,—and can a youth, who watches all this machination of robbery continuously perpetrated with impunity, be any other way impressed, than with a proud self-complacency, that he is of a more excellent order of beings, for whom those children of bondage and wretchedness are ever doomed to toil?

He mingles with his own class of persons, and as soon as his mind is enlarged, and he is competent, he is placed under a tutor for instruction in the useful and ornamental acquisitions; but *his own* "negro fellow, and negro wench," as they are disdainfully termed, remain in the same natural darkness, and grow up with all the animal passions becoming more uncontrollable, and without a single particle of moral restraint to tame their fury; while the youthful despot himself habitually learns wickedness from his enslaved associates. Is it possible, as he extends his knowledge, that the white youth can resist the deep-rooted conviction, that his coloured boy and girl and himself are of a totally separate rank in creation? can we wonder that the slave-holders struts and boasts, " I was born a gentleman, and that is my negro."

The child of the slaveholder looks abroad, and surveys a large domain. On it, he discerns that there are seven or ten white residents, who have no labour, but that which they voluntarily perform; and even that is more for relief from langour, than for the sake of exercise; intermitted and re-sumed exactly as their humour dictates: and with this solitary exception, their whole life is one incessant alter-nation of indolence, uselessness, vanity, and vice. Look at the contrast! He explores; and lo! forty or fifty or one hundred coloured persons of all ages and hues, around the house, are driven to incessant labour. To them, relaxa-tion is almost unknown. Of sufficient repose they are always deprived. Their complaints are not only disregard-ed, but most probably punished. Every varied torture urges the muscular machinery on, until its energies decay; and the unpitied victim prematurely wastes by disease, and is buried in forgetfulness, with no other emotion than regret for the pecuniary loss.

A system which naturally produces these morbid feel-ings of self-sufficiency, that one, or a few white persons shall contemn a multitude of coloured men and women around them, as if they were no more than two-legged beasts, stationed in the world solely to contribute to the rapacity of their task masters, and thereby to furnish the means of gratifying every turbulent passion, and every licentious desire of the corrupt heart, in its very spirit, must be vile; and not less abominable in its effects than it was detestable in its origin, and is criminal in its con-tinuance. This inflated arrogance extinguishes all ten-dency toward that grace of humility, which is the first principle and predominant temper of those who desire to escape from " the wrath to come;" and without which, the gracious Redeemer who was " meek and lowly in heart," hath assured us, in the benediction which he pro-

nounced upon the "poor in spirit," that "no man can enter the kingdom of heaven."

2. A *marble-hearted insensibility* is the second natural effect which slavery produces upon slave-holders.

To expect feeling, compunction, commiseration, mercy,
benevolence, and their correct kindred qualities from slave-
holders, is a self-evident absurdity. There may be partial
or temporary exhibitions of something like these mental
and moral exercises, but they are only sudden and casual
excitements; which are never displayed in their appropriate sphere. We frequently hear of liberality and kindness developed by slave-holders, but it is toward their own
associates; and obviously more for show and fame, or
from the force of example, than from principle; because
they are not manifested in the proper form, and in favour
of the legitimate objects.

Slave-holders are often eulogized for their hospitality;
and the fact implied is true, if by hospitality is intended a
willingness to feast with those who are of similar character, habits, and principles. " They make dinners and
suppers, and call their friends, their brethren, their kins-
men, and their rich neighbours, who bid them again, and
make recompense to them,"—but who ever heard of a
slave-driver's obedience to the Lord's admonition, Luke
14: 12—14, to "make a feast, and call the poor, the
maimed, the lame, and the blind" enslaved descendants of
the kidnapped Africans, who till his lands, and honestly can
claim the reward of their unintermitting fatigue and toil?

It is manifestly impossible, that genuine religious,
moral, or even merely human sensibility can exist in the
same heart where the arrogance of slavery reigns. Selfishness is an essential ingredient in that overweening esti-
mate of his own importance, which is inseparable from a
slave-holder's principles; and an unfeeling indifference,
or a contemptuous disregard of the necessities and anguish
of others; especially when the haughty notions of characteristic superiority, which slave-holders imbibe and culti-
vate, are combined with them; is as indissolubly united
with slavery, as in his view, a coloured skin is conjoined
with degradation.

The children of slave-holders observe all these proceedings from their youth; and having no other examples before their eyes, and no counteracting instructions either from the literary preceptor, or from the professed minister of Jesus Christ; most awful and condemnable silence! they grow up in a reckless unconcern to all the miseries which they behold; until the softer emotions of humanity are absorbed in the unholy conviction, that they are authorized to treat their slaves without any of those attachments, and sympathies, and reciprocities, which belong to man in his social relations: and thus according to the natural progress of evil, the mind and heart and conscience become callous to every idea of rectitude and feeling, when the subject refers to the situation and claim of the despised and afflicted slave.

The contradictory character of slave-holders in this respect is aptly illustrated by a descriptive phrase, which is common in the slave states. "He is a very kind and gentlemanly man at home; or he is a good Christian in his house and at the church; but he is a devil on his plantation." This account of slave-holders may be heard, in every direction, from Philadelphia to the gulf of Mexico, and it unfolds the abhorrent qualities of slavery, and its pernicious influence upon those who are engaged in it. Slave-driving transforms men into monsters, and leaves the large mass of that portion of society to be ranked among the *unaccountables,* who for one hour claim our respect, as valuable associates; and for the rest of the day, demand our execration as ruthless barbarians. Such however is the invariable consequence of man-stealing; and to it may be imputed all the misery which that ungodly contrivance inflicts: because to endeavour to unite slavery and benevolence, and tenderness, and "bowels of mercies, and brotherly kindness, and charity," is just as preposterous, as it would be to strive to "change an Ethiopian's skin, or a leopard's spots."

3. The third natural effect of slavery upon slave-holders is this; *They become sensual; and lose that instinctive pudicity which God, for the wisest and holiest purposes, has implanted in the hearts of mankind.*

In the houses of slave-holders, you behold young ladies elegantly attired and attended by their coloured sisters, children of the same father, and yet slaves. You recognise the driver of the carriage, the footman, and other domestics as manifestly the planter's own offspring. What effect this must have upon unrestrained youth, no person can doubt; especially when it is recollected that no relationship is admitted to exist between the coloured attendant upon the sister, and her brother, who either forces or coaxes the girl to submit to his lawless desires. All the relations of life are thus confounded in one bestial indiscriminate mixture, for the matrimonial covenant cannot exist among slaves.

Coloured boys and girls grow up together in nakedness, until they arrive at almost mature age; and in the most exposed condition, wait upon visiters, in the presence of youth, when the smallest sense of propriety would urge their exclusion; and where they remain in attendance, without any apparent idea on the part even of the females, of the glaring, shameless indecorum which every moment meets their eyes.

Young coloured women, stripped to a thin, scanty body garment, after the most offensively indecent examination, are publicly placed in scales, weighed, and sold by the pound.

" Breeding wenches," as they are shockingly termed in the slave-holder's ungodly and impure phraseology, are as .regularly nurtured and trafficked, expressly to supply the human flesh-market, as a northern farmer endeavours to improve and enlarge his stock of horses, cattle, hogs, and sheep.

On many plantations bribes are offered expressly to encourage the utmost licentiousness that children may be born; who are always for sale, provided rapacity can be satisfied; and thus all maternal and parental and pure domestic feelings wither and die.

With comparatively few exceptions, the slave plantations are a scene of promiscuous uncleanness, of the most abhorrent character, which defies all attempts to preserve the existence of decency, personal or social. The child of

Selling Females by the pound.   Page 88.

a slave-holder sees and hears this unrestricted iniquity in
every form, and all the year round. It is open to the boy
who roams about with his youthful slave, and cannot be
concealed from his sisters in their domesticated seclusion.
The influence which this loathsome turpitude, in its undisguised deformity, must unavoidably exert upon the un-
formed character of youth, who are accustomed to scarcely
any moral or religious restraint, it requires very little
perspicacity to comprehend. The ineffable abominations
and unnatural barbarities that flow from this part alone of
the system of man-stealing, which prohibits and cancels
all the divinely appointed connexions of life; which exterminates all domestic endearments and relative tenderness, and which openly encourages the utmost practicable
lewdness, all condemn this satanic contrivance to utter
and universal execration.

No topic connected with slavery requires a more complete and barefaced exposure, than the duties and transgressions which are included in the seventh commandment. The time has arrived when the true state of domestic society, and the inexpressible wretchedness of woman's degradation, as they exist among the man-stealers
must be fully developed. For this most *frightful* licentiousness, the female slave-drivers are chiefly responsible.
They would rather connive at the grossest sensuality in
their husbands, sons, fathers, and brothers, than abandon
the system which enables them to live in luxury and indolence.

One of the most remarkable anomalies of human frailty
is exhibited in the incredulity which men manifest in reference to practical truth and the evidences of ungodliness;
and also the facility with which sinners believe every fiction, when it gratifies selfishness, or flatters pride. Many
persons make extensive journeys through the south, and
having felt no anxiety to understand the character of
slavery, or through interest, having resolved to know
nothing at all of the system, they return not only ignorant,
but *false witnesses;* for they avow that the most notorious
facts are fictions; because they had not seen such occurrences: while they craftily take care not to state, that so

far as slavery is concerned, they travelled perfectly blind-
folded.

Some years ago, a Baptist minister of Vermont was appointed a delegate to a number of Baptist associations.
When he arrived in Philadelphia, he professed his intention to attend several of the associations in Virginia; and
was especially anxious to comprehend the true character
and operations of slavery. In that city he met with some
Brethren who understood the arcana of that hell-born contrivance; and by them he was warned not to be imposed
upon by the external glitter, and the comfortable drapery
of the menial attendants about the mansion-house, assumed during the meeting of the association, and then
carefully laid aside for a similar festival; but he was enjoined privately to visit the "Negro Quarter," as the miserable huts of the coloured citizens are familiarly called.
Thus adequately instructed, he proceeded on his journey.

About one fourth of the time, which he had specified for
his absence, had elapsed, when the Green Mountaineer
was at the deacon's house in Philadelphia, and accounted
for his speedy return by a statement to this effect. He
had travelled on, gradually becoming more and more dis-
satisfied with the scenes which he daily witnessed, until
he arrived about the Appomattox river, where he was received at the house of one of the slave-driving Nabobs,
on the evening prior to the meeting of the association.
The next morning after breakfast, he proposed to take a
walk, and by a circuitous route unperceived, he obtained
access to the "worn out slaves." From them he speedily
heard the heart-rending recital of their awful prison-house;
the female violations, the unceasing stripes, the direful privations, and the frenzied despotism which were ever their
inalienable portion. He also became acquainted with the
audacious measures which were always adopted to impede
among them all moral and religious instruction. About 11,
the horn resounded, and "the working hands" returned from
the field to breakfast. The hard corn dough, which a hog
can scarcely masticate, and insipid hommony which hunger itself almost rejects, were their only food; and time
until sunset would not be allowed to swallow any more

Family Amalgamation among the Men-stealers.   Page 91.

even of that unsavoury compost. The men corroborated in full all the circumstances which the elder females had described; and the Vermont preacher retired from his coloured associates, in the true *fanatical* humour which characterized the primitive puritans.

About 1 o'clock a number of ministers and delegates to the association having arrived, they were invited to a sumptuous dinner. The New-Englander was offered his choice of the whole; but his stomach was so *evangelically delicate*, that he could not eat. To all the apologies, entreaties, and apparent sympathies which encircled him, he finally ventured to make this homely reply, " My conscience will not permit me to partake of this food; while the people who work for it never taste a mouthful of necessary sustenance from one end of the year to the other. If I eat any thing, it will be a plate of that hommony, or a slice of that corn bread which the coloured people had for their breakfast." A bag of rattlesnakes let loose among them, could not more have disturbed the men-stealers.

The test was decisive and complete. Immediately after dinner, he was admonished to go away the greatest distance possible that night, as if he staid he would surely be killed; and for his own safety, he was also advised not to attend any one of the Virginia associations. As the consequence, the Christian fled from the American Sodom and Gomorrha, to detail the facts to his brethren in Philadelphia.

Men may travel to the south, and so far as slavery is concerned may continue in a dead sleep until they return; but wakeful and inquiring persons may witness in every varying occurrence, such facts as these; and they put to instantaneous silence, all the silly trash which the southern profligates, and their northern infatuated coadjutors vociferate respecting the *amalgamation* of the white and coloured races.

You put up at the Tavern of some Major or Colonel of 70 years of age; presently you are astonished to find yourself attended by a tawdrily dressed girl who appears as the tavernkeeper's daughter; as conceited, and vain, and empty as a magpie; with two or more waiters nearly or quite naked, manifestly her own brothers or sisters, only with a differently tinged skin. This puts a stranger to his full stretch of imaginative meditation; and as is often the case, he perceives, that it you could divest him of his mental associations, and clothe the girls and boys alike, they could not be known apart. The children are suckled at the same coloured women's breasts ; and except that their treatment is different during infancy, they grow up together with their common animal instincts, and equally devoid of correct moral sensibility.

That such a system must destroy all feminine purity and domestic confidence is obvious : and that such a perennial fountain of vice long since would have been dried up, if the southern women had so determined, is not less undeniable. But females, old and young, and of all ranks among the slave-holders, shamelessly boast that they never put on or took off a single article of their dress during their lives. They would consider it excessive toil, and the utmost degradation thus to dress or undress themselves ; and of course boys must be multiplied to work in the fields, while girls are nurtured for the house.

Two ladies of the first rank in Virginia affirmed, that the Northern citizens were totally incompetent to form any correct idea of a slave plantation. One of them remarked : " We are called wives, and as such are recognised in law ; but we are little more than superintendents of a coloured seraglio." When the old slave-driver is dead, the " boy" who is most like him is generally called by his title ; and you are often surprised to hear a mulatto coachman or footman denominated captain, major or colonel. You ask the cause, and are informed ; " the man is so like his father, that if it were not for the colour of his skin, he is such a chip of the old block, that you could not know them apart." This man is often the confidential manager of the house ; the coachman who drives about his father's daughters, waits upon the table ; and, in fact, is upon terms of the most intimate, and often, it is understood, of licentious familiarity with his half sisters. Hence, there is now growing up in the southern states with inconceivable rapidity, a third race of American people ; whose numbers will soon preponderate over both the resident whites, and the genuine blacks. They are the persons of the various shades between the Europeans and Africans. These citizens ordinarily possess the constitutional energy and aptitude of the black race for the southern climate, with the high temper and cunning of their white fathers. They feel neither the sullen debasement of the descendant of the kidnapped African, nor the languor and emaciation of the dissolute white. Myriads of southern white women, it is fully believed, if they dared would rather marry those light coloured young men, than the miserable profligates with whom they associate; and to this mixed race, if there be any way of reading "the signs of the times," God in his Providence, has surely given the southern portion of the United States bordering on the Atlantic, as their domicil. A remuneration to the succeeding generations, for the toil, sweat, blood, and anguish of their ancestors.

As in the slave states, a man's wealth is not estimated by his bank-stock, or the number of acres of land which he owns, but by the coloured citizens whom he has kidnapped; it necessarily follows, that every slavite will propagate slaves as fast as he possibly can, and at the least expense. Consequently, every slave farm and plantation, in various degrees, is a scene of inconceivable dissolution. There may be some men, who will not degrade themselves by an actual participation in the fornication, adultery, and incest, which inhere to almost every slave quarter: but who ever heard of a man that would not connive at all these things, and reward the father and mother, if he had so promised, for so cheaply putting another "fellow," or another "wench" within his grasp?

In the lower counties of Virginia, this white-washing system and these amalgamating processes were carried on to a diabolical perfection. A picture of one plantation will serve for the whole. I was riding alone, and had pursued my solitary route from Charlotteville during the whole day. Toward sunset my attention was arrested by a large crowd of coloured people collected close by the road. When I came near to them I halted; and instantly perceived that they were husking corn. There was a genuine slavite, the despot, strutting about with his whip, two boys of man's size, his hopeful sons; and his overseer almost incessantly resounding his commands and oaths, and cracking as a signal, the huge cart whip which he brandished. I think I counted nearly a hundred full grown coloured persons; the surrounding juniors defied all my arithmetic. There was every distinguishable shade of complexion from Congo black to that sallow, which the ingenuity of an artist can scarcely define.

While I was musing upon this unusual display of domestic purity and of American freedom, a true Virginian rode up and accosted me. "You are from a distance, stranger, I see." I replied, "Yes, and have met with a curiosity," pointing to the field near us.

"Well, that's a good one," he retorted; "but which way are you riding?" I told him where I was going to stop for the night. "I live a little distance beyond the tavern," said he, "so we will ride together."

After we were fairly started, my companion began. "What were you thinking about, stranger, when I met you?" The man had so little of the slavite's usual scowling and furious passions on his face, that I resolved if possible to obtain some information from him. I therefore replied, "I was puzzling myself to know how so many people of different colours could be collected together on one plantation. The man must have exercised some ingenuity in picking out his assortment." The Virginian burst into a roar of laughter, and said, "Well, stranger, that's a good one. Sure enough, you know nothing about our ways here near Richmond." I begged him to explain the secret to me. "Major E." he retorted, "is too cunning to buy negroes; he breeds and sells them." I asked, "But what has that to do with the twenty different shades of colours on the faces of the motley groupe?" He again laughed aloud, and then proceeded to divulge the major's process of multiplying and whitewashing his slaves.

I dare not publish the particulars of the major's bleaching manufactory; but I gathered from his statement some general views which will unravel what southern women know or connive at or encourage, that they may pass their

A Slave Plantation.　　Page 94.

days in comparative sloth and voluptuousness. The language of the Prophets Joel and Amos here rightly may be applied ; and in all the sacred solemnity of divine inspiration, they furnish a clue into the slave-trader's labyrinth. "They have cast lots for my people, and have given a boy for a harlot, and a girl for wine that they may drink." Joel 3: 3. "A man and his father will go in unto the same maid, to profane my holy name." Amos 2: 7.

It was one grand object of the major, with all celerity to clear his plantation of every *real* African, of whom he had a small party remaining. These he sold to the regular slave dealers, as soon as they exhibited symptoms of debility or discontent ; and the women of the same race were also disposed of for the southern market, when they began to show that they were "*wearing out !*"

According to my companion's account, there was a regular system established, by which it was scarcely possible for a child to be born without having some approximation to white, beyond that of the darkest of its generators; and that between the major, and his boys, and the overseer and his son, and their other artificers, he presumed that soon he would not have one real black person on the plantation.

Every inducement was held out to the "likely breeding wenches" to engender children ; and the value of the douceur was estimated according to the final tinge which the child's skin assumed. The infernal acumen which the gambling Virginian, thus thoughtlessly depicted, and the reckless unconcern with which he talked of the major as a great man in the state, and what a clever fellow he was, only proved to me the certainty of the scripture, that because men "receive not the love of the truth, for this cause, God sends them strong delusions, that they should believe a lie and be damned, who had pleasure in unrighteousness." 2 Thessalonians 2: 11, 12.

Nineteen years have passed away, and the impressions of that afternoon are indelible. The scene remains upon my imagination in all its vivid reality ; and the glowing descriptions of the Virginian horse jockey, have lost none of their convincing force. Often afterward did I scrutinize the system with the utmost accuracy ; and frequently were incidental circumstances mentioned apparently without design, which fully corroborated my travelling companion's statement. As far as memory can retrace the less important circumstances, the tavernkeeper confirmed the general view. Every item concerning his valuable stock, and his sagacious and successful methods of improving them in their personal appearance, and marketable value, was noticed merely as an article of common information, and without the smallest apparent idea or reflection, that there was any thing but what was laudable; for he and his family were represented as among the people of the highest rank and respectability. Yet it is manifest, that there is scarcely a gradation in the crime of incest, to say nothing of the minor offences, which was not constantly and openly perpetrated, if not actually before the eyes, evidently within the knowledge of his wife and daughters.

It will probably be alleged, that these exposures are so utterly scandalous, that they ought not to be published. If slavery were like any other unnatural system of turpitude, accurately known and therefore avoided by all good men, and abandoned only to the lowest profligates and incorrigible villains, the plea peradventure might be admitted. On the contrary, slavery exercises its ruthless despotism over the United States of America. It controls all our congressional legislation. It domineers in all ecclesiastical proceedings. It silences the Christian ministry. It nullifies evangelical doctrine and discipline. It is a stony hearted and iron armed monster, which from the halls of legislation, the benches of justice, and even the pulpit of the sanctuary, brandishes his whip of scorpions burning with fire and brimstone; and threatens to sweep away with his besom of destruction, all that is equal in right, holy in practice, and Christian in authority.

Besides, all the ligaments of human society in the southern states, are rapidly decomposing into nonentity; and the safety of the republic is therefore deeply endangered. With the moral aid of the northern anti-slavery citizens, two classes among the slaveholders must awake from their lethargy, combine their energies, cry aloud, spare not and never cease, till the thraldom of American citizens has been dismissed to that bottomless pit, whence the gloomy and pestiferous smoke which has darkened the sun and air of liberty originally ascended.   Those two classes of persons, are the preachers and the women ; and until they unite in the holy war against this legion of devils ; however otherwise objectionable, these loathsome pictures shall be published to excite universal indignation ; and then the loud demand for the death of this atrocious monster of sin and uncleanness will be uttered in a voice of thunder, which neither the artifices, the power, nor the numbers of the confederated man-stealers for one moment, will be able to resist.

Among all the natural effects of slavery upon the slaveholders, the sensuality and its concomitant vices with which it fills them, are the most pernicious in their present influence, and the most appalling and dangerous in their future consequences.   Every southern woman, the member of a slave-driver's family, if she had any correct feminine and Christian feeling, would live in a continuous shudder.   In the word of God, the great Creator teaches us, that female purity is the subject of his constant care, and that the violation of it, without repentance, insures his tremendous retribution.   The scriptures are replete with examples. Upon this principle, what may not the females of the south expect in the day of award.   It is vain to palliate, or bluster, or ridicule, or threaten.   The fact stands before us in all its resistless truth.   Generation after generation of the southern females, have witnessed their fellow creatures, even the children of their own fathers and husbands, living as the mere tools of unbridled lust, and often violated with a savage barbarity, of which the legal annals of crime afford no parallel.   Against this inconceivable wide spread and enormous load of guilt, the white women have never yet spoken so as to be heard.   Now therefore, let them boldly advance and say to this desolating flood, " Thou shalt go no further."

How can they expect to escape, if the Lord should ever permit our southern states to be convulsed with a resolute struggle on the part of the slaves to be free ?   What plea could they offer to a coloured ruffian against his atrocious

assault, which would not recoil upon them with overwhelm
ing force?

If there be any one aspect in which the resolute and
criminal negligence of preachers to the south, appears most
heinous and aggravated, it is in this connexion. They
know, they behold all this extending pestilence. They
must see the enemy advancing, and yet the trumpet of
alarm is dumb; and the watchman snores away fast
asleep, or sings his lullaby to the people who are about to
go into captivity. From southern preachers and from
southern women at present, there is no more reasonable
prospect of co-operation, than from Satan, the prince of
all slave-drivers.

What then shall be done? To whom shall we recur?
We must look to the northern ladies. They must cast off
their mischievous prudery, their fastidious squeamishness,
and their injurious reserve upon this delicate subject; and
covering themselves with Christian mail, and forming an
impenetrable phalanx, neither to be lampooned out of the
truth, nor to be stared out of their dignified self possession,
by infidel debauchees and profligate slavites; they must
take up the arms, which they can wield with more success
than men, and urge the southern women to join them;
until with their matronly pu.ity and authority they have
exterminated this devastating pestilence, which in connexion
with its crafty and filthy coadjutor popery, is filling the
south-western country especially, with a flood of iniquity,
that in its meanders, pollutes the furthest boundaries of the
United States.

4. The fourth natural effect of slavery is this; *Slave-
holders are always irascible and turbulent.*

This consequence of slavery is inalienable. There is
no restriction upon the power and blustering of the domestic tyrant. The courtesies of society, the dread of resentment, the fear of loss, or the hope of gain, must unavoidably repress the ungovernable tendencies of human passions, when they are brought into collision with the multitude of equals; but a slave-holder's plantation is his
world, where no law rules but his caprice, and no power
interferes with his arbitrary mandates. Hence, patience,

meekness, and all the mild virtues must inevitably be excluded.

Besides, the mainspring of the slave-machinery is the law that the slaves must be kept in rigid subjection: and consequently no inquiry is made whether the measures pursued are requisite or just; the only object is to ascertain that they will contribute to the ends desired, the intimidation of the slave, and the strengthening of the chains which already fetter the bondman.

On the slave plantations, not only men and boys, but women and girls are often scourged in rotation, not for any real, alleged, or even pretended fault, but merely for the sake of example; and that all the gang, as they are vilely denominated, may remember the lacerations and tortures to which they are momentarily subject; provided the slave-driver or his overseer, to gratify lust, or satiate revenge, or fiend-like, from sheer love of mischief, choose to direct that the lash and stripes shall be inflicted.

An officer of a church thus exhibited his tyrannical propensities, by flogging as many of his slaves as suited his irascible propensity on different mornings. I asked one of his slaves, when he had got flogged last? "O Massa," said the chuckling boy, me have not lived at home for some time, "so the rest get it instead." Of this exemplary Christian Ruler! one fact will suffice; it is a portrait many similitudes of which may be traced from Washington to the Mississippi.

S. had engaged a carpenter with his workmen, to repair and enlarge his house. After some time had elapsed, K. the builder was awakened at a very early hour in the morning, by a piteous moaning and shrieking, which harrowed his soul. He arose and quickly dressed himself; and following the sound, at length discovered a coloured woman naked to the loins, tied by the neck to the rail of a fence, and her feet similarly pinioned below; while S. was lacerating her with the cowskin or hickory rod in his hand. K. instantly commanded the brute to desist. A long and severe altercation ensued. The slave-driver maintained his sole jurisdiction over his slaves, and threatened K. that he would also punish him for his interference. The latter told him, guilty or not guilty, deserving stripes or not, he never could tolerate such merciless barbarity toward any woman, and finding all other means unavailing, except a personal trial of strength, he finally menaced him with a public exposure. This so far operated that S. consented to release the woman, who was ordered to her cabin. S. went to bed to sleep over his morning's benevolence, and K. remained upon watch.

A second occurrence of the same character, I think, with another female, happened. This was attended almost by a personal combat between the slave-driver and the carpenter. The cruelty was more aggravated, and K's. indignation more intense. The approach of day light only severed the disputants. The carpenter however, had early contrived to release the woman, and dared S. to pursue her to vent upon her his wrath. These scenes placed S. and K. in a new relation. The former was on the alert, that K. might not ascertain from the slaves, the additional agonies which they endured in consequence of the discovery which he had made; and K. was wide awake to interpose his shield, whenever an eligible opportunity offered; but as his employments were restricted to the house, he could accurately know nothing of the scenes which were enacted in the distant barns and fields.

At length, the third and final rencontre took place just before the glimmer of day break. Silently, K. appeared before S., while he was scourging a young woman, and presenting his fist; "Strike the girl again, and I will fell you to the earth." Choked with rage, S. could scarcely utter, "Stand off, or I will cowskin you worse than that bitch." K. adroitly seized and wrested his whip from his hand, and assured him, "If you offer in any way to molest me, I will knock you down, and give you some of the same stripes that you have laid upon this poor creature, cost what it may." Dreading the carpenter's muscular superiority, he sullenly watched K. release the woman, wrap her rags around her, and send her to her hovel. Without doubt, had S. been armed, or had any means existed to have procured

Flogging American Women.   Page 100.

a weapon to overpower him, the carpenter would have been murdered for his philanthropy.

Their altercation continued until the coloured people began to show themselves.   K. asked the slave-driver, " how would you like to see your wife and daughters, tormented as you do these women ? I could not stand the sight of my wife and sister thus abused, and no man shall ever treat any woman so if I know it." Having reproached him and threatened him to his full satisfaction, he permitted him to depart to his house; " Go," said K., " and repent of your cruelty, and pray God to pardon you, and not to punish you as you deserve."

During the interval before breakfast, and while S. was asleep, as if he had been an infant in innocence; the carpenter arranged all his affairs, packed up his tools in his wagon, and prepared to depart.   " Where are you going ?" demanded S. in a blustering tone.   "I am going to return home ;" answered K.   " Then I will pay you nothing for what you have done," retorted the slave-driver, "unless you complete your contract."   The carpenter left the scene of turpitude with this edifying declaration; " I will not stay here a day longer ; for I expect the fire of God will come down and burn you up altogether, and I do not choose to go to hell with you !"

I believe, however, that K. through hushmoney, and promises that the women should not thus be whipped any more, eventually returned and fulfilled his engagement.

This unvarying course of unrighteousness, is witnessed by the youth in all its gradations ; and in none probably more injuriously to himself, than in the profaneness, and dreadfully vindictive language, in which the slaveholder's exasperation is effused.   Cursing, and swearing, and blasphemy, may be impolite, or uncourteous, or even wrong, if introduced in the hearing of certain white gentlemen, and nominal Christian preachers ; but the violation of the third commandment of the decalogue, among slaves, is not considered worthy of notice ; hence, it is a common maxim with slaveholders, " damning a negro, is not cursing and swearing."

One of the most kind and friendly class of slaveholders,

9*

once called upon me for some copies of the swearer's prayer.
I remarked; "I never understood that you were addicted
to profane language." He replied, "No, I could not be
called a swearer, I sometimes cursed the slaves, but that is
thought nothing of. However, since I read the swearer's
prayer, I get choked; and cannot even do that, and I want
to try the effect of a few of them upon my neighbours."
He carried away to his great delight, a pocket full of those
tracts, for the relief of some around him of that class so
aptly described by the methodist preacher. "You are bad
citizens, you will not even pray for your country; alas!
there is a good reason for it, you cannot pray, you are
choked! you have got a negro in your throats."

The awful character and consequences of the varied iniquities which are inseparable from slavery, are too obvious
to be concealed; and it is irrefragable, that the habit of
using profane language, and of indulging in furious ebullitions of unrestrained anger, however temporary may be
the bursts of tempestous passion, as they are continually
recurring, must naturally engender the most discordant
tempers, and violent antipathies; and with few exceptions,
these are the uniform constitutional adjuncts of every slave
plantation. Indeed, the slave holder could not maintain his
unhallowed jurisdiction, without this apparent wrathful
demeanour, and all its concomitant outrages. In this unnatural and constant storm, the children are born, and
reared, and in it they die.

I was once called to write the will for a Presbyterian,
who was greatly debilitated. His wife was a Methodist;
and also one of his sons about 18 years of age. The boy
was conscientiously opposed to slavery root and branch.
We proceeded to divide the lands and all the other property
very amicably. At length we came to the slaves. I
paused and told them I could write no more; he insisted,
and dictated the manner in which these were to be appor-
tioned. Among other items, he directed that this boy, who
declared that he never would hold a slave, should have a
man and woman, and her children for his lot: but should
the testator die before the son arrived at twenty-one years
of age, and the latter would not take possession of them,

with a direct proviso against their emancipation; then the executors were ordered to sell those slaves upon the best terms, and divide the proceeds among the younger children. I assured them, that I neither could nor would write any such clause in a will for any person; that separate from all the questions respecting the character of slavery, it involved the very utmost injustice; and that it was an unnatural usurpation over the rights of his son's conscience. A severe and protracted disputation ensued. I reminded the parents of their Christian profession, and of their son's hopeful piety. I endeavoured to impress upon the sick man his emaciated condition, recalled to his memory, his early associations, when slavery appeared to him in no other light than as a fiend incarnate, and finally attempted to transfer his solemn attention to the accountability of man at the tribunal of Christ. He was in a measure docile, and not being able to evade or shake off the application of the truth; he remarked, " By our marriage contract, my wife was to have the sole management of the slaves, in fact, they are her property independent of me; and she will do as she likes with them." This brought the lady and myself into direct collision; and during the whole evening, it was as impossible to keep her in any thing like rationality, as it would have been to quell the ocean in a storm. She called my truth, "all cant, all lies, all nonsense;" &c. When her fury was so far vented, that her husband and I could put in a few words; I expressed my regret at the occurrence. "Mrs. —— if there be any truth in God's word, your profession of religion, if not directly hypocritical, must be vain. If there be any equity in the divine administration, the hope of the slave-holder, like the hope of a hypocrite, is of no more consistency than that of the spider's web, and must perish. I can comfort Mr. —— with no cheering gospel promise, for I know not one adapted to his case; and if there be any correct mode of comprehending the scripture of truth, and he should speedily depart, indulging a hope of admission to glory, I fear that he will die with a lie in his right hand; for as your own homely preacher proclaims, " You think to go up to heaven with a gang of slaves on your back. No, no! I tell you that they will

sink you down to the dungeon of damnation." Thus ended
the making of a will for a female man-stealer!

5. The fifth regular effect of slavery, as it exists in the
United States upon the slave-holders, is this; *It destroys
every correct view of equity, and fills the adherent and practitioner of the system with all injustice and knavery.*

Slave-holders often boast of their magnanimity, highmindedness, acute sense of honour, refined feelings of propriety, independence, and enlarged views of reciprocal obligation. The claim to these virtues is made, but how are
they practically exemplified? His magnanimity, highmindedness and honour, are ready to resent the smallest
unintentional affront, if he dare, in a white citizen ; and
for a similar suppositious offence, by a coloured man, provided no white person is witness, to torture him as much,
and as long, as his caprice or vengeance may dictate. His
refined feelings of propriety, are illustrated in the varie-
gated hues of his slaves of every colour, from Congo black
to the lighest shade of mulatto. His independence, is his
claimed superiority to all the laws of God and man. And
his views of recipocrity are, to pay the debts which he con-
tracts to his white associate, because he can be coerced to
discharge those obligations; but to rob all the coloured
persons with whom he has any connexion, every day of
his life, and even by his last will and testament to die a
kidnapper; and when entombed to bear the brief but ex-
pressive epitaph, " Here lies an incorrigible, impenitent
manstealer!"

Two distinct cases will illustrate this system.—For the
smallest offence, or for no fault at all, under the influence
of irritation, the slaves are raved at and punished without
mercy.

A preacher, on the Lord's day morning, frequently stripped his female slave or slaves, tied them up to the rafters
of his house, scourged them, left them there fastened, rode
to the meeting house, and after preaching, returned home
and repeated the flogging, or released them as his humour
in the afternoon dictated. Although this was notorious to
the whole surrounding country, I never heard him censured
either by a preacher, or by any other person, but a few of

the gospel fanatics, who could not discover any method to amalgamate torturing girls and preaching Christian love at the same time.

There was a church member of the same class. Mrs. H. used to boast that she was the best hand to whip "a wench" in all that country. She had a post in the yard to which she pinioned the girls, and after scourging them until she was tired, on the Lord's day morning, she then would sprinkle them with the usual mixture of salt, vinegar, &c., leave them fastened, exposed to the sun and flies, walk to the church, sit as demure as a popish nun, and after service repeat her flaying or not, according to her whim. I once expostulated with her upon the impropriety and wickedness of this course. " Mrs. H. how can you possibly whip your girls so publicly on the Lord's day morning, and disturb your neighbours going to public worship?" Her answer was a memorable specimen of slave driving and slave torturing Christianity. " If I were to whip them on any other day of the week, I might lose their work for a day ; but by whipping them on Sunday, their backs get well enough by Monday morning!" That woman, if alive, is no doubt a member still.

It is utterly incomprehensible to every reflecting mind, how a pilferer of men, women and children, can be an honest and righteous man. Slavery is a system of wholesale plunder. It commenced in " the highest kind of theft ;" and is prolonged by continual stealing. Slavery is oppression, fraud, and the forcible seizure of rights, comfort, property, liberty, and life, without cessation, and without end. Slavery is theft of the most atrocious character; it is always kidnapping ; and there is neither the name, nor the cloak, nor the appearance, nor even the pretension of integrity connected with its malignant robberies. Now, that a man can be upright during six hours weekly in his intercourse with white men, who will force him to be just towards them ; and the remainder of the seven days, be a voluntary rapacious grasper of every coloured citizen's labour whom he can rob with impunity, to squander upon his lusts and profligacy ; is a paradox, that no person of common sense, and much less no man of Christian principles, for one moment, can admit.

On my return to Virginia, in 1815, after the discussion respecting mansealing, which took place in the Presbyterian General Assembly of that year, I was informed, that there had been a great excitement during my absence, respecting a coloured man who belonged to a preacher, and I was referred to Mr. F. for the particulars. Mr. F. had been nurtured among the Friends, and although I believe not actually numbered with the society, yet he retained many of their principles and habits of life. After the usual salutation, I introduced the subject, and he spontaneously disclosed his feelings in these words, " I believe that you preachers are the greatest hypocrites in the world." I answered, " Not all of us I hope, Mr. F. certainly they are not all deceivers." Mr. F. replied, "How do I know? there's R., I thought he was the best man in the world, and look at the trick he has played me. I will hear no more of your preaching and praying, it is all hypocrisy." He finally said, that so far he could not apply his censure to me ; but he had no doubt that if there was only the chance, I should swap, cheat, and drive slaves like the rest of them.

After the first burst of his indignation had passed away, he resumed his usual equanimity, and then proceeded to recount the tale. Instead of the conversational form, I have condensed it into a narrative.

It seems that some years before this period, the preacher had exchanged a stallion horse for a citizen ; the difference in value of the two animals was paid as usual. There was an understanding at the time of the barter, that when Tom should have fully earned the price paid for him, he should be emancipated ; and with this enticing lure in prospect, Tom, to use their own expression, went to work like a negro. Merely to relieve his wife, and against their mutual principles and feelings, Mr. F. had purchased a coloured woman for domestic duties, and with this female, Tom by consent of the parties cohabited. Thus years revolved until some one of the honest Christians around, put it into Tom's head, that he had earned much more than he cost, and therefore, was justly entitled to his freedom by the contract.

Tom took proper advice, and being assured that the valuation of his labour was correct, began to talk to R. the preacher about going free. His claim was at first disregarded; then denied; and as Tom became more clamourous, he was threatened. Amid this feverish excitement months passed away, until in a momentary fit of delirious rage, Tom finding that he could not be free, resolved to mutilate himself, and with an axe chopped off the thumb and forefinger, I think, of his right hand.

This gave a new aspect to the affair. R. speedily after removed to a distance, and not caring about Tom in his then sulky humour and helpless state, left him to be cured, and to work through the winter in any way which he could. At the latter end of May, 1815, the preacher appeared to make a final disposition of Tom. He attempted to sell him in vain. By all persons, even those who had no truly just notions of their own, the man was deemed to be justly entitled to his freedom. These would not purchase. The other " Brokers in the trade of human blood," would not buy a slave thus maimed and damaged, and the slave barterer was in a quandary. The path of duty, justice, and humanity was plain and obvious, but that required the abandonment of several hundreds of dollars; and consequently, it was useless to expect that a man who had already violated his agreement, and been the cause of an irreparable injury, would voluntarily " do justly and love mercy." He knew well, that Tom would be a source of unceasing vexation around his own house, and therefore, he had no alternative but to traffic or emancipate him. The former seemed impracticable, and the latter would cost too much. A good conscience is too precious a jewel for a slave-driving preacher to possess! One method only remained, and that was to tamper with Mr. F.; and through Tom's connexion with his domestic coloured female, and his benevolent sensibilities, to induce Mr. F. to purchase the man, notwithstanding his altered condition, at the original price. When this proposition was first made to F. it was indignantly rejected. " I bought a woman against my judgment," remarked the Friend, "merely to preserve my wife's health, and she has been a burden upon my mind ever since, I will not trade in any more of my fellow creatures. Set Tom free according to your promise, and if he chooses to stay about here, I will employ him." To this plan the preacher steadfastly objected. After some additional explanations, Mr. F. proceeded, "If you will emancipate Tom, I will manumit the woman; and she shall live with me as before upon the customary wages." This proffer was scouted by the preacher with equal inflexibility. Mr. F. then added, "Take Tom away with you, and rather than separate the man and woman, I will liberate her, that she may accompany him."

But now another and an insuperable difficulty arose. The woman refused to be emancipated upon that condition; and with most provoking contempt declared, "I will not live with a preacher who has cheated my man out of his work and his freedom, and drove him in a fit of rage to cut off his thumb and finger; I would rather be Mr. F.'s slave. I will never live with that preacher." In this dilemma the affair remained; until after some days probably had elapsed, tired of the woman's lamentations at the idea of being obliged to separate from her man, wearied with Tom's unceasing importunities that F. would purchase him, with every promise of faithfulness, gratitude, and diligence to repay him; and exasperated at the unfeeling barbarity and unprincipled rapacity of the preacher, F. bought Tom, I believe, at the original price, which was paid for him in the barter for the horse.

When Mr. F. had closed his detail, he subjoined, "Excuse me, all you preachers are hypocrites, and as such, I never will have any thing more to do with you." He kept his word. He was always affable, kind and friendly as ever; after my removal from Virginia used regularly to call upon me with all cordiality; often expressed his regret at the treatment I had experienced in Virginia, expressed his indignation against R. and his flagrant iniquity, denounced slavery in the most unmeasured terms; but unless he heard my farewell address when I left Virginia, I presume has never since attended the public worship of God.

The tenth divine commandment of the moral law enjoins; " thou shalt not covet thy neighbour's wife, nor his ox, nor his ass, nor any thing that is his." The slaveholder not only covets, but actually steals the whole, and his neighbours also ; which was a crime of such infernal magnitude, that it did not seem requisite to the supreme legislator, even to prohibit that indescribably unnatural transgression. To defraud the labourer of his wages and hire, is condemned in the sacred volume, as a sin which is surely attended by the curse of God ; but this is a venial offence, compared to the other unrighteousness which is inseparably conjoined with slavery as it exists in the United States.

A preacher had a young coloured girl who was consti- tutionally unhealthy. After every attempt to benefit and to invigorate her had been tried in vain, A. the preacher sold the girl to a member of his congregation, and warrant- ed her in the usual elegant style of the human flesh-dealers, " sound, healthy," &c. with all the technical slang of that nefarious science. The fraud was instantly discovered, and the restoration of the sum paid for the " diseased slave" was demanded. This claim A. refused ; upon which a suit at law was commenced by the layman. During the continu- ance of the action, which was protracted as long as money and chicanery combined could contrive, the daughter of sorrow died. The facts were so grossly flagrant, that the plaintiff recovered the full amount of his claim, with addi- tional compensation, I believe, for damages. From this verdict, the preacher appealed to the Court of Chancery ; and after the cause had been detained in that vortex of all that is just and good, until the ingenuity of corruption could imprison it there no longer; the chancellor affirmed the prior sentence, with a remark to this effect, that exclusive of all the questions respecting slavery, or of the relative condition of the parties, which aggravated the turpitude of the case in the highest degree, a more scandalous and bare- faced specimen of swindling had never passed under his judicial cognizance. Yet with the exception of a few Christian fanatics who indulged their reveries amid " the poetry of philanthropy," I never knew that the preacher
10

lost one particle of esteem, or was considered to have acted contrary to the character of a minister of the Gospel.

The following exhibitions and practices are constantly passing in public in the southern regions, where they excite not the smallest sensibility; or rather, in which the most dignified characters in society participate, not only without any compunction or pity, but even without the least apparent emotion.

During the period of the last war, when the northern citizens were engaged in improving the breed of sheep, and also in extending the Merino race throughout the country, scenes occurred, the outrageous folly of which almost obscured their atrocious baseness. The travelling sheep owners would never trade so as to pay money in barter: and you might see those sons of cupidity, riding or walking along the road with a flock of sheep, a horse or two, and one or more coloured persons young or old, male or female, all moving together; stopping at every large plantation and in every village; and there realizing all the various processes of traffic; the citizens and the sheep equally transferable for money, horses, or other truck, if it suited the travelling merchants tariff of prices and profit.

One picture will illustrate this curious trade. A man with a flock of Merinos stopped at the door of a Methodist class-leader and offered trade. The Christian wanted a ram, but he had no cash to spare, and no useless horse. There was a coloured woman in the kitchen, a sort of supernumerary. She was ordered out in front of the house, and after a lengthened series of appraising and artifice, a ram with some sheep was turned into the yard, and the female with her bundle of clothing pursued the course which the merchant took with his four legged tribe. It should however be added, that the Methodist repented of his sin, and could he have traced the woman, would have redeemed her from bondage. This particular fact is mentioned, chiefly because it will verify the extreme obtuseness with which all the moral faculties can be blunted, when amiable enlightened American citizens can be so lost to all that is natural and just, as to exchange a woman for a flock of sheep.

A Woman exchanged for a Ram and Sheep.   Page 116.

Auction at Richmond.   Page 111.

Auctions are statedly held for the sale of coloured citizens, as a distinct flesh-market; and more frequently with the four-legged cattle. They are always advertised together, and the descriptions are in the same beastly style, " young, sound, without fault," &c. The following graphical delineation of auctions for slaves was sent me some time since from Richmond. The author is a native, and always has been a resident of Virginia. It is the picture of a master artist, glowing with " the poetry of philanthropy."

" Since my visit to Richmond, the horrors of bondage, to me always a source of bitter anguish, have been exhibited to my view on a more extended scale than I had ever previously witnessed them. Here almost every morning the crimson auction flag,—fit emblem of the purpose it proclaims,—announces on its conspicuous label, that the blood and bones of American citizens are publicly to ⁻be vended ! Here, *half covered with rags, and loaded with chains,* human beings are driven together in crowds, and by beings calling themselves human, are sold and bought. Within a few days past, I have beheld in Richmond *hundreds of men, women, and children, thus exposed in the open streets, and bartered off like brute animals !*

" Draw near to that wretched group. Great have been their sufferings; but still they have feelings, and their condition may be worse. They are to be transferred to other and unknown drivers. Their minds are revolving those hideous pictures of Carolina and Georgia cruelty, which have so truly been delineated unto them ; and they know their destination is thitherward. The whole prospect of future life to them is dismal, dark, and frightful. Soon the only tie which binds them to life is to be severed. See that convulsive embrace ! it is the last expression of connubial love, their last, long farewell.

" This is but the beginning of misery. Those visages of grief indicate the desolation of whole families, all are dragged from each other, husband from wife, mother from child, father from son, and brother from sister, never more to meet on earth.

" Hark ! those groans and shrieks and plaints of wo are

the language of wretchedness, distracted love, and wild despair. See the mournful victims of avarice, rallied under the gory banner of their new tyrants; and laden with ponderous fetters, commence their toilsome march to the land infamously wrested from the Cherokees, which they are destined to fertilize with their sweat and their blood. Behind the melancholy groups, are their merciless drivers, armed with whips, bludgeons, and pistols, in ferocious pomp. These are the almost daily exhibitions which present themselves in this land, boasting of its liberty, its benevolence, and its *Christianity*. Yet these scenes pass before us without exciting a murmur of sympathy, either public or private. With our Bill of Rights upbraiding us for our falsehood and despotism, and condemning our daily wicked practices ; we still vaunt our devotion to freedom, the philanthropy of our sentiments, and our inextinguishable attachment to the rights of man. Were it not for the human misery connected with it, this would be a most farcical absurdity ! These most ungodly, shameful, and degrading spectacles of human thraldom are almost perpetually exhibited in the public streets, without awakening a moment's censure or concern.

In the mean time, the streams of amusement flow on with an unruffled current. The hum and bustle of business, for one minute, are not suspended. The poor coloured citizen's anguish touches no fibre of sensibility, except in his own bosom, and the bosom of his fellow-sufferers.

Even the fair delicate female, whose heart should throb in unison with every pulsation of human wo, beholds this indescribable wretchedness and torture with careless unconcern. Her face is the seat of smiles and gaiety, in the presence of all this gloomy array of sorrow. *She too can talk of the cent per cent value of human flesh, with all the cold calculating cupidity which is manifested by* " the Christian broker in the trade of blood." What can be more revolting, than the *unfeeling and insulting scrutiny* of females, which is instituted by the dealers in men, among the objects of their mercenary traffic? What can be more disgusting than the *slang* with which they

discuss the marketable qualit es of human beings? What
more inflammatory to our indignation, than the frozen indifference with which they witness the unhappiness of
their victims? I have beheld these *soul-traffickers* in their
shambles, bartering the blood of their fellow citizens. A
cannibal ferocity scowled on their shameless visages. The
fires of hell glanced from their eyes. The germs of affection, hope, and happiness withered under their flash.
That flame seemed to burn back on itself with insatiate
greediness! and my soul shuddered at the cruelty of
man."

This is a recent picture of slavery in Richmond, delineated not by a "*hot-headed enthusiast*," and a "*reckless
fanatic*," but by a patriot statesmen of the first rank; who,
in virtue, intellect, and affectionate sensibilities, as far surpasses the New-York Clinton Hall mob orators and their
associates, as the brilliance of truth outshines the fogs of
error, and Christian uprightness and consistency surpass
in value the knavery of a concealed accessory in crime,
or the open perfidy of a conscience-seared Judas.

From this vivid portraiture, it appears that at those
auctions for slaves, all family bonds, and every relation of
domestic life are severed without compunction or remorse;
and the wailings of the wretched and hopeless children of
despotism and savageness only furnish amusement to the
obdurate flint-hearted *soul-traders*. Parents and children,
and lovers; and associates in misery, whose cohabitation
has been their only solace in privations, stripes, chains,
disease, and starvation, are separated to glut the avarice,
or to satiate the prodigality of the licentious slave-driver.
Is he a just man?

Let us survey another scene in this labyrinth of American tragedy. By the Bloody code of slave-laws, one white
man's evidence against a coloured citizen is sufficient to
criminate; no coloured testimony against a white witness
is admissible; and where slavery is concerned, unless
through political wrangling or from revenge, and even in
those cases ordinarily the attempt would only recoil upon
the coloured man's friend, no white man will appear as a
witness on behalf of a coloured person; and the law au-
10*

thorizes the court which condemns a man found guilty of any crime, to appraise the slave, the value of whom is paid by the sheriff of the county to the slave-holders. From this diabolical machination flow the following and similar developments of integrity, truth, justice, benevolence, and American freedom.

For brevity's sake, we will call the slave-driver Brown. This man has a restive, sturdy slave, who is too wise and too noble spirited for his degraded condition. Finding that no power can coerce the slave to submit to the vile sway exercised over him, Brown goes to a magistrate, swears to the commission of some crime which places the coloured man within the jurisdiction of the highest court assigned for the trial of slaves. There, without any other evidence than notorious barefaced perjury, known probably to all the magistrates, he is condemned, valued, and driven off to the Penitentiary. Speedily after Brown has received the stipulated sum from the state for the loss of his slave who had been condemned as a felon; he proceeds to the governor, pretends great commiseration for the hapless condition of the unfortunate wretch, and both to relieve the state, and show mercy to the criminal, Brown offers, if the governor will release him from the Penitentiary, that he will take the criminal out of the state, so that he shall no more trouble it. Glad to empty the prison, and send out of the state such adepts in crime, as he supposes, the governor releases the slave, and Brown drives off his prize to the next state, sells him as a valuable working hand for an increased price, warranted; and returns home with his dollars, boasting how he has befooled the court, and tricked the Governor.

The following narrative was received from a Preacher, who I believe, held not a slave; and whose mind was probably like that of many others, who had been born in Virginia, almost dead asleep to any thing connected with slavery, except in its grosser and more revolting wickedness. At that time the Preacher resided with a Magistrate, who was an officer of a Christian church. He called upon me one Saturday evening, in no small perturbation;

and informed me, that he had witnessed this exhibition of judicial equity and power.

A travelling slave-dealer had that afternoon met with a strong, able-bodied coloured man, and having ascertained his master, made the farmer such a tempting offer, that it was irresistible. But what pretext could be alleged for severing the man from his woman and children? The slave-merchant suggested a complaint to the magistrate against the slave, which would insure a sentence of 39 stripes; when he would appear and offer to remove the slave out of the state, if the owner would sell him, and the magistrate remit the punishment. The plan was adopted. Some petty crime was alleged; all the man's protestations of innocence, and incidental statements which proved that he was not guilty, were unavailing; he was ordered to be stripped and receive 39 lashes upon the spot. At this juncture, the American citizen-trader appeared, and proffered to purchase the man, provided they would release him from the scourging; and to give security to the Magistrate, that within a certain period, he should be transferred to another state. The magistrate recommended the adoption of this measure; and hoping all the parties would agree, consented to postpone the punishment until the Monday ensuing.

The preacher intimated that he had no doubt the magistrate was privy to the whole iniquity. "How," said the servant of the sanctuary, "can I preach to these people to-morrow?" I replied, "Very well; go and thunder the doctrine of retribution in their ears, till by the divine blessing you cure or kill them." The poor creature, tortured between the abandonment of his only earthly associates, and the dread of the 39 stripes, which he knew would be most mercilessly inflicted, at last sullenly consented to go to Carolina or Tennessee; and on the Monday morning after, heart-broken, he commenced his journey most probably to a premature grave.

Free coloured persons are often united to female slaves. As soon as practicable they purchase the emancipation of the woman and their own children. A difference of 100 or 150 dollars in price is made, if the female be pregnant, unless the man chooses to wait the result of her delivery; or consents to some conditional stipulation, by which in case of the life of the child, the man thief shall obtain an additional bonus. Yet the manager of this accursed traffic, the receiver of this price of blood, this worse than prowling Arab, who sells the children born in his house, and the trader of another citizen's wife and infant, even before it is born, professes to be a Christian, and declares that he is not a kidnapping Ishmaelite, but an honest man; what nefarious transaction then possibly can be ungodliness?

An officer of one of those synagogues of Satan, called a church, which was composed of men-stealers, detained in his accursed man-trap, a coloured woman, who cohabited with an American citizen, who by their own infernal laws was FREE. I think she had three children, and was bearing the fourth. During a late period of her pregnancy, this exemplary son of mercy so scourged and lacerated her, that the existence of both the female and her anticipated offspring was endangered. In consequence of the uproar which this Christian's barbarity occasioned, even among the female slave tyrants, Jack, as the man was called, was advised to make a resolute attempt to obtain the liberation of his wife. The plan succeeded, so far, that B. the slave driver finally agreed to sell the woman, and the three children, I believe, for 600 dollars to their own husband and father; with the proviso, that if the unborn child survived the birth, a certain short definite period, the man-stealer was to receive 100 dollars more; and this sum at the period referred to, a preacher of one denomination was paying by instalments to a lay church officer of another sects There is religion for you! of the genuine slave-driving stamp; equally as sublime and good, as that which rules the congregation in Virginia, who hold a gang of slaves, rent them to various Egyptian task-masters, and from the ungodly proceeds, pay their minister his salary. How a man can preach, and knowingly receive the wages thus feloniously griped from the poor and defenceless children of sorrow; money saturated with their tears, begrimed with their blood, procured through their stripes, and cursed with their anguish, is a problem which no mortal can solve,

They must recur to the author of the iniquity, Satan, who stands by grinning; claps the Judaslike preaching hypocrite on the back, and says, "Go on at that, brother!"

The above citizen Jack had become free in divine providence; but his back was a transcendent curiosity. From his neck to his loins, it appeared in furrows like a ploughed field, and the whole equally unimpressible and hard. In point of feeling and softness, the raised flesh in rows, and the bone covered with nothing but the skin, were equal. I asked the brother, how his back could possibly have attained such an extraordinary character? His reply was, " Master ——," I forget his name, or I would publish it at length to immortalize him, "used to take the hickory sticks and the cow-skins; first he would whip the flesh up, then he would beat it downwards, and when he was tired, he would put on the salt, pepper, mustard and vinegar. So he followed on, till he made my back just as you see it.' I inquired, "How did you get free?" His answer was uttered with great devotional sensibility. " The Lord in heaven knows how that was done; Jack could never find out; but it is safely recorded, and now Jack will have his wife and children free too."

The man-thief who was receiving 100 dollars annually from Jack the preacher, held a mortgage or title to the woman and all her children, by which in case the payments were not made, he could seize her, and sell her to the highest bidder to obtain the balance claimed by his atrocious rapacity.

The pursuit and seizure of a *runaway* slave, as he is disgracefully denominated, is equally as *direct and ruffian* kidnapping as it is to sail to Liberia, raise a *palaver*, with "*rum, guns, and gunpowder*," storm a village, then steal every defenceless African in the vicinity, and ship them to Charleston or Savannah. Every public officer who aids to arrest, and every Magistrate or Judge who delivers his sentence, by which the coloured citizen who has escaped from the American " house of bondage," is again forced to return to " the land of Egypt," to experience all its terrors and anguish, and to wither and die amid its inexpressible toils and tortures, is not only guilty of wilful and corrupt per-

jury; but he is a daring violator of the divine command
ment, Deuteronomy 23: 15, which peremptorily enjoins:
"thou shalt not deliver unto his master, the servant who
is escaped from his master unto thee." That divine censure rests upon them all: "when thou sawest a thief, then
thou consentedst with him," Psalm 50: 18; and they may
well dread the infliction of the divine judgments, Obadiah
14, 15. "Thou shouldst not have stood in the crossway
to cut off those that did escape: neither shouldst thou
have delivered them up in the day of distress. As thou
hast done it, shall be done unto thee; thy reward shall return upon thine own head." Wo be to some American
judges, and their inferior myrmidons, if the Lord should
ever permit their own daring injustice and iniquity to recoil upon themselves.

The constitution of the United States does not justify the
delivery of slaves who have escaped from their thraldom to
their former kidnappers. That instrument speaks of persons " held to service," and the implication is by their own
contract; and who therefore by violating it, have committed a fraud, and should be enforced to execute their
agreement; such as apprentices, hired workman, &c.
But a slave is no more " held to service," in strict English
parlance, than a horse who is fastened in a stable by an
iron chain, with his four legs completely fettered. The
laws of Congress upon this subject, are now, as they always
have been, utterly null and void; being directly opposed to
the supreme law of Jehovah; and no Christian ever did or
possibly can conscientiously execute them. They are a
flagrant violation of the rights of man; they are an insult
to common sense; and they are an indelible disgrace to
our republic and the world. Away with them!

Every magistrate or judge, when a coloured citizen is
thus brought before him, if he had the fear of God before
his eyes, and was not instigated by the devil, for all lawyers
thus profess to believe in God the Judge, and the devil the
prompter of all mischief; every magistrate or judge, should
simply inquire, whether a citizen, coloured or white is of no
importance, had been forcibly seized in the high road,
without crime or the semblance of judicial authority; and

if that fact were ascertained, he ought at once to release the coloured innocent citizen, and send the white kidnappers to jail without bail; and every magistrate or judge, who does not thus administer justice, violates his oath, and neglects the duties, which by the law of God he is imperatively bound to execute.

Nothing can more evidently display the unblushing hypocrisy of all slave-drivers without exception, than one series of constantly occurring criminality. Coloured citizens, in the fulfilment of the first law of God and man, escape from their vassalage; and Christians so called, not less than infidel scorners, will ransack every nook and corner of the republic to restore that free born citizen to their hellish captivity; for NO CHILD CAN ENTER THE WORLD A SLAVE! The man-thief will devote time, toil, and expense with the utmost profusion and good-will, to recover the fugitive, and for what purpose? that he may pour out his wrath in tormenting, and slowly murdering the object of his vengeance. At the same time, he pretends, to whine out his *cant* over the evils of slavery; and with genuine Satanic hypocrisy, professes his willingness to extirpate the odious wickedness of kidnapping. Are not those slaveholders, especially if they are professing Christians, undisguised counterparts and followers of Judas?

Alas! our metropolis and all parts of the southern states, are guilty of legalizing still more atrocious outrages and iniquity; crimes of such nefarious magnitude, that they were never perpetrated except by slave-drivers. Freemen, who indisputably never were subject to the despotic code of the modern Egyptian task-masters, are seized on the public roads, or in their habitations, immured for a short time in a filthy dungeon, in the nearest jail of misery; and for which audacious wickedness, the sheriff and all his subordinate myrmidons are equally condemnable; then sold out for prison fees, or rather for legal robbery; manacled, and bought for transportation to a distant state, by the original man-thief. This most detestable and complicated ungodliness is universally and notoriously practised, and sanctioned by custom and law in the district of Columbia, and in all the slave dealing districts south of the Potomac; and if not actual participants in the unholy craft, the municipal officers connive at the man-stealer, and promote his open unnatural felony. The tale of a white man thus forcibly seized, tied to the tail of a horse, dragged to a loathsome jail, and trafficked like a stray brute, would fill the country with alarm and wrath; yet kidnapping a coloured citizen, because he is " guilty of wearing a dark kin," not only in the slave-driver's code, but in our federal ungodly legislation, so far from being a heart-rending robbery, is a laudable display of superior cleverness ; and these men-stealers, with their official coadjutors, legislators, magistrates, and sheriffs, affirm, that they are all excellent Christians and Republicans : who then are hypocrites and ruffian pirates ?

Nothing is more common than for two of these white partners in kidnapping, Satan like, to start upon the prowl ; and if they find a freeman on the road, to demand his certificate, tear it in pieces, or secrete it, tie him to one of their horses, hurry off to some jail, while one whips the citizen along as fast as their horses can travel. There by an understanding with the jailor, who shares in the spoil, all possibility of intercourse with his friends is denied the stolen citizen. At the earliest possible period, the captive is sold out to pay the felonious claims of the law, bought through jugglery, by this trio of man-stealers ; and then transferred to some of their accomplices of iniquity, the American citizen traders, who fill every part of the southern states with rapine, crime, and blood.

In addition to this astounding turpitude ; another appalling wickedness frequently is enacted ; which defies all accurate description ; and which, if the least genuine human and Christian sensibility predominated in our country, would " make every man's ears who heareth it to tingle." Slaves are articles of gambling. Men, women and children, often the dissolute lawless profligate's own adulterous progeny, are transferred from one domestic tyrant to another, by the turn of a card, or the shake of the dice, or the fleetness of a horse, or any of the other numerous modes of fraud and robbery, which these debauched gamesters have invented to swindle each other with impunity ; yet forsooth, " they are all honourable men." This was done in Washing-

Kidnapping.   Page 120.

ton not long ago; and I presume, is still practised even by members of Congress. If these are dignified citizens, by what epithet will you describe a horde of peculating, predatory freebooters?

These direful abominations, however, are almost pardonable, when contrasted with another ordinary practice among slave-drivers. They not only violate all their conjugal vows without any remorse, for the sake of increasing the stock of marketable human cattle; but then, especially, to use their own most loathsome phrase, if "they are likely wenches," they will sell their own female offspring at a higher price, on account of their lighter colour, and their improved form.

I knew a member of the Legislature of Virginia, with a large family, who speedily after his arrival in Richmond, bought a mulatto girl, scourged her mercilessly until she was forced to submit to his sensuality, removed her to his residence, and had several children by her. To pay a judgment awarded against him for having with others buried and almost murdered a traveller alive, because the stranger would not gamble with the knaves; for this same son of Belial read the prayers over him, and in equal mockery, they fired three rounds at his grave; the woman and the children were seized. He raised the money to pay the sheriff, by a conditional transfer of the woman and his own children; but being an adept in this hopeful science, I believe he finally contrived, by some of the quirks of law, of which he was a practitioner, to cheat both the man-stealer from whom he bought the girl, and also the Ishmaelite to whom he pretended to sell her and his children.

Sometimes, the mother and the junior tribe are disposed of in a lot, but more frequently the females are sold for "breeding wenches," and yet, these same unnatural slave-dealing monsters, boast of their honour, highmindedness, and justice; then what is pollution, debasement, and villany?

All this fearful wickedness, the man-stealer's child witnesses from his infancy, in unceasing variety, and permanent action. No instructor admonishes him of the atrocious "iniquity of their sins." This evil spirit he imbibes, and these crimes as far as his situation admits, he perpetrates,

11

after the example of his neighbours and associates. In this course he lives; and in the love and practice of this ineffably odious wickedness, he enters eternity. Yet by courtesy, he is denominated a gentleman, probably a Christian; for unless there are two white witnesses to prove his transgressions, he cannot be convicted. Who then can be a miscreant, and a servant of Satan?

6. The sixth natural effect of slavery upon slaveholders, is this; *It renders men violent in cruelty.*

The facts which already have been specified, plainly determine; that slavery is a most agonizing system; even if its unnatural enormities and exactions did not more immediately affect human existence. But the barbarity of slave-driving never relaxes, until it terminates in the death of its anguished and wo-worn victim. Who can calculate the myriads of murders which have been committed, by the process of slow-paced famine? by diseases consequent upon the deprivation of essential clothing? by the torturing scourge? and by the more deliberate butchery, as well as in the sudden bursts of malignant fury?

Some years since, a man in Virginia, after a long trial was acquitted for the unrelenting and undisputed killing of a young woman, who had died from the mortification of her lacerated body, during several weeks of excruciating protracted torture. Her body and her legs were literally cut in pieces. A more barbarous slow paced malignant murder can scarcely be found recorded even in the annals of manstealing. The facts could not be denied. He was acquitted on two grounds. The woman had not received, as far as the evidence stated, more than the number of stripes which by law he was empowered to inflict at one time, and she had not actually expired under the lash. It was also maintained in his defence, that the woman was his property as much as his sheep, and that he had a legal right to do as he would with it. One of the counsel for the ruffian slavedriver, in his speech, expressed his surprise at any judicial investigation for whipping a slave to death; for said he, "in that part of Virginia where I was born, it would be considered the greatest insult possible, to take any notice of a gentleman for killing a Negro!" That lawyer's state-

ment is no doubt correct; for even in the case of the wo-
man-killer referred to, there was great difficulty in procuring the formal investigation which elicited the facts, and
the examining court were so intimidated, it is supposed, by
the opposition of the slave-drivers, that they dared not to
transfer the murderer to the higher court for trial and punishment. One of the counsel assured me, that he aided
in the villain's defence, solely to expose the unspeakable
iniquity of the Virginian code of laws respecting slavery.

This butchering iniquity is so frequent, that when a
slave is missing, citizens who are not men-stealers may
" guess;" but they dare not express their suspicions or even
their knowledge.

A few years ago, in Maryland, a most barbarous planter
was killed in a fit of desperation, almost in self-defence, by
four of his slaves, whom he had threatened to half murder
for not performing some work within a given time, which
it was absolutely impossible for them to accomplish. It
was discovered, while the unfortunate culprits were in
prison, that with the commission of every other atrocious
outrage upon their female companions, within a few years,
that slave-driver had deliberately butchered twenty or more
of his slaves, their relative associates, with circumstances
of almost incredible horror. The four men were murdered
by law, as a sacrifice to the popular clamour. These
crimes are not perpetrated where a white man can be evidence ; and the climax of all the heaven daring, hell born
wickedness of slavery is this; that a coloured person's
testimony is not received against a white man; not even
from a female for the violation of her person : or for an
attempt to kill, or the actual commission of murder.

A minister of Virginia informed me of this fact, which
occurred in his own congregation. " A member of my
church," said the brother, " has lately whipped a coloured
young man to death. Nobody saw it but the rest of his
slaves. What shall I do?" my reply was ; " I hope you
do not mean to continue him in your church." " How can
we help it ? the minister remarked ; " we dare not call him
to an account ; for as we have no legal testimony, he would
sue all the officers of the Church for slander and ruin us."

Their Communion season, I believe, was on the second Sabbath following. I addressed his wife. " Mrs. —— what do you think of this Christian ; do you mean to sit at the Lord's table with him ?" " Not I ;" she answered, " I would as soon commune with the devil himself." The murderer passed off, not only unpunished, but also even unnoticed, either by ecclesiastical discipline, or the civil authority.

If the infernal secrets of the kidnappers' prison-houses, their plantations, could be divulged ; and all the tortures, scourgings, rapes, maimings, barbarity, pollution, and massacres with which they are begrimed, *black and bloody*, could be unfolded, the record would be like the ancient roll of the Prophet Ezekiel, " written within and without, lamentations, mourning and wo."

Some time since, a coloured woman was put in the jail of Lexington, Kentucky. She was charged with having set fire to her tyrant's barn, &c. ; and upon the trial was convicted, and sentenced to death. Her execution was respited on account of her pregnancy. During her detention in the prison, her unhappy and delicate condition awakened the attention of some ladies of that town, who visited her in her cell ; and in endeavouring to impress her mind with a proper sense of her guilt, they elicited the cause why she had committed the offence. The unfortunate creature's narrative was to this effect.

A young man, a slave on a neighbouring plantation, and she had become faithfully attached, and were permitted by her master to cohabit together. After a lapse of some time, her driver fixed his adulterous eyes upon her, and demanded her compliance with his sensual desires. She refused. He insisted ; whipped her unmercifully for *her disobedience to his orders ;* and finally, partly through her incapacity in her emaciated state longer to resist him, and partly by force, accomplished his infamous design. During this procedure, the ruthless felon had prohibited her lover from appearing about his house. When she began to recover from the effects of her scourgings, her companion was again permitted to visit her. The honest affectionate creature told him the story of her sufferings and of her debasement ; and besought him to continue his tenderness and his regard towards her, assuring him that in the midst of all her stripes and defilement, she had been only and unreservedly his faithful partner both in heart and person. He received the information with distrust ; even the marks of the cruelty which she had endured did not pacify him · and finding from her confessions, that the ravisher often was connected with her, the coloured man sullenly left his formerly beloved associate, stating, that he would not give away his love any longer to a woman who was so disho-noured ; whether it was involuntary on her part, or with her consent. Finding that all attempts to recover his af-fections and company were unavailing, in a state of frenzied exasperation with her master, at her complicated wrongs, she went out of the kitchen with a firebrand, and set fire to the barn, which with its contents were con-sumed.

This was the substance of the piteous tale, which the condemned woman told the ladies in her dungeon. The white man, in common parlance, was a respectable and influential citizen ; and the ladies reminded the delinquent, that attempts to exculpate herself, by criminating her master with such a heinous offence, would only render her situation the worse, and every endeavour to save her life more hopeless. She maintained the truth of her state-ment with undeviating pertinacity ; and avowed her con-viction, that her ravisher would not have the hardihood to deny her narrative in the presence of those ladies.

At length, feeling indignant at this brutal mode of exter-minating all feminine sensibilities, the ladies resolved, if possible, to ascertain the truth of the woman's tale. The coloured man first was secretly examined. He confirmed it in all its points, so far as her excuses to him had been offered for her unwilling infidelity, and stated to the inquirers some other common facts which occurred between the planters and their female slaves, which he alleged in justifi-cation of his doubts of her attachment, and of his ceasing any more to visit her. From some of the other female slaves belonging to the same gentleman, I believe, the ladies obtained additional information which finally pro-
11*

duced the full conviction in their minds, that the woman's
statement was not only true, but that the worst part of it
had not been communicated to them.   They therefore resolved if possible to save her life, and procure her freedom.

They had no easy task to accomplish.   The station of
the villain who had originated these evils; the difficulty of
combating a white man for crimes perpetrated in private
and without any legal evidence ; the probable opposition of
their own husbands; and the unconquerable prejudices
of the whole mass of society around them, all were arrayed
against their effort; but they determined to effect, if possible, their benevolent design by union and perseverance.
From whatever cause, whether political collisions, or dislike arising from personal disputation, or envy, some of
their husbands manifested a willingness to aid their wives
in their merciful object.   The grand difficulty was this; to
obtain such an acknowledgment of the facts from that de-
stroyer of female happiness, that the ladies might be enabled to appeal to the governor with the assurance of success.

It was contrived, if practicable, to induce the wretch to
visit the daughter of wo in her dungeon.   This solicitation
he steadfastly rejected.   When, however, the time of her
delivery approached, another attempt was made for that
purpose ; and he was asked, whether he was willing that
the poor creature, for in her agitated state, she might not
survive the hour of nature's sorrow, should die without
his pardon ?   This manoeuvre was successful ; and he promised at a certain hour to visit her, accompanied by some
of those gentlemen whose wives had soothed the woman's
anguish, and consoled her in her heavy affliction.

When the gentlemen and the slave-driver arrived at the
prison, to the manifest surprise of the latter, they found
several ladies present, robed in all the sternness of matronly
dignity and purity.   After a little preliminary blustering,
the woman scourger asked his slave ; "Are you not sorry
for having set fire to my property ?"   She feelingly replied,
" I am very sorry for it."   Some other unimportant remarks
followed, when one of the ladies inquired ; " What induced
you to set fire to Mr. ——'s barn ?"   The coloured woman

then narrated the circumstances, precisely as she had before stated them. When she had finished, another lady
remarked to this effect; " Such a hideous story cannot be
true, you are only speaking falsely of your master." During this whole time, the ladies and their husbands were
scrutinizing the varying features of the slave-holder, and
saw clearly enough the evidence of his guilt indelibly depicted on his countenance. The woman answered, " What
I have said is all true, and master cannot deny it."
    From this direct attack there was no escape. The wo-
man torturer began to talk largely of his property, his power
over his slaves, the dangerous impropriety of other persons interfering between the master and his coloured people,
his right to manage his plantation as he pleased, the villany
which the woman had committed in burning his barn, and
that he had done nothing more than all his neighbours always
did, with a long strain of similar ungodliness. The persons
present heard him to the end with great patience, and did
not pretend to dispute any one of his most vile principles.
One of the ladies merely told him, that their sole object was
to relieve an unfortunate creature in a very delicate condition,
and under the sentence of the highest punishment which
the law can inflict; and that the statement which she had
made, if true, and they should fully believe it, unless he
denied and disproved her account, so palliated her offence,
that they should exert their influence with the governor for
her pardon and release. The coloured woman finding herself thus supported, solemnly reiterated the truth of her
narrative, and defied her tormentor to deny its accuracy.
Whether the man-stealer directly admitted the facts, as
detailed by his victim, I do not remember; my impression
is, that he substantially corroborated them; boldly pleading
his rights, and that the female slaves ought thus to be sub-
servient to their masters, for the benefit of the plantations,
and to increase their attachment to their owners. As soon
as the ladies retired from the prison, they devised their plan,
and obtained an interview with the governor, who at once
reversed the sentence of the law, and as a commutation for
her sufferings, I think, in due legal form, immediately
enrolled the emancipation of the victim of lust and cruelty.

Slavery was begun in avarice and barbarity. From the first preparation of the slave vessel in Europe and America, through all its multiplied anguish and wailing, till the slave's decease in hopeless bondage, its character is the same. In some few instances, its horrors may be mitigated, but its uniform and essential predominating quality is blood, *human blood!* Like " the horse-leech, it cries, give, give !" and it is one of those things which is " never satisfied, and saith not, it is enough."

One of the most decided and inflexible opponents of man-stealing in this republic, is a gentleman of Virginia, who was born amid slaves ; nearly all whose early knowledge was obscured through that blinding system ; and all whose associates, whether by natural or matrimonial relations, are in various degrees infected with the leprosy of slavery. Some years ago, during a solemn and momentous discussion on the extension of slavery in the United States, he thus remarked. " My hostility to slavery springs from my attachment to justice and freedom. All my early habits and associations were calculated to blind me with prepossessions in its favour; but before I had passed the limits of boyhood, I read the history of our Revolution, the declaration of Independence, and the Virginia Bill of Rights, and *the scales fell from my eyes.* With the opinions I entertain on this subject, if ever I give a vote in behalf of human bondage, I should myself be unworthy of freedom."

That patriotic orator and philanthropist, although he did not deem it advisable on that occasion to unfold all the means which had aided his correct discernment of the truth, yet he communicated to me the following specimen of " *eye salve,*" with which in junior life his eyes had been anointed, that he might see the genuine character of that American bondage, which in the two ensuing paragraphs, he so eloquently describes. Let it be remembered, this is not a " reckless incendiary," this is not a " hair brained firebrand," this is not a " rabid agitator ;" but a thoughtful, amiable, enlightened and judicious legislator.

" My heart sickens. Whence these unwonted emotions ? Their source lies in the consideration, that it is necessary, even in this land overflowing with the benedic-

Torturing American Citizens.　　Page 129.

tions of heaven, illumined by the light of science, and the celestial splendours of Christianity—this land bought with the blood, and the lives of patriots, and pouring forth hosannas to the God of our fathers and our freedom, for the hallowed boon of liberty—that, even here in this land, it becomes necessary to oppose a deliberate and voluntary extension of the crimes and horrors of slavery; that in this Columbian Republic, thousands of freemen whose hearts leap at the sound of freedom, when applied to individuals and to nations blessed with a complexion like their own, should exist; whose utmost energies are exerted to enlarge the dominion of human bondage, and whose souls kindle into rage against the man, who has the humanity, the justice, and the independence to plead the cause of beings, who are *men, animated with the breath, and stamped with the image of the deity, who are free from crime*, but whose misfortune it is, to have had a different tinge shed upon them, by the influence of an equatorial sun !

" Slavery, like ' the pestilence that walketh in darkness,' spreads ruin and calamity wherever it passes. It scatters poison upon the morals, petrifies the sensibilities, and exasperates and corrupts the passions of all its participants. It contaminates the fountains òf health, kindles the flames of domestic contention, breeds effeminacy and indolence, multiplies artificial wants, introduces into society every kind of luxury and intemperance, and finally gnaws like a canker into the very core of the government, until it saps the vitals of national strength and happiness."

Of this infernal machination, the graphical portrayer, whose picture is thus set before us, detailed the ensuing fact; remarking, "from that exhibition I walked away, the resolute, and unalterable enemy of slavery, in every degree, and under whatever form it might disguise its most abhorrent cruelty and abominations."

"When I was a boy,' said my beloved friend, "on a short ramble from my father's house, I encountered a neighbouring farmer, who had a coloured citizen tied to a large log or a tree lying on the ground. The man was lying on his face uncovered, from his neck downwards. His driver had been lacerating him most mercilessly, until his back was one entire mass of blood and flesh cut up in pieces, which were commingled and slowly amalgamating together. To complete the tortures of his writhing victim, who could scarcely move on account of the tightness with which his hands, neck and feet were bound to the tree; the citizen-flayer caught a large cat, and so fastened the animal, that in endeavouring to get loose, the cat's talons continually tore the slave's already gory back, until the villain's vengeance was glutted; when he released the cat, administered the usual plaster, *salt, pepper, vinegar,* &c., and ordered the son of anguish to resume his labour."

Well might the witness of such a specimen of American freedom declare, "my heart sickened. Its regular pulsations were interrupted, and it felt as if the cold touch of death were about to congeal its vital streams!"

Probably, some persons will object, that these are only isolated instances of uncommon and infrequent barbarity, perpetrated by those infuriated sons of Belial, whom Jehovah mysteriously permits to curse the world. This view is totally incorrect. The foregoing facts develop slavery in its unvarying and universal attributes, as it is always and every where practised. "Murder will out," says the old proverb; and in spite of all their artifices to conceal their flagrant iniquities, the God of Providence, as he did with the Jewish Prophet, Ezekiel 8: 3—18, occasionally permits a Christian explorer to see "the great abominations which" American men-stealers "do in the dark, who fill the land with violence, and provoke the Lord God to anger."

The history of the African coast, of the middle passage, and of the West Indian islands; and of the subsequent introduction of that diabolical iniquity into the Northern and Southern American continents; is one perennial, heart rending catalogue of those desolating wide-spread massacres, which are inseparable from slavery. Blood and endless multiform barbarity are its grand aliment. Slavery and cruelty cannot be disjoined; consequently every slaveholder necessarily must be inhuman. Its hideousness may be modified in exhibition; or it may exist in different degrees; according as social circumstances, or the physical

or mental constitution of the slave-driver may exert its influence; but the peculiarly ostensible features are paramount; and cannot be obliterated: for there is indelibly
inscribed upon this whole mischievous conspiracy against
God and the rights of man, and unless they repent of their
unequalled wickedness, upon its ungodly impenitent artificers, " BLOOD, DEATH, and DAMNATION !"

7. One more natural effect of slavery upon slave-holders
must be mentioned. *It is the prolific source of all infidelity
and irreligion.* These are both the tree and the fruits of
slavery; the tree is corrupt, and of course the fruits are
evil, " by their fruits we know them." They first blind
the eyes to all that is good, then they nurture all that is
unholy; and thus by their reaction, they engender and multiply other " things, which are not convenient;" until the
slave-holders are " filled with all unrighteousness."

A Christian observer in the slave driving states, will incessantly behold the following developments of infidelity
and irreligion, in all diversified exhibition—here, disguised
in a hypocritical garb of exterior decorum; and there,
avowed in all their criminal deformity, and palpable turpitude.

" The fear of the Lord is the beginning of wisdom," say
the inspired oracles. That fear includes profound reve-
rence for his majesty; fervent affection for his authority,
works, and benevolence; devout attention to his requisitions; and faithful obedience to his commandments. It is
impossible to conceive how these dispositions can be sincerely felt and cultivated by a slave-holder. We do not
pronounce concerning the actual moral relation of any
man with his Creator and Judge. The Lord hath rules
of judgment, in his infinite wisdom, beyond our ken; and
the slave-holder may be acquitted at the dread tribunal of
Christ. Our concern is only with a correct interpretation
of the Holy Bible; and according to divine revelation,
every attribute of the Godhead is insulted, and all the laws
of God are violated by the slave-dealer; to whom, in this
case may justly be addressed the pungent expostulation;
especially to those slave-holders, who profess to be Christians, " a son honoureth his father, and a servant his mas-

ter; if then I be a father, where is my honour? and if I be
a master, where is my fear? saith the Lord of hosts unto
you, that despise my name." Malachi 1: 6.

This destitution of the fear of God is generally accompanied by a scornful rejection of the bible altogether, as is
the case with the overwhelming majority of slave-drivers;
or the merely nominal fruitless acknowledgment of its
divine origin and authority; or as is exemplified by professors of Christianity, a total negligence of all those passages which denounce slavery, and a flagrant perversion
of their spirit and design, if possible, to twist them into a
justification of that iniquity which they infallibly condemn.
Thus the divine code which has been imparted to mankind
by our gracious Creator, as "the light of our feet, and the
lamp of our path," is entirely nullified, and the resplendency
and healing of the beams which emanate from "the Sun
of Righteousness," are obscured; and men grope in tangible night, and engage in "the unfruitful works of darkness," without fear, and without compunction.   Indeed,
nothing can be more enigmatical, than the inconsistency
of slave-drivers, who retain a book in their houses, the instructions of which they profess to believe, and all whose
intention, doctrines, and precepts, they perpetually and
wilfully violate: for the bible and slavery are totally irreconcilable, being separated by the impassable gulf.

As a natural result, the worship of God, domestic, social
and public, is either partially or wholly discarded. Genuine
Christian prayer and slavery cannot be conjoined.   What
can be more shockingly absurd, than the petition; "forgive
us our trespasses, as we forgive them who trespass against
us!" uttered by a slave-driver in the presence of his slaves,
whom he robs, starves, and scourges; and whose tears,
tortures, and blood daily cry to Heaven for retribution?
What more awful, than the general exclusion of slaves even
from domestic worship, where the form is so inconsistently
maintained?   What more criminal, than the death-like
silence of Christian ministers of all denominations in the
southern states, upon the various topics of slavery, its unrighteous principles, its corrupt motives, its diabolical acts,
its incestuous defilements, its sleepless barbarity, its daring

impiety, and its desolating curse? Preachers of the Gospel, so called, resident south of the Potomac, and many to the north of that river, who are their brother coadjutors, either are "possessed of a dumb devil" on this subject, or they only quote the scriptures, Satan-like, to falsify their meaning, and to defend the heaven-defying abominations, which so loudly call for the just vengeance of their dishonoured and insulted master, Jesus the friend of sinners, who came " to preach the gospel to the poor, to heal the broken-hearted, to preach deliverance to the captive, to set at liberty them who are bruised, and to seek and to save that which was lost." " Wo unto you, blind guides, who strain at a gnat, and swallow a camel! Wo unto you, who shut up the kingdom of heaven! Wo unto you, hypocrites! Ye make clean the outside of the cup, and of the platter, but within they are full of extortion and excess! Even so ye also outwardly appear righteous unto men, but within, ye are full of hypocrisy, and deceit! How can ye escape the damnation of nell?" Matthew 23; 13—23.

The next consequence of this deplorable violation of all evangelical prescriptions is this: slaves are prohibited from all instruction, and excluded from the means of grace in every form. No infant school gladdens the hearts of the coloured prattlers; no Sunday school cheers them with " the light to life;" no Bible unlocks to them the " treasures in heaven, which neither moth nor rust can corrupt, nor thieves break through and steal;" no sabbath proclaims to them the " glad tidings of great joy," with all the " unsearchable riches of Christ;" and no trumpet resounds to them the Jubilee's joyful sound. If a slaveholder proclaims pure gospel truth, every sentence which he utters, speaks his own reprobation ; for the instruction of the slaves, and the existence of slavery, can hold no more " fellowship, than righteousness with unrighteousness; and no more communion than light with darkness."

This opposition to all the means of spiritual and moral improvement among the slaves, cannot be extirpated unless by the immediate extinction of the whole system. A striking illustration of this principle occurred some time since. A black man of undoubted piety desired admission to

12

Christian membership and privileges. The minister was afraid to recognise him as a Christian brother, because as he alleged, " no person scarcely around me supposes that a negro has a soul to be saved; and although Jacob is one of our best believers in Jesus, I should only secure to myself violent censure and incurable hatred, did I admit him to the communion."

Slave-dealers lamentably are consistent; they first brutalize the coloured people, then stigmatise them as irrational animals, and then force them to exemplify the melancholy adage, " like brutes they live, like brutes they die." But to whom will the Lord, the Judge, announce in his wrath, their "blood I require at your hand?" The blind watchmen. Isaiah 56; 10. This deprivation of religious knowledge is not less illegal, and unconstitutional, than it is contrary to the gospel.

What must unavoidably follow from this mass of infidel principles, and this scornful neglect of all the institutions of religion? Nothing else, than increasing hardness of heart, and " searedness of conscience as with a hot iron," in the slave-driver. It is the natural course of sin in its infatuated votary. The slaveholder refuses the light, and therefore like "the fool, he walketh in darkness." He gradually becomes more and more wedded to his lusts, in proportion as he has indulged them. His avarice, inordinate sensuality, haughtiness, and impetuous domineering, all augment with his increased sphere for the display of them, and with his years, until he neither " fears God, nor regards man," further than as his worldly interest, or ever shifting expediency may oblige him. Every slave-driver's plantation verifies this humiliating fact, and, if their vices have not prematurely shortened their earthly pilgrimage, their latter days ordinarily are appalling manifestations of the dreadful progress which iniquity unopposed makes over all the moral faculties, until it leaves the guilty perpetrators indifferent to the past, thoughtless of the present, and reckless of the future, even when they are on the verge of receiving " the wages of sin."

The contrasted lives, the eulogised virtues, and the apparently happy departures of the comparatively small number of persons, who are emblazoned before the world; admitting them all to be genuine and correct, which is incredible, are so "few and far between," that they only tend to make the otherwise "palpable obscure," more visible; and certify, that the loss of the moral sense, and a stupified conscience, are the unavoidable effects of that system, which "steals, sells, and holds human beings as slaves."

It is also indisputable, that the slave-dealer's life of iniquity, is generally attended with a death in manifest impenitence and sin. All the efforts of Christian charity, cannot obliterate the long-continued robberies, the heart-rending shrieks, and agonies, and the constant internal resistance to the light and truth, which have marked the man-thief's course. His death-bed emits no cheering evangelical retrospect, and no ray of that freedom which belongs to the children of God. He has been a kidnapper and a slave-driver, and he grasps his stolen fellow-citizens to the last. The produce of his thefts he bequeaths to his heirs of the same character and dispositions, and who most probably, like the brethren of Dives, will follow him to the "place of torment." Admitting that a Christian may extenuate his holding slaves, while he lives; a doctrine, however, which is totally incompatible with divine truth, how he can die and transfer them as property, is a mystery which defies all human solution. Every deceased American slaveholder since the fourth of July, 1776, died a man-thief, and a mist of darkness hovers over his grave, which no fire of Christian love, that "hopeth all things," can possibly dissipate.

If we advert to the history of men-stealers generally, of whatever name or class, Solomon's inscription may be affixed upon the tomb stones of them all, both ecclesiastical and civil, at least in the United States, subsequent to the declaration of Independence. "I saw the wicked buried, who had come and gone from the place of the holy, and they were forgotten in the city where they had so done." Ecclesiastes 8; 10. Washington alone seems likely to survive the sepulchre of oblivion; but he was a father to his coloured people when living, and at his death, they were all emancipated. Of all the other dead American slave-drivers, "the course of time" is illustrating the rapid fulfilment of that startling prophecy, Proverbs 10; 7. "*The name of the wicked shall rot.*"

The period has arrived, when slavery must be entirely abolished. To tolerate its abominations for one hour, extends a pestilence throughout the union, adds fuel to the volcano which is ready to burst forth in all its devastating fury upon the republic, increases a mass of moral corruption, which now is mortifying in the body politic, and with the most open provoking effrontery, calls for the vengeance of heaven, and the retributive curse of God upon our guilty country. What citizen, with a sane mind, can possibly suppose, that the righteous Arbiter of Providence much longer will permit a horde of oppressors, haughty, presumptuous, "past all feeling, without natural affection, implacable, unmerciful," profligate, unrighteous, turbulent, religious persecutors, cruel, impious in principle, and filled with all practical ungodliness, to doom two millions of our fellow immortals, free born American citizens, to every contrivance of misery and vice here, and to hell hereafter; only to gratify their atrocious hard-heartedness and lusts, and to glut their insatiate thirst for despotism and blood?

The only effectual and Christian method to destroy the natural effects of slavery upon the slaveholders, and thereby to remove the danger and the curse of kidnapping, with all its concomitant ferocity, anguish and crimes, from our country, is evident; instantly, universally, and altogether, to "proclaim liberty to the captives, to loose the bands of wickedness, to undo the heavy burdens, to break every yoke, and to let the oppressed go free." Amen!

ABOLITION OF SLAVERY.

No KIDNAPPERS IN PUBLIC OFFICE! No MENSTEALERS IN
THE CHURCH OF CHRIST!

SLAVERY is the disgrace and curse of the United States:
and no question of more importance to the citizens, can be
propounded for discussion than this; By what mode can
the direful pest be eradicated?

. The history of the period which has elapsed since the
fourth of July, 1776, assures us that all arguments which
can be deduced from reason, consistency, justice, and religion, are nugatory. The noblest faculties of the human
mind have exerted all their energies in vain; for slave-
drivers continue as practically unconvinced, as though no
illumination had ever beamed upon this melancholy topic.
All appeals to the moral sensibilities of men, have been
equally unavailing; for so debased and stupified is their
conscience, that without a blush, ministers of the gospel,
officers of the Christian churches of every name, and
nominal disciples of Christ of all ranks in civil society,
prolong the kidnapping system, and unite in "the trade of
the bodies and souls of men."

For them in vain does genius lavish all its ample treasures of intelligence; and for naught does oratory pour
forth all its eloquent illustrations of the primary clauses of
the Declaration of Independence, and the infallible social
canons of the several Bills of Rights enacted by our different confederated republics. Hardened by avarice, and
seared by long practised iniquity, their consciences feel
not; although they are convinced that their discordant professions and practice are the scorn of tyrants; the disgrace
of freemen; and the lamentation of all sincere friends of
the rights of man, and of every Christian Philanthropist.

Long has equity proposed her resistless claim to the immediate and the entire abolition of slavery. The thunders
of avenging justice, and the invitations of pardoning mercy
are equally despised by those infatuated sons of crime
and oppression, the kidnappers. They vociferate inces-

12*

santly respecting the injustice of emancipating their slaves
without a full pecuniary equivalent; that is, unless a thief
is paid to desist from stealing; but to propound unto them
that the man-stealer shall refund to the slave any portion,
however small, of the plunder which they have continually
amassed from the pitiable objects of their stripes and robbery, instead of convincing, only excites their rage; and
they would feel no remorse at torturing, or even murdering the honest man who will urge upon them, as the only
acceptable sacrifice which they can present unto God, that
they shall "do justly, and love mercy."

In the southern states, all the orators who ever lived
would discourse upon the duty of reciprocal justice, without the least impression; unless they made the direct application to the system of man-stealing.

A slave-holder will expatiate upon liberty, honour, righteousness, and all their kindred virtues, until a person who
hears him, could almost suppose that he was an absolute
stranger even to the very terms, tyranny, baseness, injustice, and their allied vices,—for he seems to have not the
least perception that there are probably fifty or a hundred
of his fellow-citizens detained by himself in the most cruel
and iron bondage, in connexion with whom he never exhibited any decorum, or right, or philanthropy.

More true still is the allegation in reference to religion.
Christianity exercises no legitimate sway over any slave-
holder. The planter may not be an image-worshipper;
and he may not be profane, or a dissolute Sabbath breaker,
and thus violate the four primary commands; but he is a
man-thief; and his slaves curse and swear without rebuke,
and are forced *not* "*to keep* holy the Sabbath-day." He
may not absolutely dishonour his own father and mother;
but without remorse, he cancels all the domestic relations
of the coloured men, women, and children, whom he has
kidnapped into misery without end. He may not kill a
white man from fear of the gallows; but he feels no solicitude for the sudden or slow-paced murder of the inoffensive coloured citizen, whom he detains in his accursed
man-trap.

As for the four last of the moral laws, given by the Lord

to Moses, on Mount Sinai, multiform uncleanness, continual stealing, perjury, deception, and false witness without intermission, and that covetousness which is idolatry, are so essential to a man-stealer's domain, that without them, *slavery* would instantaneously disappear.

Whether or not every individual slave-driver is a practical violator of the seventh commandment is of comparatively little importance; he connives at the sins, or sanctions them. Therefore, since every motive and argument which can be adduced, in all their authority and solemnity, during nearly sixty years, have been tried without effect, to induce these God-robbers to abandon their crimes, and to desist from man-stealing; it is now become an imperative and sacred duty, to ascertain whether any other means can be adopted, which shall persuade or coerce these Felons to " repent and turn from their wicked ways," that God may " turn and heal our land."

It is often alleged, that time will cure the evil; and that it is preferable to transfer the fulfilment of their obligations to emancipate their slaves to their oppressors. This position is not less absurd than it is mischievous. Every citizen of the United States, on the fourth of July, 1776, and since that period to this present hour, actually attests, that " all men are born free and equal," with undisputed liberty to pursue that course, which in consistency with the immunities of others, shall best promote their own happiness. Not only nearly every individual of all the adult generation then living, but even the large majority of their immediate descendants have departed from this earthly pilgrimage. The third race are also rapidly hastening to the tomb; and what have they done? They have multiplied their human cattle in a very extraordinary ratio; they have tightened the fetters of their wretched captives: they have increased the horrors of their miserable bondage; and they have rendered the emancipation of our coloured fellow-citizens more hopeless; and as far as their power extends, indescribably less practicable to be accomplished than at the termination of the Revolutionary war.

During this whole half century, they have been shouting

in praise of liberty; boasting of American freedom, and the rights of man; and despising almost all the other nations of the world on account of their submission to the yoke of their cruel despots. Is it not therefore manifestly preposterous, or rather is it not a proof of hallucination bordering upon insanity, to indulge any expectation, that these persons, who, during so long a revolution of years, have resisted public merited contempt for their duplicity, the claims of reason and justice, and the tremendous curse which the law of God denounces against the impenitent workers of iniquity; will now voluntarily "cease to do evil, and learn to do well;" unless some argument which hitherto has not been propounded, and some measure that yet has not been executed, shall be put in operation to arrest their transgressions, and to counteract the unspeakable and continuous agonies which they inflict?

During the time when the topics connected with man-stealing were the prominent themes of discussion with the small Christian band in Virginia who opposed slavery; and when its merciless and odious exhibitions were ever before their eyes, the question was often agitated among these stern advocates for full and prompt emancipation—what is the most certain and efficient method to exterminate the abhorrent system of man-stealing?

Two schemes only could be devised which appeared to possess the smallest recommendation, or which could produce any decisive influence upon the result. It was a perilous attempt then, even to disseminate the doctrine; and much more to exemplify it in practice. But it was resolved, at all hazards, to fulfil the authoritative claims of the divine law, and to comply with the faithful dictates of an enlightened conscience.

All the varieties of slave-holders may be classified in two distinct bodies. They are either men of the world, in the scriptural sense of the term, or they are professed disciples of Christ. Luxury and worldly ambition are the grand pursuits of every slave-holder; and to obtain them, they perennially sacrifice all the sensibilities of humanity and religion. To this it will be retorted—remember the large donations which are contributed by the southern

churches to benevolent institutions, as a proof of their philanthropy and religion. With the deepest pungency and
mortification is that fact recollected; nor is it less regret-
ted, that their presents are even received for any avowed
holy purposes. Greatly to be deplored is that unhallowed
combination in our country, which so influences our northern Christian citizens, that they will accept the spoils
of kidnappers, as suitable votive offerings to the treasury
of brotherly love, or Christian zeal—for all the gifts of the
hordes of southern men-stealers to the fund of evangelical
service, are most painfully, but instructively delineated by
the prophet Isaiah; chapter lxvi.; verse 3. "He that
killeth an ox is as if he slew a man; he that sacrificeth a
lamb, is as if he cut off a dog's neck; he that offereth an
oblation, as if he offered swine's blood ; and he that burneth
incense, as if he blessed an idol. They have chosen their
own ways, and their soul delighteth in their abominations."

Whatever individual exceptions may exist to the general rule is of no consideration in reference to our argument; but these words convey the correct Christian esti-
mate of the slave-driver's pretended, but eulogized generosity.

The question now returns for our examination—By
what means can the beneficent object of anti-slavery societies, the universal abolition of man-stealing, most ce-
tainly and speedily be accomplished ?

The answer will comprise two views of the subject—
the former as it includes civil society; and the other as it
refers to ecclesiastical concerns, or to the Christian church.

I. By what method can slavery be extinguished, through
the opposition which can be made unto it by citizens acting
only in their social relations?

Every slave-driver, under any pretext whatever, is absolutely as incapable, as he is unworthy of a public office in
the United States : and every citizen who votes for a slave-
holder to fill any public office violates his duty, and is
virtually guilty of subornation of perjury.

These doctrines will be considered even now, as they
were nearly twenty years ago, when they were first pro-

mulged, as startling, and very revolting positions; but they are infallible truths, which no enlightened honest man will dare to impugn.

It is due to those slave-drivers in the southern states, who are merely profligate infidels, to acknowledge, that they never attempt to justify slavery upon principle. The nominal Christians are the only persons who strive to sanctify their man-stealing, by the sacred volume. The former plead their present difficult situation, and their *incapacity*, that is a very pernicious misnomer, it should be, their *unwillingness*, to remedy their peculiar condition, and the danger of emancipation, and prudence in the adoption of means, and the expediency of a general movement upon the subject, and the propriety of waiting until all the slave-drivers are agreed. As if the wildest lunatic who ever raved, could fancy, that a large horde of widely scattered kidnappers, will all simultaneously and voluntarily coalesce, at once, to become honest men, and to restore their ungodly spoils, while their honour, opulence, and enjoyments are augmented and retained solely by their legalized felonies!

These men desire only present honours and enjoyments! The acquisition of the latter, no person ought to interrupt, provided the man who attempts to obtain worldly comfort does not infringe upon the laws of society: but elevation to office in this republic involves totally different principles. American citizens are amenable to God and the world, for the men whom they elect to fill the dignified and influential stations of our federal and state governments.

The candidate when he enters upon public office, swears, that he will obey the constitution of the United States, and of course, that he believes the principles upon which our social fabric is avowedly founded. Hence, no slaveholder can take this oath consistently, in the true and legitimate meaning of the terms; and therefore, he is either ignorant of his duty, which is ample disqualification for office, or he is guilty of wilful and corrupt perjury.

Among persons of this character, all the holier obligations have little or no influence. The oath of office, by the greater part of the southern men-stealers, is deemed to be merely a stupid form, invented by ignorant fanatics, and which is complied with, because the honours and emoluments cannot be obtained without a submission to the requirement. As to any supposed bond of fidelity, further than as it may serve the public interest, when their own personal aggrandizement is also secured, not one out of a hundred of the whole of the slave-driving Confederacy ever supposed, that the official oath imposed any additional test, or implied any other claim, than that which is voluntarily displayed.

All this is consistent, but then, it is a tissue of deliberate equivocation, exactly analogous to the man-stealer's notions of honesty, and the precise counterpart of the atrocious falsehood which he utters, when he declares, that his coloured fellow citizen's child whom he has stolen, and the money which he obtained as the price of his own offspring, are his honestly gotten property.

It is vain to reason, argue, or to persuade these men who " love darkness rather than light, because their deeds are evil." You must apply more coercive machinery, and boldly and peremptorily announce, and from your resolution never swerve, that *no slaveholder shall receive your vote.* In principle, he is a merciless tyrant, by his constant profession, he is a shameless deceiver, and in his unvarying practice, he is the most abhorrent of all thieves. How any enlightened, patriotic, and virtuous citizen can vote for a perjure kidnapping despot to rule over him, either as a legislator, or an administrator of the law, is a " Mystery of iniquity," which no one but Satan, the original contriver of his own hell-born work, slavery, can possibly explain.

This resolution in practice, thanks be to God ! cannot be exemplified in the eastern and northern states : but the principle must float upon your banner of emancipation, and be resounded throughout the United States, until it shall rouse, into concentrated action, all the honest and consistent citizens of our Republic.

A beginning must instantly be made. The efforts already commenced, by petitioning Congress for the abolition of slavery in the District of Columbia, must be repeated, with renewed vigour, with enlarged numbers, and in a more thundering tone. The Federal Legislature is controlled by the kidnappers ; who, like the unjust judge, "neither fear God nor regard man ;" and who yet at last may grant to persevering importunity, that which could be obtained, neither by the wailings of sorrow, nor by the demands of justice. This "continuance in prayer," will be also of great importance, because it will attract public attention, until the act shall be passed, that slavery shall no longer disgrace that portion of our country which belongs to the whole federal union.

It would be irrelevant here to consider the principle for which we contend, in reference to the only two public officers, the President, and the Vice President, to whom this doctrine can apply in the non-slaveholding states, because, nothing is more detestable, than the ever fluctuating expediency, by which all sins and corruption can be justified. We stand upon holier ground. Our oracle is this, slavery is wickedness in every variety, and " only evil continually," and *all slaveholders without exception,* are "*men-stealers, sinners of the first rank, and guilty of the highest kind of theft.*" Therefore, slavery ought instantaneously to be abolished. One of the two only effectual means, according to human judgment, to secure this desirable result, is this ; to eject from public office all those who are its chief abettors, and who will ever resist all measures to exterminate the ungodly machination ; except they shall ascertain, that their ambition and their sensuality cannot be gratified, unless by assenting to the demands of the Christian fanatics.

There are honest, wise, patriotic, and conscientious citizens in ample numbers, to execute all the duties of our republican government. Voluntarily, therefore, to select men, who upon their admission into the office, perjure themselves, and all whose acts testify, that they have no clear or upright perceptions of the difference between truth and error, honesty and theft, cruelty and love, good and evil, is equally absurd, as it would be for a man to choose for his confidential domestic, the greatest villain who was ever condemned to the Penitentiary, in preference to a diligent, long tried, and inflexibly faithful friend.

The banner of truth and liberty must be unfurled, and all American citizens must adopt this motto, *No slaveholder shall fill any public office.* His detestable principles, his falsifying declarations, and his systematic robbery, all disqualify him to be a legislator, magistrate, or judge among men who know their rights, and who are determined to retain them. For every kidnapper, with similar willingness, would steal a white girl as a coloured female, if it could be effected with impunity.

Some years since, a white boy about seven years old, was stolen from his parents. He was tattooed, painted, and tanned. Every other method was also adopted which wickedness could devise, to change the exterior appearance of the unfortunate creature, into one uniform dark tinge. In this wretched and forlorn condition, he grew up to maturity; driven, starved, and scourged, like the coloured people with whom he was obliged to associate. He was a genuine non-descript, neither of the white, Indian, nor African species of man. At length, some friends of freedom compassionating his anguish, mercifully contrived to procure his escape to his parents in Ohio, who had lost this boy about twelve or fourteen years previous, when about to remove from Virginia, and of whom no vestige could be discovered. Like the Patriarch Jacob, they had been constantly bewailing their child, without however the additional pungency of knowing the desperate sufferings which were his constant portion.

The kidnapper was a pretended Christian, and when it was communicated to him, that the youth was in safety under the protection of his family, he cursed and reviled all those persons who had aided in his flight, as notorious knaves, who had united to rob him of his property, and threatened them with the punishment of the civil law : for it is one of the most flagrant crimes in the slave-driver's catalogue of iniquity, to encourage and assist a slave to escape from his fetters and agony.

No doubt exists that many Indians, are now retained in slavery in Georgia, upon the same principles, and in the same manner, and any attempt on their part to fly from their tortures, would secure their instant death. The grand objects of the chief kidnappers in that state, in their outrageous assaults upon the Cherokees and Creeks, have evi-

13

dently been, not only to dispossess them of their lands, but
also if their Albany accomplices could effectually have aided
them, to have reduced those Aborigines of the American
soil, to unconditional and endless personal servitude.

They who have enacted the death-dealing code of diabolical legislation, which fills the loathsome statute-books of the
slave states, concerning colored persons; with equal alacrity
and delight, would frame another series of laws, adapted to
the white citizens, marked with that same injustice, pecu-
lation, perjury, blood, and all diversified crime, which now
render the system of government in the southern portion
of our Republic not less loathsome, than it is damnable.
No alternative remains, but resolutely to withhold our
votes from the most atrocious criminals as public officers.

2. The effect of this VETO, however, will be of little essential importance, unless it is accompanied, and sanctioned
by a more influential measure. The great and efficient
prop of man-stealing in the United States, is founded upon
its connexion with the Christian church, and thence it must
be extirpated. According to the existing practice, ere long
all our extensively associated ecclesiastical bodies will
become not only virtually, but actually " Synagogues of
Satan."

Even now, the nominal members of all the large affiliated
religious communities in the United States, are despotically
controlled in all their proceedings, by the preaching kidnappers. This fact is verified by one continually recurring
circumstance, which forms a fearful anomaly otherwise totally inexplicable.

At the meetings of the numerous ecclesiastical assemblies,
and in the newspapers and other public documents, which
are issued among the various denominations of Christians,
with the utmost propriety, we hear loud and reiterated lamentations over the prevalence and evil effects of intemperance, gambling, sensuality, profaneness, sabbath-breaking,
and their concomitant vices : but where will you discover a
hint whispered against man-stealing, and all the multifarious horrors, anguish, and crimes of which it is the prolific
parent ?

Why is this atrocious system of iniquity, with all its in-

Taming a Boy.   P. 145.

separable drunkenness, knavery, uncleanness, blasphemy, rejection of God, dishonour of the Sabbath, and murder of men, tolerated with impunity? Why, upon this subject of kidnapping, are the public meetings of the Christian churches, " silent as death, still as midnight?" Why? because they "love the praise of man more than the praise of God." Why? because the slave-drivers have usurped stations of high dignity and authority in the land. Why? because by their continual robberies of the defenceless, poor and oppressed coloured citizens, whom they have deprived of their labour, liberty, and pursuit of happiness, for the sake of honour, influence and power, those God robbers, and man-stealers will occasionally contribute, from the mass of superfluous wealth which they have stolen, a donation for a charitable, or a professedly religious purpose. Thus, a whole life of incessant violence, unrighteousness, and criminality is obscured from our vision, and the guilty slave-driver, with all his enormities, in direct contradiction to every hallowed dictate of divine revelation, is metamorphosed into a Christian of the highest standard. " For this thing, the earth is disquieted." All slaveholders, and their time serving coadjutors, who pretend to be disciples of Jesus, and who when they see a man-thief, consent with him, are graphically delineated by Agur.   Proverbs 30; 12—14. " There is a generation that are pure in their own eyes, and yet are not washed from their filthiness! There is a generation, O how lofty are their eyes, and their eyelids are lifted up! and there is a generation whose teeth are as swords, and their jaw-teeth as knives, to devour the poor from off the earth, and the needy from among men."

How can this desolating curse effectually be extirpated?

Every slaveholder, peremptorily and without delay, must be excommunicated from the church of God.

It is of no importance, what titles, what office, what station, or what rank, the slaveholder may hold, or what apparent virtues, or talents he may possess, and develop. To all these specious pleas, and to all this anti-christian whitewashing, there is a concise, significant and irrefutable reply ;— *He is a man-stealer.* But as a man-stealer is the very highest criminal in the judgment of God, and of all rational uncorrupted men, he cannot be a Christian, and therefore, it is an insult to the Lord Jesus Christ, the head of the church, to record the most notorious criminal, as an acceptable member of " the household of faith."

This is both the root and offspring of modern American slavery. Had the various Christian denominations in the United States, immediately after the close of the revolutionary war, honestly promulged evangelical truth, and faithfully preserved the order of the Lord's house upon this momentous subject, no slave would now exist, to implore the curse of God in his retributive vengeance, upon our slave-dealing republic.

The nominal Christian churches in the United States, are responsible unto the Judge of all the earth, for the prolonged existence, and the amplified extension of slavery in this country. To the pretended professors of that period, appertain the indelible disgrace of having proclaimed the principles of civil and religious liberty as their own birthright, and of having simultaneously affirmed, the most debasing thraldom both of body and mind, of heart and conscience, for the coloured portion of the citizens. They are chargeable with having avowedly adopted the holy oracles, as the standard of their faith and practice, and yet with allowing the perennial abrogation of them, by all the wretched transgressors who steal, sell, and make merchandize of their brethren.

Such deliberate, unblushing, and publicly transacted hypocrisy, by large numbers of men in the very face of the world, cannot be parallelled, except in the proceedings of the council of Trent, or of some other of those ecclesiastical assemblies, over which Satan presided, that he might establish, and perpetuate " the mystery of iniquity."

This doctrine will doubtless receive those unmeaning retorts, " uncharitableness, severity, harshness," and all the other collateral canting terms, which are used by " Scribes and Pharisees," and applied without judgment. We are searching after evangelical truth only, and that proclaims in a loud and resistless voice, that a slave-driver, whatever he may be in the decision of Jehovah, cannot exhibit one solitary claim or title to the privileges of Christian communion, as a member of the confraternity of them, who " love the Lord Jesus Christ in sincerity," who " know that they are passed from death unto life, because they love the brethren of the household of faith," and who are part of that mystical body the church, " where there is neither Greek nor Jew, circumcision, nor uncircumcision, barbarian, Scythian, bond nor free, but Christ is all and in all."

The grand, and it is childishly supposed, the irrefragable pleas against the description for which we contend, are these : The comparative smallness of the number of those who will adopt the system of exclusion, and the want of general concert ; and the apparently terrifying opposition which cannot be surmounted. These pretexts are altogether unavailing. It is the old device of Satan to plant obstacles in the way of all good, and to imbue us with that " fear of man, which bringeth a snare," instead of putting our trust in the Lord, and finding in him promised safety. According to this evasion, the holy apostles were idiots, glorified Martyrs, were lunatics, and the immortal Reformers, were disturbers of the world. The men who declared our national independence, admitting this absurdity, were infatuated, and the founders of the Temperance Reform, deserve to be execrated. But as this is too silly even to be uttered, therefore, the other allegation is equally invalid and mischievous.

There must be a beginning, and to the Christians of New England especially, to the descendants of the Puritan Pilgrims, is reserved, the honour of commencing upon a large arena, and of effectually carrying on the warfare which shall expel man-stealing from all connexion with the American churches. However plausible may be the pretexts, and however ingenious and urgent may be the excuses, they must categorically denounce the profession of Christianity in alliance with slaveholding as *pestiferous hypocrisy*. They must sternly prohibit all slave-driving preachers from officiating in the sanctuary, or leading in any devotional exercises. And they must copy the high and holy example of Jesus of Nazareth, the head of the church ; who when he saw that the Jewish disciples of Mammon, had

13*

transformed " the house of prayer into a den of thieves," cast them all out of the temple.   Thus the northern and eastern Christians must unsparingly act: they must eject every man-stealer, without exception, from " the communion of saints," instantly and forever.

If we desire to eradicate a rotten tree from longer cumbering the ground, it is folly merely to lop off the withered branches.   The axe must be laid to the trunk, that the whole useless mass may be cleared away together.   Thus it will be of no use to exclude private individuals or lay officers of the church from membership, while preaching negro scourgers are honoured as messengers of the Gospel of peace.   Every one of them must be silenced, and no more be permitted to enact that mournful theological farce before the world, which combines the preaching of the revelation of justice and mercy, with the ever enduring practice of all diversified unrighteousness and cruelty.

Every Christian society must commence this work of reformation for themselves.   It is madness to pretend to stay for conventions, assemblies, conferences, synods, presbyteries, or associations to begin and consummate this glorious object.   If we wait for any fundamental or extensive amendments of ecclesiastical abuses, and religious corruptions from *them ;* the patience of Job, and the meekness of Moses would be exhausted, and not only Methuselah's long protracted term would revolve to its end, but " the sun himself will grow dim with age, and nature sink in years."   No reformation in the church of God ever began with its ministers, in their collective capacity.   The alarm was sounded probably by one or more separate and isolated individuals.   The common people " heard the word gladly," seized the weapons of moral and spiritual war, and eventually forced that radical renovation, which otherwise would have been denied as unnecessary, or delayed as long as priestcraft could have cajoled its silly and enslaved votaries.

Who can indulge any rational expectation that the ecclesiastical bodies in the southern states, will ever seriously undertake the extermination of slavery from the church of

Christ, as long as they remain organized according to their present system, and while they are composed of characters similar to those which at present constitute them ?

Walk into an Episcopal convention south of the Potomac, and from the chairman to the doorkeeper, it is almost certain that they are all slave-drivers, or what is tantamount, the disproportion of the honest Christians to the kidnapping tribe may be assimilated to Gideon's three hundred chosen warriors of the Lord God of Israel, against the Midianite army, " as grasshoppers for multitude." Now to expect that such a body as this, resolved to continue their peculating enormities, as long as the civil law permits them to escape the rightful abode of all men-stealers, will boldly denounce man-stealing, as the most heaven defying crime, and honestly promulge that divine truth, which declares that every perpetrator of it, who assumes to be a Christian, is a scandalous hypocrite, is equally wise as to anticipate the very highest self denying act of pure and undefiled religion from a conspiracy of resolute hardened robbers.

Enter a Baptist association about the Roanoke, where, although the assembly has no ecclesiastical authority, yet the members might discuss an abstract question, and having determined it according to their judgment, might recommend their decision to the consideration of their churches. Who are present ? The chairman, the clerks, and messengers, except northern delegates, are all hardened menstealers. Most probably, not one is named on the roll, who does not drive, scourge, and starve those defenceless sons of anguish, his fellow citizens, whom he has kidnapped, until the fictions of romance lose their interest in the thrilling horrors, which those dens of human misery, their slave-quarters, like the dungeons of the Popish Inquisition, if permitted, could recount. That man who hopes for reformation from such a confederacy of land pirates, manifests no more common sense, than if he were to look for a fraternal embrace in a bear's gripe, or the kiss of love from a hyena's jaw.

Many of our northern Baptists, to their honour, refuse to admit any slaveholder to their communion ; yet, they *lack one thing.* They admit the preaching men-stealers into their pulpits. This great evil destroys all the lesser good, and proves that they are partial in themselves respecting persons, contrary to the faith of the Lord Jesus Christ. To eject an obscure layman from the Lord's table is of small influence; because the fact is not known probably, except to the minister and deacons: but to announce openly from the pulpit or the chair, before a large expecting assembly, that a president, or a professor in a college, a D.D. S.T.P. L.L.D. whose fame is blazoned through all the land, cannot and shall not be permitted to appear in the pulpit, or on the platform at our philanthropic anniversaries, because he is a notorious man-thief, would bring the controversy at once to an issue. That evangelical medicine would either kill or cure the mortified culprit. He would depart to his home, and sign the deed of emancipation, and then return to his friends, and be hailed as a penitent upright Christian, and exemplary ambassador of Jesus the Son of God, or he would continue in his slave torturing occupation, until he passed away from earthly disgrace and obscurity, into the tomb, whence no good man ever wishes to resuscitate the remembrance of a slave-driver.

Visit a Methodist conference in lower Virginia, or Carolina, or Georgia. As the ministers are always moving, it is possible, that some of them are not personally chargeable with the actual guilt of kidnapping. Therefore, "they have no cloak for their sin." They have even less excuse than the other, for their compromising with slavery. What is their creed of faith? They declare that no man ever had a "sincere desire to flee from the wrath to come," who is concerned in the traffic, or the enslaving of men, women and children. Consequently, at the very threshold, by their own discipline every slaveholder is denounced as unworthy of the Christian name, and his profession of religion, if he assumes it, is virtually declared to be stark naked hypocrisy, while he is debarred at once from admission into their societies. Notwithstanding, the southern methodist preachers, are as dumb respecting slavery, as if they were "*choked with a curly headed quail stuck fast in their throats*," or as if that direful curse, like " the world before the flood," was so distant and incomprehensible a subject, that it is scarcely necessary ever to bestow upon it a cursory remark.

During nearly fifty years, have the Methodists solemnly told the world in their book of discipline, that every slave-driver is " in the gall of bitterness, and the bond of iniquity," that as long as he holds slaves, he can give no evidence of genuine repentance, faith, good works, and of a consistent Christian profession ; and, nevertheless, almost all their local preachers, stewards, class leaders, and members, besides many of their travelling ministers, from Baltimore to the gulf of Mexico, are men-stealers, and in Georgia, they are not only slave-torturers, but they also blasphemously attempt to justify their nefarious hypocrisy by the holy scriptures. Well are they described by the apostle Paul, Titus 1 ; 16. " They profess that they know God, but in works they deny him ; being abominable and disobedient, and to every good work reprobate." As long therefore, as this unblushing hypocrisy is tolerated, justified, and decorated by Christian titles, it is a perversion of all rationality, to anticipate, that the Methodist conferences will denounce man-thieving, because such a decree would be tantamount to an order, to burn all their classpapers, and to lock up all their houses of worship.

Examine a Presbyterian ecclesiatical meeting at Richmond or Raleigh, a presbytery or a synod, and what will you behold ? The moderator and clerks, ministers and elders, obdurate men-stealers, resisting the truth, and denying their own solemnly attested exposition of the eighth commandment, which declares of man-stealing, " this crime among the Jews, exposed the perpetrators of it to capital punishment, Exodus 21 ; 16 ; and the apostle classes them with sinners of the first rank. The word, comprehends all who are concerned in bringing any of the human race into slavery, or in detaining them in it. Stealers of men, are all those who bring off slaves or freemen, and keep, sell, or buy them." This doctrine, had been published by the Presbyterian church during twenty years, as their authorized standard opinion of slavery, and yet the general assembly of 1816, audaciously denied their own infallible doctrines, and wickedly expunged the above evangelical truisms from the constitution of their church, expressly, that they might propitiate the southern men-stealers.

But belonging to the southern presbytery or synod, probably there is scarcely a church member, who is not a barbarous slave-driver, from whom an old Egyptian task-master, if he were permitted again to enter the world, might take lessons in the art of cruelty and oppression. These are the men, who are described by the prophet Ezekiel, who " have set up their idol in their hearts, and the stumbling-block of their iniquity before their face, who are all estranged from God, through their idols," their slaves. They will persecute, slander, lie, suborn perjury, swear falsely, rob and murder, if they dared, any man who exposes the crime of man-stealing, and faithfully applies God's holy word to their atrocious iniquities. In these abominations they have lived—exchanging horses for men—bartering women for sheep—scourging females in the last stage of pregnancy, until from fear of the consequences, they have transferred the lacerated creatures to their husbands, for a conditional extra price, to depend upon the health and life of the expected child—putting their slaves to death by slow-paced torture, and exemplifying "the iniquity of their sin," by every species of knavery and barbarity, which this detestable traffic originates and prolongs. Can any man in a sound mind expect, that these confederacies of men-stealers will address a pastoral letter to their pseudo-churches, all of whom constitute but one vast confraternity of criminals, " sinners of the first rank," as they themselves declared in their own confession of faith, " guilty of the highest kind of theft," to prohibit the traffic and retention of their fellow-citizens in slavery ?

A preacher in the slaveholding states, especially, if a few coloured persons should be present in the assembly, will introduce the subject of theft, and it is no less melancholy, than wonderful to a judicious and thoughtful hearer, to remark how earnestly he will warn the congregation against dishonesty ; especially servants not to purloin from their masters, while during the whole harangue, he seems to be

altogether unconscious of the astounding fact, that if the
famished coloured man picks a chicken, *he* and his *elders*, and
brethren kidnap every infant whom they can seize; and if
the wearied hungry labourer, from the mere cravings of
nature, devours a young pig, they steal all his wages,
with his children, wife, and himself.

No man in the southern states preaches the gospel of
Christ in its fulness and truth.   There is no ecclesiastical
body now in existence in that portion of our Republic, at
whose meeting, a minister, before a promiscuous auditory
in a place of public worship, in either of the cities or large
towns, would dare to read as a theme for discussion the
words of the prophet Zechariah.   " Thus saith the Lord
my God, feed the flock of the slaughter, whose possessors
slay them, and hold themselves not guilty; and they who
sell them, say " Blessed be the Lord, for I am rich! and
their own shepherds pity them not."   The slave-driving
ecclesiastics would not permit the prophet Zechariah, or
the apostle Paul, to proclaim their own divinely inspired
instructions; and if the Lord Jesus Christ himself would go
among them, and "preach deliverance to the captive," they
would be like the people in the synagogue of Nazareth
" filled with wrath, they would thrust him out of the city,
and lead him to the brow of the hill, that they might cast
him down headlong."   No man could proclaim for half an
hour the solemn truth contained in that exquisitely apposite
passage of scripture; and if any northern philanthropist
would go to Richmond, Charleston, or Savannah, and there
read that text; ere he had faithfully expounded its sacred
truths, as long as Stephen argued before the Jewish council,
the men-stealers would " gnash their teeth, cry with a loud
voice, run upon him with one accord," and if they did not murder him in the house of prayer, he would be butchered without remorse at the door; unless Providence interposed, and
kept him secretly in his " pavilion from the strife of tongues."

It has been proposed, that a general congress of all the
Christian denominations should be held by delegates, expressly to adopt a simultaneous and uniform plan for the
extirpation of slavery from the church; but at present, the
scheme is impracticable.   There is a worldly spirit of unholy

amalgamation predominant in the modern churches, with a
solicitude to incorporate large numbers, vast wealth, and
extensive influence with each religious community, and a
discordant sectarianism incompatible with evangelical
brotherly love. Every attempt to combine Christians in
one grand effort for the extinction of slavery, as yet, must
be totally ineffectual. Conventions, assemblies, conferences, synods, associations, and presbyteries, in various degrees, all are governed by the maxims of carnal policy, and
swayed by the wiles, or intimidated by the bullying menaces
of the men-stealers; so that from them, no hope of amendment can rationally be indulged. Therefore we must act
for ourselves, every individual in his own sphere ; and each
single Christian society must proceed according to its own
convictions of duty ; thereby to set an example to the
world, that their " light may so shine before men, that
others seeing their good works may glorify our Father who
is in heaven." To the antislavery ministers and Christians, belongs this magnificent work. It is their privilege
to commence, and to give a continuous impulse, by doctrine
and example, to the extinction of this abomination which
deluges our country with the vilest crimes, and their consequent curse.

To wait for regeneration from the slaveholders themselves,
is idiotism; and it is not less visionary to rest in sloth, until
we have secured, as we suppose, ample and efficient co-operation. " The plague is begun ;" myriads of our fellow
citizens are perishing in ignorance and torture ; and while
we hesitate, the ungodly confederacy of men-thieves augments and becomes more powerful.

Blow the trumpet, and sound the alarm in Zion ! Unfurl
your holy banner. Your watch word must be, *Immediate,
unconditional, and universal emancipation !* The motto on
your standard, " *No kidnappers in public office, and no men-
stealers in the church of Christ.*

You must expect all obloquy and all opposition ; but
the command of Jehovah is the same as that which was
given to Moses, amid unparalled difficulties, " Go forward !"
" If the plague," or the cholera " had rewards and honours
to bestow," says Frapolosarpi, " they would find apologists ;

but in defending the poor and the oppressed, as we must struggle against power, riches, and frenzy, we may expect nothing but calumny, injuries, and persecutions." You will have to wrestle against principalities, against powers, against the rulers of darkness of this world, and against spiritual wickedness in high places; wherefore take unto you the whole armour of God." We have one certainty attached to the struggle. The battle will be arduous, and the conflict severe: but the victory is certain, and cannot be very remote.

Erelong, you shall unite in the rapturous shout of triumph, resound the Hallelujahs for your success; and with heartfelt devotional exultation, reverberate the inspiring chant of Paul, that holy apostolic emancipator; "Thanks be unto God, who hath given us the victory through our Lord Jesus Christ."

Nothing is more common among men-stealers, and especially among the nominal Christian kidnappers, than this retort. "We admit that slavery is a great evil, as well as yourselves, and we shall be glad to be delivered from it." That however is a direct and wilful falsehood. And hypocritically they pretend very harmlessly and modestly to inquire, "How can we escape from it?" To this insnaring question, and all similar palaver, the Virginian Methodist preacher's forcible reply, in only two words, is full and decisive; and far superior to a cyclopedia of eloquent erudition—"QUIT STEALING!" Let slave-drivers desist from kidnapping, and slavery will for ever be destroyed. But as the very terms of this summary process are always most galling to the men-stealers, and are inapplicable to our northern citizens, we must adopt the other course, and when we are asked, by what means slavery can be totally abrogated in the United States? We answer, only by a general determination on the part of every patriot, not to vote for a slaveholder for any public office; and by the inflexible resolution of every Christian to have no church fellowship with slave-dealers, and not to tolerate a kidnapping preacher.

That recent occurrence, which was published in the common journals of intelligence, illustrates this point. A coloured girl, as was her highest bounden duty by the law of God, fled from her kidnapper, and in providence escaped to the vicinity of Philadelphia.   There, after some months had elapsed, she was discovered by one of those biped white blood-hounds, called " slave catchers or negro hun-ters," and eventually was delivered up to her preaching despot, and forced back to Richmond.   The abolitionists indignantly described this fact in proper language of repro bation.   To repel the righteous censure which his detestable criminality had provoked, the Richmond preaching kidnap-per published a canting, fulsome, and deceptive explanation respecting the evils of slavery ; his repugnance to the odious system; his kindness to the female whom he had stolen, for he had bought the girl, knowing her to have been kidnap-ped ; but " the receiver is worse than the thief," because he rewards him for his felony ; and his desires for the im-provement of the wretched condition in which the coloured people are at present placed.   To this " all deceivableness of unrighteousness," the refutation is prompt and easy. When the girl was at 275 miles distance from him, where she could not be a slave ; and in circumstances of comfort, with good expectations ; why did not the preaching man-stealer secure the advantages which she had providentially obtained, by breaking her yoke, and to save her from all future danger, why did he not legally record, that the op-pressed should go free.   His philanthropy is in unmeaning delusive words, without sincerity.   To denominate such a man a gospel preacher, and his hearers, who sanction such a woman-stealer, Christians, is to utter self-evident and most mischievous contradictions.

One duty only remains to us; if possible to cleanse the government, and to purify the sanctuary.   We have the means in our own hands; the ballot box at elections, and Christian discipline.   These remedies are of the very pa-cific character of Christianity.   They demand neither political wrangling, nor fierce polemics.   They are pure, peaceable, and decisive.   The mere promulgation of these two principles of action by all anti-slavery Christians, as their deliberate resolve, and as the declaration of the course, which in future they will pursue, in reference to this momentous subject, will strike dismay into the hearts of all the varied tribes of men-stealers.

Already the professed disciples of Jesus in the North Western States are severed from those in Kentucky and Tennessee, not only by the river Ohio, but by the gulf which will soon be impassable. The narrow tottering bridge by which they yet maintain a slight intercourse, speedily will be ingulphed in "the bottomless pit;" and the barrier of separation will be drawn, according to the spirit and claim of Jesus Christ, the king of philanthropists; which commands all his servants that love him and follow his example, to "have no fellowship with the unfruitful works of darkness."

This subject must not sleep. It must be introduced on all occasions, and as paramount to every other social consideration.

It is stated of Cato, that in the ardour of his ambitious zeal for the prosperity of the Roman republic, he closed every harangue which he made in the Senate house, whatever was the subject before the Conscript fathers— "and I also am of opinion that Carthage must be destroyed." This should be the appendage to all our political, and to all our ecclesiastical deliberations—and I also declare, that *American kidnapping must be abolished*. As long as this loathsome iniquity exists in our republic, every section of the Federal states must be at discord.

Slavery alone is the chief, if not the sole cause of all the agitations which now perplex and disturb the body politic. Its peculiar demands are so utterly adverse to all the best interests of our citizens, and so totally incompatible with all that constitutes national prosperity and harmony ; that no permanent concord among the different portions of our country, and no lasting security for the stability of our national institutions can rationally be anticipated, as long as that direful curse shall exist.

Slavery must be immediately destroyed, not merely because it is fraught with political evils which endanger our common welfare; but also, because *it debases the moral character and influence of our citizens.* From the frequent intercourse which exists between all the districts of the

Union; through the artifices of the men-stealers, the pure sensibilities of our citizens, who have never breathed the poisoned air of slavery, and who have never been contaminated by its morbid infection, are exceedingly defiled. Many persons either conceive of slavery as a slight evil, which may be tolerated; or they palliate its multiplied enormities, until in the estimation of those who are seduced by those fallacious delineations, the death-dealing pestilence appears to be transformed almost into a blessing. To dissipate this pernicious delusion, slavery must be displayed in all its abhorrent genuine features and terrific effects: so that they who participate in the unholy system shall be denounced as disqualified for every public office; and man-stealing itself, with its guilty felonious perpetrators, shall be continually exhibited to the world as meriting only universal execration.

Slavery must be destroyed, because *it is ruinous to immortal souls.* The southern infidel kidnappers contend that Christianity is only priestcraft; chiefly because, that like themselves, men called preachers of the gospel, and the professed disciples of him " who went about doing good," steal, buy, sell, drive, starve, scourge, and torture their coloured fellow citizens, whom they have wantonly enslaved, with equal injustice and ferocity as the avowed servants of Satan.

They will openly admit that the gospel and slavery are absolutely irreconcilable; and thence they conclude, that the book is not true, or that they who pretend to preach it, and they who avow their faith in it are flagrant deceivers; for if they were sincere, they could not hold slaves. The argument is invulnerable. No slave-holder can adduce any title to be a Christian. A preaching man-stealer is one of the most efficient tools which Satan employs to effect his soul-destroying operations in our country. You must therefore remove the mask which these pretended disciples of Jesus so long have worn; and the lying tongues of all unfaithful teachers must be silenced, by peremptorily excluding them from the church, according to the injunctions of Jesus, the Son of God, and his apostolic servants.

Christian Anti-slavery Brethren! You perceive your

duty. In the fear of God perform your obligations. From this moment solemnly resolve, by divine grace, that you will never abandon your efforts to demolish slavery; and as the only efficient method to secure that glorious result—that you will exert all your combined energies to hinder slave-holders from being elected to any public office—and as you conscientiously abhor that falsifying system which ranks men-stealers as Christians, and kidnappers as ministers of the gospel;—that you will not acknowledge them to have any " part or lot in the matter."

Men and brethren. If such be the origin, character, defence, and effects of slavery, such its contradiction to sound reason, such its opposition to the rights of man, such its aversion from every affectionate sensibility, and such its condemnation by the word of God, how can you participate in its wickedness? Is it not almost incredible, that citizens of the United States, the only land of civil and religious freedom, should have established a system of servitude which extinguishes every personal right, nullifies every sacred obligation, and that Christians should maintain this atrocity? Tell it not in Gath. Messias' disciples profess that they are probationers for that kingdom and glory, to which God has called his children. But adaptation is indispensable to our admission at heaven's gate. Can any rational mind believe that a man, who has passed his threescore years and ten, in the spirit and practice of all the merciless oppressions which are the invariable concomitant of slavery, is capacitated to engage in the devotions, to exemplify the righteousness, or to manifest the love which reign in the boundless regions of eternal felicity?

That worship of God upon earth he restrained, that equity he never cultivated, that charity he always counteracted. A meetness for paradise, he has consequently not attained. How can the Christian church longer tolerate so shameless an absurdity as a profession of religion, and eternal man-stealing? How did the devil ever persuade men that a slave-holder was a Christian? This is a problem totally incapable of solution, by any human ingenuity or wisdom. The officers of the church are chiefly censurable. Of

two sects of Christians, the public formularies expressly
reprobate slavery as the highest crime which can be perpetrated, and any connexion with it as an ample evidence
that the parties are not followers of the Lamb. This is
their FAITH: what are their works? Publish it not in
Askelon.

You are now all called to repentance. Preachers, elders,
exhorters, deacons, leaders, and professors: how can you
deny your own creed? how can you falsify your own faith?
how can you profess that slavery is the highest crime against
God and man, and practise it? how can you promulge that
a slave-holder is the most guilty thief, and notwithstanding,
yourselves continue to steal, and affirm that you are sanctified? how can you declare that "upon the principle
of equity, no man can be a slave-holder, that all slave-
holders are men-stealers, the devil's dogs and children,"
and nevertheless, yourselves be characterized as merciless
flesh merchants? how dare you most solemnly admit your
own faith, promise to comply with it through all opposition
and persecution, and notwithstanding, neither admonish
the guilty, nor inculcate the truth, but engage in man-
stealing, and sustain the citizen-thief in his religious profession?

The church of God groans. It is the utmost Satanic
delusion to talk of religion and slavery. Be not deceived:
to affirm that a slave-holder is a genuine disciple of Jesus
Christ, is most intelligible contradiction. A brother of him
who went about doing good, and steal, enslave, starve,
scourge, and torment a man, because his skin is of a different tinge! Such Christianity is the devil's manufacture to
delude souls to the regions of wo.

You are Christians! you profess that you feel bowels of
misery, and hold in free-born slavery the descendants of
stolen Africans! Your Christianity is a nonentity. You
are a class-leader! you ask your class-mate how he has
lived during the past week? he informs you of his peace
of conscience and love of God; and you saw him half-
murdering his servants, you know that his dependant is
naked, without food, houseless and miserable; do you believe him? You are a deacon! You converse with a pro-

fessor: he assures you, that he endeavours to obtain
heavenly bliss, conformably to the example of the friend of
sinners; but you are certified that as a magistrate, he
swears, " all men are born free," and nevertheless, detains
his Christian brother in slavery: no man can credit such
absurd contradictions. You are an exhorter, you are at a
prayer meeting, you ask your friends to engage in the exercises; they plead for the mercy, pardon, love, benevolence,
and approbation of God, because they manifest those affections in their intercourse with men, and notwithstanding hold slaves! can you subjoin an AMEN to such hypocrisy?

You are an elder, you avow before the church and the
world, that you believe the book which condemns slave-
holding or man-stealing as the utmost iniquity; and yourself unmercifully lacerate coloured women in the last state
of pregnancy; or tan the servants whom you have flayed
with salt, pepper and vinegar? Who can place the smallest
confidence in you?

You are a preacher, you have the bible as your light, and
as your sole remuneration. That book informs you, that
slavery is the acme of all unrighteousness; and notwithstanding you are a slave-holder! That book teaches you,
that the worst of all sinners is the church officer, who engages
in the iniquity which he ought to reprove, and connives at
the transgressors whom he should admonish: Yet, you
are either a kidnapper or his defender!

Longer to abet such inconsistency, to support such absurdity, and to continue in such guilt, must affix a death-
warrant to the existence of the church. It is absolutely
impossible that religion can flourish among men-stealers:
and every mode except an immediate expulsion of obdurate flesh-dealers from the professed family of Christians, is
a sanction of the crime.

Remember, church officers, your awful responsibility.
The illumination of the sacred volume is around you. Can
you rest in peace, with the conviction that men are deluded,
and you enlighten them not? Can you risk the scrutiny of
the bar of God, with the condemnation of impenitent slave-
holders transferred to your negligence and intimidation?

Who can calmly assert, or who himself believes, that slavery is either equitable, merciful, or devotional? Who dare to profess himself a Christian, and be connected in any form with man-stealing? Slave-drivers sow to the flesh, of the flesh they reap corruption. Will you venture your everlasting felicity, upon a perhaps; upon an unfounded hope that so many have not been deceived; when that perhaps, that hope are both declared by the book, to originate in that "covetousness which is idolatry," to exist through deceitfulness, and to end in Tophet?

You procastinate! The enemy of souls urges you to cry to-morrow. He advises the adoption of prudent and moderate reform; knowing that such amendment insures him more certain conquest. He excites dread, by the menace of worldly displeasure, and the varied reproaches and privations which accompany it: you listen, and assent to his seductions, and thus the evil augments. The duration of all terrestrial vanities hastens to its close. In the result, you are individually interested. Who can calmly anticipate righteous retribution upon the basis of man-stealing? who can peacefully contemplate the exchange of worlds, with the never-ceasing horrors of domestic oppressions unexpiated? who can fearlessly await the judgment of the Son of Man, with the diversified iniquity and hard-heartedness of slavery recorded against him?

The doctrine which our Lord inculcates, in his narrative of the wondrous events that will occur on the day of our resurrection, is tremendous condemnation to the merciless and the unjust. Every Gospel affection is totally extinguished, by the principles whence slavery flows, by the tempers which are its inseparable companion, and by the dispositions which it invariably engenders. The approbation which the Son of Man will express of all those who exemplified Christian philanthropy in their intercourse with their fellow-creatures, as strongly argues the reprobation which oppressors may expect, as if they had already heard the awful irrevocable denunciation, "Depart, ye cursed, into everlasting fire, prepared for the devil and his angels."

Christians! How long will you tacitly or openly sanction, or actually engage in a system which includes every practicable iniquity? Can you conscientiously believe, that a slave-holder exhibits that assimilation to the meek and lowly Jesus, which is indispensable to an enjoyment of the inheritance of the saints in light? Are you prepared to answer all the demands, which equity may propound at the final examination of the last great day, when the enormities of slavery are weighed in the balance of the Judge? If so, persevere—but if not—be alarmed, and instantaneously desist from all participation in this ungodliness. Kiss the Son, lest he be angry. Pluck out the right eye, cut off the right hand, and amputate the right foot; though thy slaves be equally precious as these necessary corporeal members; *Emancipate them.* It is more profitable to thee, to pass through life in penury and scorn, and at death, to enter the paradise of the blessed, than to enjoy all earthly good, and at thy mortal dissolution, to be plunged into the abyss of wo—where their worm dieth not—and the fire is not quenched.

A SHORT SERMON TO PREACHING MEN-STEALERS.

The subject of our discourse is recorded by the Prophet Zechariah, chapter 11, verses 4 and 5. " Thus saith the Lord my God ; Feed the flock of the slaughter, whose possessors slay them, and hold themselves not guilty ; and they who slay them say, blessed be the Lord, for I am rich ; and their own shepherds pity them not."

As hardened sinners are not fond of long sermons, especially when they are conscious of their truth and application to themselves, I shall proceed without any introduction into the very marrow of the subject.

I. We have the character and condition of the American coloured citizens exactly described ; they are " the flock of the slaughter." Because, 1. Coloured people are not accounted as human beings. 2. They are treated in all respects as if they were an inferior order of cattle to horses and dogs, except as they can augment wealth and luxury, and minister to sensuality. 3. It is considered the greatest insult in the world, among the unfeeling and hardened slave torturers to take any notice of a gentleman's killing a slave. They are a body of two-legged animals, only kept to be starved or worked to death, or to be killed by toil, or torture, or outrage, or violation.

II. The conduct of American slave-holders is plainly declared, " Whose persecutors slay them and hold themselves not guilty; and they who sell them say, Blessed be the Lord, for I am rich."

1. They are engaged in a most ungodly traffic, like the people of old, who are condemned by the other prophets. Joel 3; 3. " They have cast lots for my people; and have given a boy for a harlot, and sold a girl for wine that they may drink." This is the constant practice among slaveholders. Amos 2; 6—8. " Thus saith the Lord; they sold the righteous for silver, and the poor for a pair of shoes; that pant after the dust of the earth upon the head of the poor, and turn aside the way of the meek; and the man and his father go in unto the same maid to profane my holy name." These are the constant practices of almost all slave-holders.

2. They mix impiety with their wickedness. They become rich by their man-stealing and man-selling, and then pretend hypocritically to thank the Lord that He has blessed them in their most felonious mode to obtain opulence. This is true of all slaveholders; they accumulate wealth by continuous robbery; and yet many of them profess to be followers of Jesus Christ, who went about doing good, the prince of philanthropists, and the godlike liberator. Our text, therefore, teaches us, that all profession of the Christian religion by such slaveholders, is impious hypocrisy.

3. The slaveholders are as cruel as they are corrupt and deceitful, for they slay the flock. The work of murderous death is always going on in the slaveholding districts, either more suddenly or with lingering tortures. No earthly

record is kept of the human bloodshed and of the human lives sacrificed to the relentless demon of slavery. The Lord holds the catalogue, and at the head and foot of the direful scroll, is the dreadful indictment written with American and Christian blood, " Their possessors slay them, and hold themselves not guilty !" They are not only robbers, hypocrites and murderers, but practical atheists, who commit the most nefarious crimes, and yet plead not guilty. Thus they despise the law of God, and maintain, notwithstanding all their superlative wickedness, that they are innocent. They virtually deny all morality, and discard the divine government of the world. They abrogate all religion, and even adduce the name of God and their hypocritical profession of divine truth as a sanction for their inordinate depravity. This is the character, in different degrees, of all the slaveholders who curse the church and the world.

III. The conduct of the pretended shepherds in reference to slaves ; that is, of American preachers in the southern states, is pungently denounced, ' Their own shepherds pity them not.' It is one of the most extraordinary principles of slavery, that ministers of the gospel, so called, of nearly all denominations who reside in slaveholding regions, are slaveholders, who will " sell the righteous for silver, and the needy for a pair of shoes." It is self-evident, that the preachers have no pity for slaves ; they neither comfort them, nor plead for them nor instruct them ; and all attempts to teach them by oral doctrine only, is no better than solemn mockery. Like the Papists, they will not permit the coloured citizen to learn to read or to possess the scriptures ; and all the knowledge which they acquire by a white preacher's discourses is both deceptive and insulting. No man dare to preach the whole gospel south of the Potomac and the Ohio.

In no aspect does the appalling and atrocious criminality of man-stealing develop its merciless and destructive horrors with more repugnance to intelligent Christians, than in the daring impiety with which it tyrannises over the understanding and consciences of men ; and in that profound ignorance in which it imprisons all its victims. If no other cause for its extirpation could be alleged, that total destitution of all moral and religious instruction, which ever marks its impious and detestable supremacy, should consign it to the deepest execration.

This is the hallowed ground, on which Christian philanthropists can securely stand and combat, and defy all the envenomed arrows and "fiery darts of the wicked." The claims of Jehovah are always imperative and ever obligatory that we should "send out the light and the truth" among "the people who sit in darkness." This duty especially belongs to all preachers of the gospel. Their peculiar office, their solemn vows, and their inconceivable responsibilities all urge upon them the inflexible discharge of this high and momentous service; and yet no class of persons in society, not even the Jesuit priests, who minister in the idolatrous temples of that " Mother of harlots and abominations of the earth, Babylon the great," more resolutely endeavour to obscure the rays of the Sun of Righteousness, and to extinguish the candle of the gospel, than American preaching slave-drivers.

Every preacher in the southern states, almost without exception, in reference to the dissemination of the pure truths of divine revelation in all their amplitude, is living in an obdurate and unceasing violation of the solemn vows which he made, and of the important duties which he voluntarily assumed when he was inducted into the office of the Christian ministry. His base neglect of the divine requirements comprises two heinous sins, and involves the most perilous and fearful consequences to immortal souls, both in this life and in that which is to come.

All the dead and all the living preachers, who have ever resided among the slavites, and who have maintained the silence of "a deaf and dumb spirit" upon the subject of slavery, are distinctly chargeable with these two unspeakably aggravated transgressions.

1. They have not only directly approved or connived at "sinners of the first rank," but with few exceptions, they themselves have actually been guilty of "the highest kind of theft." To these pretended "prophets that prophesy lies, prophets of the deceit of their own hearts," who carry " human blood on their skirts, and who have the price of

souls in their pockets," may justly be applied that most
pungent expostulation of the Apostle Paul, Romans 2;
17—24, "Behold, thou restest in the law, and makest
thy boast of God, and knowest his will, and art confident
that thou thyself art a guide of the blind, a light of them
who are in darkness, an instructer of the foolish, a teacher
of babes, who hast the form of knowledge and of the truth
in the law.   Thou therefore who teachest another, teachest
thou not thyself?   Thou that preachest a man should not
steal, dost thou steal?   Thou that makest thy boast of the
law, through breaking the law dishonourest thou God?   For
the name of God is blasphemed among the Gentiles through
you."

If there be any body of men to whom the gracious Redeemer's melancholy description applies, it is to preaching
slave-drivers, and to those who sanction the men-stealers
with their direct approbation or defence, or smooth prophesying ; and their exact fraternal counterparts, the Roman
priests, those "unclean spirits like frogs which come out of
the mouth of the dragon, and out of the mouth of the beast,
and out of the mouth of the false prophet."   Hear the infallible Judge!   Matthew 5; 19, 20.   "Whosoever shall
break one of these least commandments, and shall teach
men so, he shall be called the least in the kingdom of
heaven.   Except your righteousness shall exceed the righteousness of the Scribes and Pharisees, ye shall in no case
enter the kingdom of heaven."

To understand the pertinent and precise application of
these words of Jesus, who " taught as one having authority ;" we must examine some of the principal characteristics
of those ancient " hypocrites."   " They made the commandment of God of none effect by their tradition, teaching
for doctrines the commandments of men."   Matthew 15;
6, 9.   " Full well they rejected the commandment of God,
that they might keep their own tradition."   Mark 7; 9.
"They shut up the kingdom of heaven against men."
Matthew 23; 13.   "They took away the key of knowledge : they entered not in themselves, and them who were
entering in they hindered."   Luke 11; 52.   "They tithed
mint, and anise, and cummin, and rue, and all manner of

herbs, and omitted the weightier matters of the law, judgment, mercy, and faith, and the love of God." Matthew
23; 23. Luke 11; 42. " They were blind guides, who
strained at a gnat, and swallowed a camel!" Matthew
23; 24. " They made clean the outside of the cup and
platter, but their inward part was full of extortion and excess, ravening and wickedness." Matthew 23; 25. Luke
11; 39. " They laded men with burdens grievous to be
borne, and themselves touched not the burdens with one
of their fingers." Luke 11; 46. " They devoured widows'
houses, and for a pretence made long prayers; therefore
they received the greater damnation." Matthew 23; 13.
" They were a generation of vipers, who being evil, could
not speak good things. Matthew 12; 34.

This is the graphical delineation by " Jesus, who knew
all men ;" and that man who does not instantly discern all
the ostensible features of the whole motley tribes of modern preaching slave-drivers, must be the very " *Blind man*"
delineated by the poet.

> " The fool who doubts, who asks for clearer proof,
> Must hoodwink'd be indeed, and darkness love."

The canting hypocrisy of these traitors to the cause of
truth and piety is thus developed. They justly censure
with all apparent asperity, the various flagrant crimes
which disturb the harmony of the social compact; but
they never condemn the monster which engenders the
whole of them. General denunciations of sabbath-breaking, intemperance, gambling, uncleanness, profane language, and the dissipated profligacy so rife in all the slave
states are heard almost without emotion, and with little or
no application by the auditory. These orators should pass
through the vestibule, and lucidly unveil the secret doings
in the coloured people's quarter. They ought to unfold in
all its frightful deformity that " ungodliness and unrighteousness of men, which changes the truth of a God into a
lie ;" and which exemplifies almost in all its minutest
scenes, the modern revived enactment of that revolting Pagan moral tragedy, of which the Apostle Paul has furnished

the hideous outlines, and the direful catastrophe. Romans 1; 18—32.

If there be a truth deducible from the volume of divine inspiration, and from the past history of the United States, it is this fact. The preachers of the gospel are the grand delinquents, upon whom are chargeable the establishment, the prolongation, and the present existence of man-stealing in this republic. Admit that the British kidnappers and the British government of that period are criminal to the utmost extent which has ever been alleged against them, for originally introducing the African slave-trade into their colonies, their sin neither exonerates the receivers of the stolen men, nor diminishes their turpitude for participating in their piratical spoils.

When the first cargoes of the Africans were brought to our shores, had the settlers peremptorily refused to buy them, all the power of the British government could not have induced the lawless banditti who were engaged in that plundering traffic to have continued their costly and dangerous marauding expeditions. The villany would have been finished at once, if there had been no accomplices ready to remunerate them for their risks and expenditures. Even supposing that the common people were so besotted, that they could not discern the difference between a human being and a quadruped, that stupidity cannot be affirmed of the preachers in the United States, at any period since the landing of the Puritans at Plymouth. No man believes, that if the ministers of the gospel in America had " lifted up their voice like a trumpet, and shown the people their transgressions, and their sins," Isaiah 58; 1, and " sounded an alarm, till all the inhabitants of the land had trembled," Joel 2; 1, that slavery could ever have been commenced or perpetuated in this boasted land of freedom.

At the period of the declaration of Independence, or at the successful termination of the revolutionary contest, or at the adoption of the Federal Constitution, had all the preachers fulfilled their high and imperative duty, with undaunted perseverance, slavery must instantly have been abolished by universal acclamation. Even now would all the ministers in the southern states simultaneously emancipate their own enslaved fellow citizens, and then arrange with their northern brethren, to preach seven sermons on seven successive Lord's days, in every house of prayer throughout our Union; if not before, on the seventh sabbath, the whole enraptured church of Christ would resound with a modern illustration of one of the most splendid events recorded in the annals of the world. Joshua 6; 15—20. "It came to pass at the seventh time, when the priests blew with the trumpets, Joshua said to the people, ' *Shout !*' for the Lord hath given you the city. So the people shouted with a great shout, and the walls of Jericho fell down flat." The accursed Jericho of American slavery would no more be able to withstand the blowing of the gospel trumpet seven times throughout our republic, than the walls of the Canaanitish city could resist the mandate of "the captain of the host of the Lord." Therefore all preachers, and especially those to the south, are pertinaciously adhering to a palpable dereliction of their duty, against their own sternest conscientious convictions; and consequently, when "the Lord of those servants cometh and reckoneth with them," Matthew 25; 19, 26, 30, they may assuredly expect that their Lord, in spite of all their falsifying excuses, will answer and say unto them, "Ye wicked and slothful servants, cast the unprofitable servants into outer darkness; there shall be weeping and gnashing of teeth."

2. The slave-driving Preachers not only tacitly or openly approve of all the enormous wickedness of which man-stealing is the prolific source, as it is practised by their confederates in piracy; but they also destroy all those restraints which the God of Providence and of grace has appointed to impede the prevalence and progress of corruption in the world. Christianity has been revealed expressly, that by its sublime doctrines, its lofty motives, its authoritative injunctions, its cheering promises, and its terrific menaces, men may be induced, through divine assistance, to abandon the service of sin unto death, and to "yield their members servants of righteousness unto holiness." The knowledge derived from "the oracles of God" is the only appointed and effectual means by which this transforma-

tion of the human heart and character can be attained :
for men are sanctified through the word of truth. This
truth the modern successors of the ancient Scribes and
Pharisees, the preaching slave-drivers altogether take
away from their coloured fellow citizens; and thus are
justly involved in the indignant censure denounced by
Johnson, upon those men who, fifty years ago in England,
counteracted the extension of the blessings of universal
education.

" If obedience to the will of God," wrote that moralist,
"be necessary to happiness, and the knowledge of his will be
requisite to obedience, he who withholds that knowledge
cannot be said to love his neighbour as himself. He that
voluntarily continues ignorance, is guilty of all the crimes
which ignorance produces; as to him who should extinguish the tapers of a light house, might justly be imputed
the calamities of shipwreck. Christianity is the highest
perfection of humanity ; and as no man is good, but as he
wishes the good of others, no man can be good in the
highest degree, who wishes not to others the largest measure of the greatest good. To omit for a year or a day the
most efficacious method of advancing Christianity, in
compliance with any purposes that terminate on this side
of the grave, is a crime of which the world yet has had no
example, except in the practice of slave-dealers, *a race of
mortals whom no pious man wishes to resemble.*"

To conceal this hideous turpitude, a mischievous imposture has recently been attempted. The preaching slavites
have professed to open a sort of schools for the *oral* instruction of the coloured citizens. This incomparable theological tragi-comic farce is only matched by that Jesuitical imposture, a Popish Sunday school. To hinder the children of
Papists from being instructed by Protestants on the Lord's
day, the priests of Babylon in many places have appointed
a meeting on the Sabbath afternoon for children and others
to attend. There, the Massman first delivers a short harangue, in which he praises the holy church, proclaims the
power of the priests, urges the necessity of believing and
doing all that he utters, and curses all Protestant heretics.
Then he asks a question ; but as the wretched children of

15*

ignorance are utterly unable to reply to it, he makes the answer, and then teaches the infants, parrot-like, to repeat it.   The four principal questions will serve as a specimen of the whole impious and abominable foolery.

" Who said the first mass?   Jesus Christ."

" What is mortal sin?   Not to obey the laws of the church."

" Why should you confess your sins to a priest? Because he is in the place of God, to forgive our sins."

" What will become of all Protestant heretics and of them who disobey the pope and the priests? They will all be burned in hell forever."

This is antichristian enough even to satisfy the father of lies himself; but it is not one jot more base and deficient in religious truth, than the soul deceiving " strong delusions," with which the slavites attempt to gull the coloured people, and befool the northern citizens; thereby to blind their eyes to the existing ignorance, degradation, and wretchedness of American free born slaves!

One of these exhorters enters his school so called, probably offers what he calls prayer, which can be nothing else than inconsistency and mockery. . For instance, he prays the Lord to send his Spirit, which is liberty; and all his toil is for bondage.   He petitions the Lord to give salvation, while he is resolved to hold the people in slavery without redemption.   He invokes the Lord to instruct the people with his wisdom, and steals from them the sacred volume, and all the legitimate means to understand it. He supplicates the Redeemer to heal all their spiritual diseases, and yet he adds to their bodily tortures.   He implores God to give them the unsearchable riches of Christ, while he is continually stealing all their earthly wages and comforts.   What is all this but a blasphemous burlesque and undisguised diabolism?

He proceeds to instruct them in religion, and he tells them to be contented in their condition, to obey their masters in all things, not to steal chickens or young pigs, nor to touch any thing which their *kind* masters do not give them. He tells them, that Jesus Christ was meek and lowly and poor, and a servant of all men, who had not where to lay

his head; that Peter, Paul, James and John, and the other
apostles were like their Lord; and in fact makes it appear
to the apprehension of the coloured people, who are willing
to believe his insulting trash, that the gracious Redeemer
and his primitive disciples were much like American slaves.
Always dreadfully threatening them with the curse of God
if they are turbulent, or lazy, or wish to become free;
and above all, if they attempt to run away, then, according
to his account, from hell at last they cannot escape.

The questions and answers are framed and adapted to
the above model; and of course all the notions which a
slave imbibes are circumscribed by time and sense. Like
the Popish lessons, all his pretended religious acquirements
are of little more value than the rays of the sun during a
total eclipse. The system of theology which he is taught,
is not less concise than deceptive. To obey his ruffian
kidnapper is to please God; to take away his own chicken
to satisfy his hunger, incurs the divine wrath; to endeavour
to become a Christian freeman is only to fall into the devil's
clutches; a desire to learn to read, that he may search
the scriptures, is rebellion against God; a solicitude
to enjoy his birthright privileges, and to love and serve
God with all his heart, and mind, and strength, and soul,
is a sin, which can only be atoned for by more pitiless
severity and harsher privations; and the most distant
thought of emancipation incurs not only the temporal
penalty of scourging or maiming, but without repentance,
insures their eternal condemnation.

Such is the character and the substance of all the pseudo-
religious instruction communicated *orally* to the coloured
citizens in the southern states. Like those God robbers
their confederates in crime, the priesthood of Babylon, they
"are departed out of the way, and have caused many to
stumble at the law. They have corrupted the covenant
of the Lord of hosts. Therefore also the Lord has made
them contemptible and base before all the people, according as they have not kept his laws. Have you not all one
father? Hath not one God created you? why do you
treacherously every man against his brother, by profaning
the covenant of your fathers? The Lord will cut off the

man that doth this, the master and the scholar. Malachi 2; 8—12.

Thus these preaching slavites have acted. They do treacherously with the coloured citizens, by despotically and impiously refusing to teach them the elementary acquisitions by which they might search the scriptures; and they profane the covenant of their fathers, by virtually denying the fundamental principles, through which our Puritan ancestors emigrated from Britain; by daringly subverting the doctrinal corner stone of the declaration of Independence, and by scornfully obliterating the infallible axioms of their own Bill of Rights.

Why do they thus " corrupt the covenant?" Why do they thus "cause many to stumble at the law?" Alas! the sole reply which can be given to these inquiries is this : like their accomplices in this worst species of sacrilege and heaven robbery, the Romish monks and friars, they take away the key of knowledge, and defraud the coloured citizens of " the pearl of great price, and the light of their feet and the lamp of their path," that they may not accurately discern the extent of the injustice which is inflicted upon them ; and through the resistless voice of Jehovah speaking in his word, may not burst their odious shackles and become free.

But this notorious and self evident fact inconceivably aggravates the nefarious criminality of this multitudinous tribe of these legitimate successors of Judas. They hypocritically plead that the civil law precludes them from preaching the whole truth of the gospel, and that it also prohibits them from teaching the coloured citizens to read and write. Why do they not act as Martin Luther did, when he burnt the pope's bulls, decretals, and canons? Why do they not burn in Christian scorn, accompanied by believing prayer and thrilling chants of praise to Jesus, the most high liberator and emancipator, the whole code of infernal legislation respecting slavery? Why do they not say to the Neros and Domitians who legislate for them, as Peter and John boldly answered the Jewish Sanhedrim; " Whether it be right in the sight of God to hearken unto you more than God, judge ye." Why? Because " their

heart goeth after their covetousness." Why? Because
" they love the praise of men more than the praise of God."
Why? Because they are "afraid of them that kill the
body; but do not fear him who hath power to cast into
hell." Why? Because they "consent not to the wholesome words of our Lord Jesus Christ, but are proud and
destitute of the truth, supposing that gain is godliness." 1
Timothy 6: 3—5. "From such," says Paul, "withdraw
thyself and turn away!"

Preachers publicly and as readily exchange men for
horses, and women for sheep, or sell and buy and traffie
boys and girls, as any other class of men-stealers! In the
Negro quarter belonging to preachers, the slaves live with
no more religious instruction, equally destitute of food and
clothing, and labour as incessantly, and are scourged as
often and as barbarously, as on the neighbouring farms
and plantations, of which the domestic despots are avowed
sons of Belial. In the southern states of this union, almost
all the settled preachers of every sect are what the Apostle
Paul himself, terms them, " men-stealers;" without the
smallest particle of commiseration for the coloured citizens.
They possess not one sentiment of compassion for them,
more than that which Pharoah and his task-masters had
for the Israelites.

In reference to the American coloured people, slave-
holders exemplify all the doings of those ancient sinners, of whom the Apostle Paul declares; " that they
who commit such things are worthy of death, and they
not only do the same, but have pleasure in them that do
them; traitors, heady, high-minded, incontinent, fierce,
unholy, without natural affection, covenant breakers, false
accusers, implacable and unmerciful."—Romans 1; 28—
32. This is the general character of all slave-holders;
and that preachers partake of it is proved by their with-
holding almost entirely all moral and religious instruction
from the victims of their ungodly despotism. They have
no feeling for their tormented bodies, and no solicitude for
their perishing souls. Hence, about two millions and a
half of our native citizens in the United States are living
in a state of brutal degradation, with their understand-

ings darkened, " having no hope, and without God in the world ;" passing on to eternity as if they were animals without souls, while the preachers of the Gospel, *to them,* are only guides to the dungeon of eternal despair !

IV. The duty of all preachers is enjoined—"thus saith the Lord my God, feed the flock of the slaughter." Comfort, instruct, and nourish the people doomed to wretchedness and torture. This is the injunction of God, to all you preachers. It is paramount to all earthly legislation. The principles of the gospel are abandoned ; the discipline of the Christian church is sacrificed ; the very character of pure and undefiled religion as a system of love and holiness is destroyed ; and the duty of the evangelical ministry is perfidiously neglected by all descriptions of preachers in the southern States. In reference to slavery, you are Achan in the camp of the Israelites. You are no better than Judas betraying the cause of the Lord ; or the chief rulers who loved the praise of men more than the praise of God · or Demas who for the love of the present world forsook the apostle. You disobey your Lord and Master ; and if there be any truth in the doctrine of retribution, when the Master of the servants cometh and reckoneth with them. you will be denounced as wicked and slothful servants. You men-stealing preachers, and you their dough-faced coadjutors, hear the word of the Lord, Zechariah 11 ; 8. " Three shepherds I also cut off, and my soul loathed them and their soul also abhorred me."

Jehovah here emphatically declares that you abho the Lord. It does not signify what your pretensions may be. You may boast, " the temple of the Lord are we.' You may make long prayers, and sound a trumpet befor you, and love to be called of men Rabbi ; but you bin heavy burdens on men's shoulders, which you will no move with one of your fingers. Notwithstanding al this, your souls in secret and in truth abhor the Lord ; o. you would obey his commandments. Look at this descrip tion, all you ecclesiastical men-stealers and your abettors God declares that your refusal to obey his divine injunctior to " feed the flock of the slaughter," is because your souls abhor him. Who can doubt the truth of God's declaration when your disobedience verifies the infallible truth? Therefore, remember the Lord's declaration, "My soul loathed them." The Lord loathes you for your hardness of heart, your cruelties, your robberies, your impiety, your ungodly wealth, your want of human sensibility, your destitution of all Christian love, your rejection of all pastoral commisseration and sympathy, your hardened defiance of his authority, and your resolute contempt of his sovereign mandate. Therefore he reminds you of an example by which you may take warning—" Three shepherds also I cut off in one month." Whoever they were who thus experienced the Judge's displeasure, they were far less criminal than you. Preachers in America live in the midst of gospel sunshine, profess to be actuated by those sacred principles which admit the rights of conscience, civil freedom, and religious liberty; are bound by their own vows to " preach the gospel to the poor, and deliverance to the captive, to cry aloud and spare not, to lift up their voice like a trumpet, and show the people their transgression and their sins, that they may loose the heavy burdens, let the oppressed go free, and break every yoke." You see myriads of American citizens, your fellow immortals, drawn unto death and ready to be slain, and yet you forbear to deliver them." Proverbs 24; 11, 12. The Lord commands you to blow the trumpet and warn the people; and yet you will not comply; the people are taken away in their iniquity, and the Judge of all the earth declares to you, Ezekiel 33; 6, " their blood will I require at the watchman's hands." Deceive not yourselves by any delusive subterfuges.

In vain, Isaiah 28; 15, 17, " will you make lies your refuge, and under falsehood hide yourselves. The hail of the Lord will sweep away your refuge of lies, and the waters will overflow your hiding-place." You are like Jonah, refusing to deliver the message of the Lord, and you already experience and know, that " they who observe lying vanities," as you constantly do, " forsake their own mercy." If God spared not the ancient hard-hearted shepherds, but cut them off, take heed, lest he spare not you, in your insensibility and rebellion. Remember also another word of the Lord, Zechariah, 11; 7, " I will feed the flock of the slaughter, even you, O poor of the flock. And I took unto me two staves; the one I called Beauty, and the other I called Bands : and I fed the flock." *Thus the Lord declares that the slaves shall be emancipated.* Jehovah is the great exemplar of all Abolitionists. He exterminated slavery in Egypt to Pharoah's cost ; he abolished it in Babylon, but Belshazzer and the soothsayers were removed ; and if you will not feed the flock of the slaughter, he will feed them— but you shall be cut off. God will make them Beauty *honourable,* and Bands, *strong ;* and will feed, enlighten, support, supply, and strengthen them ; and then wo be to you, " false prophets, who come in sheep's clothing, but inwardly are ravening wolves !"

Watch over the flock of the slaughter and do the duty of Christian ministers. " Sinners as you are, one cannot but have pity on you. The parable of the rich man requires your consideration. He fared sumptuously and died, and lifted up his eyes in torment ! May God preserve all men-stealing preachers from being his companions !" You preachers are the existing cause of the wickedness and curse of slavery in America ; and as long as we have myriads of men-stealing ministers and professors, so long will all our churches be justly chargeable with being one half hypocrites, and the other half confederates. God pardon and convert all preaching slaveholders, and their dough-faced brethren, for Christ's sake !—AMEN.

APPENDIX I.

MAN-STEALING AND SLAVERY

PRESBYTERIAN AND METHODIST CHURCHES.

" AT a meeting of Delegates to form a National Anti-slavery Society, convened at Philadelphia, 4th December, 1833:

" *Resolved :*—That George Bourne, William Lloyd Garrison and Charles W. Denison be a committee to prepare a synopsis of Wesley's Thoughts on Slavery ; and of the anti-slavery items in a note formerly existing in the Catechism of the Presbyterian church of the United States ; and of such other similar testimony as they can obtain, to be addressed to Methodists, Presbyterians, and all professed Christians in this country, and published under the sanction of this convention."

In conformity with this appointment, the committee have selected from the records of the Presbyterian church every article of general interest which adverts to this momentous subject. They have also combined with those discussions, all that is universally admitted as obligatory in the Methodist discipline, with every thing material in the tract of John Wesley respecting slavery.

The general ignorance not only of the citizens at large, but also of the Presbyterian and Methodist churches, and their immediate adherents, of these authentic documents, renders their republication indispensable. The persons who are actually enumerated as in the communion of those two churches, with other attendants on their worship, who are directly influenced by them, probably comprise one million of the adult population of these States. The vast moral power which is thus wielded over our republic, combined with the inconceivable responsibility of

16

those who manage machinery productive of such unspeakably influential results, demands that it should be exercised legitimately, and for the holy purposes of human improvement according to the authoritative prescriptions of the Christian religion.

In reference to slavery *in the abstract*, both those churches agree. They join in unequivocally condemning the whole system as most corrupt in origin, of the vilest characters and as accompanied with the most direful effects upon its victims, and with everlasting punishment to the impenitent workers of that iniquity. Now, only let us suppose that an overwhelming majority of this million of adults would simultaneously declare, that within their moral and religious communion and influence, man-stealing should instantly terminate; and that every man among them who would not immediately cease, as John Wesley characterizes them to be a *"lion; a tiger, a bear, and a wolf,"* should be excluded from their churches; and that henceforth no slave-driver should be acknowledged as a Christian—slavery in the United States would be smitten in the fifth rib, so that it would require not the second stroke; but would speedily expire, amid the hallelujahs of Christians, who would witness and hail the last struggles of the infamous and odious dying Monster.

The ensuing extracts therefore, from the authentic standards of the Presbyterian and Methodist Episcopal churches, are earnestly recommended to the deliberate examination of all persons who are anxious to remove the evil of slavery from our republic; and especially to the serious and prayerful scrutiny of all Christians of every denomination. They afford abundantly instructive matter for careful reflection. They teach us that Christian professors will solemnly and repeatedly avow in the most public forms, their belief and adherence to Christian truth; and at the same time, that they will wilfully and constantly violate all its sublime commandments. They exhibit ecclesiastical bodies in a very mournful aspect, as asserting undeniable verities; and then obliterating their own creed; as proclaiming the mandates of divine revelation to be obligatory, and yet themselves practically nullifying them; and instead of manfully upholding Christian truth, as shifting, shuffling, time serving, and turning about, just as the demands of worldly wisdom and covetousness, the clamours of carnal policy and sensual indulgence, and the schemes of diabolical expediency, urge them to deny equity and justice; and to extenuate or sanction every diversified crime which flows from man-stealing.

No documents upon slavery of equal importance, it is believed, can be exhibited to the American churches and citizens. These are not the ebullitions of modern controversy drawn forth by the recent excitements. They are the grave, cold, and almost unfeeling declarations of men, who were governed in their expressions even by the criminals whose actions are condemned, and against whom their regulations only could be enforced. Yet no modern anti-slavery partizans, not even the Convention who formed the American Anti-slavery Society, have exceeded the Presbyterian General Assembly in hideousness of display, and the Methodist Conferences in unequivocal condemnation. The most powerful passages in the Declaration of the American Anti-slavery Society equal not John Wesley, the oracle of Methodism, in pungency of censure and reproachful epithets. It is therefore essential to recur to fundamental principles; and to make known to all classes of citizens, the sterling doctrines, the indignant denunciations, and the authoritative injunctions of the Presbyterian and Methodist churches upon this grave topic; with the genuine spirit and effects of man-stealing, and the true character and doings of all slave-holders.

New-York, January 11, 1834.

PRESBYTERIANISM AND SLAVERY.

Opinion of the Synod of New-York and Philadelphia in regard to Slavery, and its abolition, in 1787.

"The Synod, taking into consideration the overture concerning Slavery, came to the following judgment:

"The Synod of New-York and Philadelphia do highly approve of the general principles in favour of universal liberty that prevail in America, and the interest which many of the states have taken in promoting the abolition of slavery. They earnestly recommend it to all the members belonging to their communion, to give those persons who are at present held in servitude such good education as to prepare them for the better enjoyment of freedom. And they moreover recommend that masters, wherever they find servants disposed to make a just improvement of the privilege, would give them a peculium, or grant them sufficient time, and sufficient means of procuring their own liberty at a moderate rate; that thereby they may be brought into society with those habits of industry that may render them useful citizens. And finally, they recommend it to all their people to use the most prudent measures, consistent with the interests and the state of civil society in the countries where they live, to procure eventually the final abolition of slavery in America.

This "judgment" was also republished as the decision of the General Assembly of the Presbyterian church in 1793.

The second annunciation of the sentiments of the Presbyterian church upon the subject of slavery, was made in the year 1794, when the "scripture proofs," notes, &c., were adopted by the General Assembly. Their doctrine at that period is stated in the *note* b, *appended to the one hundred and forty-second question of the larger Catechism, in these words:*

" 1 Tim. i. 10. The law is made for man-stealers. This crime among the Jews exposed the perpetrators of it to capital punishment; Exodus xxi. 16; and the apostle here classes them with sinners of the first rank. The word he uses, in its original import, comprehends all who are concerned in bringing any of the human race into slavery, or in retaining them in it. Hominum fures, qui servos vel liberos abducunt, retinent, vendunt, vel emunt. Stealers of men are all those who bring off slaves or freemen, and keep, sell, or buy them. To steal a freeman, says Grotius, is the highest kind of theft. In other instances, we only steal human property, but when we steal or retain men in slavery, we seize those who, in common with ourselves, are constituted by the original grant, lords of the earth. Genesis i. 28. Vide Poli synopsin in loc."

The subject was also introduced into the General Assembly, in 1795, but without any effect, and without producing any impression. From that period, twenty years elapsed before man-stealing was again noticed in that ecclesiastical body. The following extract is found in the Digest, page 339; and it partially illustrates the views of those who constituted the majority of the Assembly at that period.

Advice given by the Assembly, in relation to Slavery, in 1815.

" The committee to which was committed the report of the committee to which the petition of some elders, who entertain conscientious scruples on the subject of holding slaves, together with that of the Synod of Ohio, concerning the buying and selling of slaves had been referred, reported; and their report being read and amended, was adopted, and is as follows :—

" The General Assembly have repeatedly declared their cordial approbation of those principles of civil liberty which appear to be recognised by the Federal and State governments, in these

United States. They have expressed their regret that the slavery of the Africans and of their descendants still continues in so many places, and even among those within the pale of the church; and have urged the Presbyteries under their care, to adopt such measures as will secure at least to the rising generation of slaves, within the bounds of the church, a religious education; that they may be prepared for the exercise and enjoyment of liberty, when God, in his providence, may open a door for their emancipation. The committee refer said petitioners to the printed extracts of the Synod of New-York and Philadelphia, for the year 1787, on this subject, republished by the Assembly in 1793; and also to the extracts of the minutes of the Assembly for 1795; which last are in the following words:—

" 'A serious and conscientious person, a member of a Presbyterian congregation, who views the slavery of the negroes as a moral evil, highly offensive to God, and injurious to the interests of the gospel, lives under the ministry of a person, or among a society of people, who concur with him in sentiment on the subject upon general principles; yet, for particular reasons, hold slaves, and tolerate the practice in others,—Ought the former of these persons, under the impressions and circumstances above described, to hold Christian communion with the latter?'

"Whereupon, after due deliberation, it was *Resolved;* that as the same difference of opinion with respect to slavery takes place in sundry other parts of the Presbyterian church, notwithstanding which, they live in charity and peace, according to the doctrine and practice of the apostles; it is hereby recommended to all conscientious persons, and especially to those whom it immediately respects, to do the same. At the same time the General Assembly assure all the churches under their care, that they view with the deepest concern any vestiges of slavery which may exist in our country, and refer the churches to the records of the General Assembly, published at different times; but especially to an overture of the late Synod of New-York and Philadelphia, published in 1787, and republished among the extracts from the minutes of the General Assembly of 1793, on that head, with which they trust every conscientious person will be fully satisfied.

"This is deemed a sufficient answer to the first petition; and with regard to the second, the Assembly observe, that although in some sections of our country, under certain circumstances, the transfer of slaves may be unavoidable, yet they consider the buying and selling of slaves by way of traffic, and all undue severity in the management of them, as inconsistent with the spirit of the gospel. And they recommend it to the Presbyteries and Sessions under their care, to make use of all prudent measures to prevent such shameful and unrighteous conduct."

It is worthy of remembrance, that during the debate upon the petitions referred to in the above unintelligible advice, the note subjoined to question 142 of the larger Catechism was first publicly introduced upon the slavery question, in the General Assembly

16*

The reading of it astonished all parties. The friends of equal rights and of Christian truth were surprised that they had overlooked or forgotten so authoritative à testimony ; and the preaching slavites were exasperated with indignation, and immediately began to conspire together for the erasure of that note, and of the doctrine which it proclaims, from the standards of the Presbyterian church.

The answer of the Synod to Ohio and the petitioning elders satisfied no persons ; especially as it did not encourage church officers to fulfil their evangelically prescribed duty. It was opposed upon these principles :—Conscientious men cannot hold communion with those who are always practising that evil which is "highly offensive to God and injurious to the interests of the gospel." It was maintained that all the records of the General Assembly had been totally unavailing ; that preachers, elders, and church members bought, sold, worked, starved and flayed their slaves as much, and even more grossly than their infidel and irreligious neighbours ; and that to talk of living in Christian "charity and peace" with men who always exhibited a direct inconsistency with the spirit of the gospel, and who were ever guilty of "shameful and unrighteous conduct," is voluntary delusion, and openly criminal. It was also avowed, that by the Confession of Faith, and the prior decisions of the General Assembly, every slave-holder who pretended to be a Christian, was a *stanch hypocrite*, who ought *de facto* to be excluded from the church : and a protest to this effect against the preceding deceptive and two faced declaration, was presented to the Assembly ; every argument in which protest, the history of the subsequent nineteen years has verified beyond dispute.

One result of the above discussion was an exhibition of as extraordinary a specimen of ecclesiastical chicanery as probably can be found in the annals of the Protestant churches ; thereby proving the truth of Article III. Chapter 31, of their own Confession of Faith : "All Synods or Councils may err, and many have erred ; therefore they are not to be made the rule of faith or practice." Whether the decisions of the General Assembly of 1816 ought to be a rule of faith or practice, can be easily determined by a consideration of these two facts, in reference to slavery.

The following question was propounded for the decision of that Assembly. "*Ought Baptism, on the profession and promise of the master, to be administered to the children of slaves ?*" A more complete burlesque upon sound theological doctrine, and a more base desecration of a Christian ordinance can scarcely be conceived. What did the General Assembly answer to this absurd inquiry ?

"It is the duty of masters who are members of the church to present the children of parents in servitude to the ordinance of Baptism. It is the duty of Christ's ministers to baptize all children of this description, when presented to them by their masters."

In other words, it is the duty of preaching slave-drivers to baptize the stolen children of American citizens upon the Christian profession of the criminal, who has kidnapped both the parents and their offspring !

The second fact is still more outrageous. It is found in the "Digest of the General Assembly," page 126, thus entitled :—

"*Resolutions in regard to the scripture proofs and notes by the Assembly, in 1816.*"

"The Presbytery of Philadelphia proposed an inquiry to the Assembly 'relative to the notes found in the book containing the Constitution of the Presbyterian church.' To this demand the Assembly replied. The minute is extended to a considerable length, and contains a variety of other matter totally irrelevant to our present discussion. Those parts only are quoted which unfold their 'mystery of iniquity.' Speaking of the notes they thus announce :

"These notes are no part of the constitution. The notes which now appear in the book were approved by the General Assembly, and directed to be printed with the proofs in the form in which they now appear. These notes are explanatory of some of the principles of the Presbyterian church. The notes are of the same force while they continue with the other acts of that judicature, but subject to alterations, amendments, or a total erasure, as they shall judge proper."

Disregarding the flat contradictions in these sentences, it is only necessary to recollect, that the notes are scarcely any thing else than texts of scripture, with a very few concise explanations; and yet according to that Assembly of 1816, they were authorized to alter, amend, or erase those notes, that is, "the oracles of God," as they judged proper. This was their antichristian assumption ; now watch their act.

No Christian will have the hardihood to contest the scriptural accuracy of the note to question 142 of the larger Catechism. In truth, it is nothing more than a few sentences, to show that the Lord's gift to man, at creation, is utterly abrogated by that crime which the law of Moses punished with death ; and which the apostle Paul enumerated with the most atrocious wickedness. Had that Assembly *nullified* fifty or one hundred other notes, whatever might have been thought of their piety, at least they would have been consistent. This was not their design, all their object was to erase that part of the word of God which denounces *men-stealers, and man-stealing.* This was their decision, omitting a clause which has no connexion with the subject of slavery :

"*Resolved :*—That as it belongs to the General Assembly to give directions in regard to the notes which accompany the constitution, this Assembly express it as their opinion, that in printing future editions of the Confession of this church ;—the note connected with the scripture proofs in answer to the question in the larger catechism, 'what is forbidden in the eighth commandment ?' in which the nature of the crime of man-stealing and slavery is dilated upon, *be omitted.*—In regard to this omission, the Assembly think proper to declare, that in directing it, they are influenced by far other motives than any desire to favour slavery, or to retard the extinction of that mournful evil, as speedily as may consist with the happiness of all concerned."

Upon this proceeding of the Assembly of 1816, it is only requisite to observe, that the Assembly "thought proper to declare" that which is notoriously untrue. Every person who was present at the General Assembly of 1816 knows that the erasure of the above note was done avowedly to *"favour slavery, and to retard the extinction of that mournful evil."* The resolution was adopted expressly to propitiate those confederated kidnappers, who are nominal Christians; and also to remove an insurmountable barrier to the condemnation of a minister, who, in his public discourses had exhibited the total contradiction between Christianity and man-stealing; and maintained that every professor of religion who is a slave-driver, is an open deceiver. This most important topic was also discussed in the General Assembly of 1817; and to prove the infallibility of Councils, they virtually decided in flat opposition to their predecessors of 1816, and also to their immediate successors of 1818.

It thus appears that the subject of American slavery engaged the attention of the General Assembly in different forms during four years in succession, 1815, 1816, 1817, 1818. Since which period the whole of the Presbyterian church have been sound asleep upon " the highest kind of theft"—and while the " sinners of the first rank" have multiplied and extended their man-stealing on every side, Presbyteries, Synods, and General Assemblies have been "silent as death, and still as midnight!" except when to gratify the Christians! who wish to transport to *their own country!* the " feeble, diseased, aged, or worn out slaves," they have adopted some *two-tongued* minute respecting the Colonization Society.

Circumstances in 1818 imperiously required that the General Assembly of that year should contrive some mode to conceal their erasure of their own long announced creed of faith, and their servile compliance with the clamorous demands of the unusual horde of men-stealers, who for special purposes of iniquity were gathered together on that occasion.

The following article, except a few immaterial omissions, was finally issued as their act. Having accomplished all their design, under ecclesiastical forms, and with the nominal sanction of the whole Presbyterian church, the slavites tacitly permitted the ensuing philippic to be placed upon the records, and to be published to the world. They well knew that by the southern churches it would not even be noticed, much less practised. Many Presbyterian ministers and myriads of their members have never heard of the existence of such a document—while among the eastern and northern churches, they only intended by it to blind their eyes to the true character and wickedness of slavery, and to silence their outcry and disquietude respecting their being participants with their guilt, or connivers at their man-stealing. Their object has been attained. From that period, those sinners have pursued their man-thieving with additional alacrity, and to an indefinite extent; and the northern churches, until very recently, have scarcely noticed their increased and continually aggravating turpitude. Nevertheless, the General Assembly of 1818 thus unequivocally execrated slavery, and all its adherents. At the same, time they most criminally then acknowledged, as they still do admit, these flagrant transgressors to their communion, and to fill every office in their churches. This act is found in the "Digest of the General Assembly," page 341. A few unimportant sentences only being omitted

"*A full expression of the Assembly's views of slavery in* 1818.

"The General Assembly of the Presbyterian church, having taken into consideration the subject of slavery, think proper to make known their sentiments upon it.

" We consider the voluntary enslaving of one part of the human race by another, as a gross violation of the most precious and sacred rights of human nature; as utterly inconsistent with the law of God which requires us to love our neighbour as ourselves; and as totally irreconcilable with the spirit and principles of the gospel of Christ, which enjoin that all things whatsoever ye would that men should do to you, do ye even so to them." Slavery creates a paradox in the moral system—it exhibits rational, accountable, and immortal beings in such circumstances as scarcely to leave them the power of moral action. It exhibits them as dependent on the will of others, whether they shall receive religious instruction; whether they shall know and worship the true God; whether they shall enjoy the ordinances of the gospel; whether they shall perform the duties and cherish the endearments of husbands and wives, parents and children, neighbours and friends; whether they shall preserve their chastity and purity, or regard the dictates of justice and humanity. Such are some of the consequences of slavery; *consequences not imaginary,* but which connect themselves with its very existence. The evils to which the slave is *always* exposed, often take place in their *very worst degree and form;* and where all of them do not take place, still the slave is deprived of his natural rights, degraded as a human being, and exposed to the danger of passing into the hands of a master who may inflict upon him all the hardships and injuries which inhumanity and avarice may suggest.

"From this view of the consequences resulting from the practice into which Christian people have most inconsistently fallen, of enslaving a portion of their brethren of mankind, it is manifestly the duty of all Christians, when the inconsistency of slavery with the dictates of humanity and religion has been demonstrated, and is generally seen and acknowledged, to use their honest, earnest, and unwearied endeavours, as speedily as possible to efface this blot on our holy religion, and to obtain the complete abolition of slavery throughout the world. We earnestly exhort them," the slave-holders, " to continue and to increase their exertions to effect a total abolition of slavery.—We exhort them to

suffer no greater delay to take place in this most interesting concern, than a regard to the public welfare truly and indispensably
demands.

"As our country has inflicted a most grievous injury on the unhappy Africans by bringing them into slavery, our country ought
to be governed in this matter by no other consideration than an
honest and impartial regard to the happiness of the injured party,
uninfluenced by the expense or inconvenience which such a regard may involve. We therefore warn all who belong to our
denomination of Christians, against unduly extending this plea
of necessity; against making it a cover for the love and practice
of slavery, or a pretence for not using efforts that are lawful and
practicable to extinguish the evil.

"Having thus expressed our views of slavery, and of the duty
indispensably incumbent on all Christians to labour for its complete extinction, we proceed to recommend, with all the earnestness and solemnity which this momentous subject demands, a
particular attention to the following points.

"We recommend to all the members of our religious denomination, to facilitate and encourage the instruction of their slaves in
the principles and duties of the Christian religion, by granting
them liberty to attend on the preaching of the gospel; by favour-
ing the instruction of them in Sabbath schools, and by giving
them all other proper advantages for acquiring the knowledge of
their duty both to God and man. It is incumbent on all Christians to communicate religious instruction to those who are under
their authority, and the doing of this in the case before us, so far
from operating, as some have apprehended that it might, as an
excitement to insubordination and insurrection, would operate
as the most powerful means for the prevention of those evils."

The Assembly here subjoin a note, which proves that the quiet-
ude of the island of Antigua, when the slaves of the neighbouring
West Indian islands had been in commotion, was owing to the
religious instruction of the Moravian Missionaries. To which may
since be added, the examples of Demarara and Jamaica. This
document of the Assembly is thus closed: "We enjoin it on all
church Sessions and Presbyteries to discountenance, and as far as
possible to prevent all cruelty, of whatever kind, in the treatment
of slaves; especially the cruelty of separating husband and wife,
parents and children; and that which consists in selling slaves to
those who will either themselves deprive those unhappy people
of the blessings of the gospel, or who will transport them to places
where the gospel is not proclaimed, or where it is forbidden to slaves
to attend upon its institutions. The manifest violation or disregard of this injunction, ought to be considered as just ground for
the discipline and censures of the church. And if it shall ever
happen that a Christian professor in our communion shall sell a
slave who is also in communion with our church, contrary to his
or her will and inclination, it ought immediately to claim the
particular attention of the proper church judicature; and unless
there be such peculiar circumstances attending the case as can

but seldom happen, it ought to be followed without delay, by a
suspension of the offender from all the privileges of the church,
till he repent and make all the reparation in his power, to the injured party."

This is the last formal act of the General Assembly of the Presbyterian church upon the subject of slavery—and it contains the
essence in smoother language, of all that the anti-slavery fanatics
have ever promulged.

That ecclesiastical body proclaims, that slavery *grossly violates
the most precious human rights ;* that it is *utterly inconsistent with
the law of God, of brotherly love, and reciprocal equity ;* that it is
*totally irreconcilable with the spirit and principles of the gospel of
Christ ;* that it *leaves the slaves without the power of moral action ;*
that *slaves are deprived of their natural rights, degraded as human beings, exposed to all the hardships and injuries which inhumanity and avarice may suggest ;* that *without these frightful
evils, slavery cannot exist ;* and that these direful effects of man-
stealing are experienced by the slaves in their *very worst degree
and form.*

This appalling delineation of slavery was not made by "reckless incendiaries, foul calumniators, blood-thirsty cut-throats, and
rabid agitators," as Presbyterian ministers and elders have characterized some of the most noble philanthropists in this republic;
but this is the picture of slavery drawn by a body, of which the
preaching slave holders directed and controlled every movement
and resolution. Such is their theory of slavery; what is the infernal system in practice, according to those slave-driving nar-
rators?

The slaves *enjoy no instruction ;* are *prohibited from all relative
endearments ; cannot preserve their personal purity and honour ;
realize all kinds of cruelty ;* are *lawlessly separated from all their
congenial and beloved companions,* the association with whom
was the sole relief for their constant wretchedness; and are
trafficked without remorse, only to suffer additional anguish. And
to crown this whole mass of iniquity, we are oracularly assured,
that *Christian professors sell as slaves members of the church, unto
the most woful bondage !*

This is not a catalogue of slave-holders' crimes drawn out by
"visionary enthusiasts, wild fanatics, sly malignant hypocrites,
and mischievous incendiaries," as the defenders of the New-York
mob, and their infidel minions described the only consistent
friends of freedom, of the rights of man, and of Christianity; but
these are the atrocities of slavery avowed by clerical slave-holders
to extenuate human bondage, to cloak over their own ungodliness; and by this farce of recording a stigma upon slavery on
their minutes, to terminate the uneasiness and denunciations of
the Northern and Eastern Christians.

After sixteen years have revolved, what has been done? What
Presbyterian professor has used his earnest and unwearied endeavours to efface this blot on our holy religion?" where is that
"most virtuous part of the community" of slave-drivers who

" abhor slavery, and wish its extermination," who have increased their exertions to effect a total abolition of slavery? Where is the preaching or nominal Christian man-thief, who is not always " extending the plea of necessity as a cover for the love and practice of slavery, and a pretence for not using efforts to extinguish the evil?" Where is the Presbyterian preacher, elder, or professor, who encourages " the instruction of slaves in the principles and duties of the Christian religion," as the Lord and his apostles taught the word of truth? There is scarcely such a man between Washington and the Caribbean gulf, or the Atlantic and Mexico, south of the Potomac and the Ohio.

Where is there a Sabbath school for the coloured citizens? Not an *oral* school, such as the slave-driving deceivers have contrived to conceal their turpitude, and blind the northern citizens; but a Sabbath school similar to those in almost every congregation in New-York or Massachusetts? In this respect Ichabod is written upon that entire portion of the United States.

Where are the church Sessions or Presbyteries, who dare to call before them men whose every act is one unceasing round of all multiform cruelty to slaves? Do not professors now sell Christian slaves to Georgia or Louisiana in preference, because their superior excellence, and their religious principles procure a higher price even from the *citizen-pedlar*, who in " his trade of blood" roams from New-York to Milledgeville, buying slaves, when he cannot kidnap freemen, and transforming every district through which he passes, into a scene of mourning and wo, in its moral attributes and agonized sensibilities, the civil warfare only excepted, the exact counterpart of that African *Aceldama*, whence the coloured people were originally stolen? Where is that church Session, or that Presbytery who will cite the most infuriated and malignant slave-driver to answer for his hellish cruelty or his piratical traffic? Where?

Since the unanimous adoption of the preceding " full expression of the Assembly's views of slavery, in 1818"—the only case approximating to it, is that of John D. Paxton in Virginia; who several years ago fulfilled the Assembly's requirements; instructed his slaves, and then emancipated them : for which philanthropy he was calumniated as vilely as if he had been a horse-thief, by all the men-stealing professors around him ; and speedily coerced to abandon the congregation before whom he had acted such a noble example of Christian benevolence. Mark the contrast! John D. Paxton, for complying with the recommendation of the General Assembly, was driven from his pastoral charge amid universal hatred; and the Richmond slave-catching preacher, who hurried away three hundred miles distance, to kidnap a coloured girl, not only escaped with impunity, but he is justified and honoured, because he is a brazen-faced obdurate " sinner of the first rank, and guilty of the highest kind of theft."

From a secret of a portentous character, which has lately been disclosed, it is also manifest that there is no design on the part of those who contrive to govern all the ostensible preceedings of the

General Assembly of the Presbyterian church, and thereby of that whole denomination, to interfere with the question of slavery upon evangelical principles.

A person on behalf of a slave holder, addressed the following letter to the editor of the Philadelphian—and as a supplement to the preceding documents, to show the utter discrepancy between good professions and evil practices, the article, a little abridged, is extracted from the Philadelphian of the twenty-third of January, 1834. Its contradictory tenets and misstatements require no elucidation.

QUESTIONS ON SLAVERY.

"I have lately received a letter from a communicant of the Presbyterian church in South Carolina, who is the owner of a number of slaves which comprise the principal part of his estate, and of which he became possessed, partly by inheritance, and partly by marriage. He says the General Assembly have repeatedly declared that the holding of slaves is inconsistent with the spirit of the gospel. And although he feels anxious to regulate his course of life according to the Principles of Christianity, and the rules of the church to which he belongs, yet he cannot think that pure justice would require of him to set his slaves at liberty, and reduce his own family to beggary and ruin. Even though he were disposed so to act, the laws of his native state forbid his setting his slaves at liberty, unless they are sent out of its jurisdiction. Humanity would, in such a case, also require a temporary provision for them, after they were set at liberty.

The General Assembly have also declared, that where any member of the church holds slaves, it is his imperative duty to give them sufficient education to enable them to become good and peaceable citizens, and to have them instructed in the way of the Lord Jesus Christ.

Now the laws of his own state, and those of Georgia, in which part of his estate lies, prohibit, under severe penalties, the instruction of slaves.

Here again, my friend 'is at fault.' His conscience and the rules of the church direct him to have them instructed. But if he do so he subjects himself to a prosecution under the laws of the state in which he lives.

He would fain know what he shall do. If he sets his slaves at liberty—he obeys the rules of the church, but violates the laws of his state, and reduces himself and family to beggary. If he obeys the laws of his state, and prohibits their instruction, he violates the rules, and subjects himself to the censure of the church, and acts contrary to the dictates of his conscience. .

An answer is solicited through 'The Philadelphian.'—HOWARD.

REPLY TO HOWARD.

Your friend and his family must turn day-labourers, earn their own bread by the sweat of their brow, become poor, beg, starve, or be crucified, rather than commit any one known sin. The certainty of impoverishing himself is no excuse for not freeing his slaves, if it is his duty to free them.

The General Assembly has ever acted in relation to this business; in resisting all the violent movements of absolute, immediate, universal and unconditional abolitionists.

To the last Assembly were sent an overture and a bundle of pamphlets for distribution, designed to show that every slaveholder ought to be excommunicated from the Presbyterian church: the overture was excluded from the house by the Committee of Bills, and the pamphlets were used as waste paper.

He who steals a man and makes him a slave is one of the worst of thieves and oppressors.

He who purchases a man thus enslaved is as great a criminal as the man-stealer.

Those who originated the system of slavery in our country, and those who perpetuate it, fall under the same condemnation.

It would be very just for the laws of the several states to subject *slave-traders* to punishment.

A man may inherit the relation of master to slaves, or he may become thus related to slaves inherited, or previously possessed by his wife.

In this case he should act the part of a friend, a patron, a father to these slaves; and should strictly compensate them for their labour according to their earnings, and his ability. If his slaves choose to be free from him, and can effect their freedom by removing from him, he should rather rejoice in it, than remove a finger to prevent them from obtaining their emancipation.

The laws of those states which forbid any man to emancipate or to instruct his slaves, are contrary to the laws of God, and the rights of man; and should be, in every constitutional way, resisted, and in every safe way evaded.

A person who has inherited the relation of master to slaves has no right to sell them to another without their consent. He should treat them as hired servants. The general law of benevolence requires all men to take all reasonable measures for banishing slavery from the world.

The political, civil, pecuniary, and religious interests of our country would all be promoted by converting every slave into a well instructed, industrious free labourer. As patriots and Christians, all American citizens ought to desire and promote the elevation, and final emancipation of all coloured people."

Two points are worthy of peculiar notice in this reply by the stated clerk of the General Assembly of the Presbyterian church. 1. He is as "wild a *fanatic*," and as "rabid an agitator" as the abolitionists whom he condemns: for he declares that all those who originated, and who perpetuate slavery, are "THE WORST OF THIEVES!" This includes all the doctrine and requirements of the "absolute, immediate, universal, and unconditional abolitionists." We only assert, that *the worst of all theft* ought not to be tolerated one moment, and that "*the worst of all thieves*" ought instantly to be impeded from perpetrating their outrageous felonies. 2. The stated clerk also *officially* informs us, that an overture was sent to the last General Assembly respecting slavery which was excluded from that body by the Committee of Bills. In other words, they determined not to fulfil their own enactments. By what right and authority a bundle of pamphlets sent for distribution among the members of the General Assembly, as every individual's own and exclusive possession, were withheld from them by the moderator and clerks, is utterly inconceivable. Those pamphlets belonged to the ministers and elders alone, for whose perusal they were kindly transmitted; and no men but the confederates of "*the worst of all thieves!*" would have dared thus to purloin the property of others; by clandestinely detaining pamphlets sent for the use of the members of the General Assembly from their rightful owners, and by using for waste paper the offering of Christian affection.

From this authentic survey of the Presbyterian doctrines upon slavery, when compared with their total abrogation of them in practice, every person must instantly discern the hypocritical inconsistency which has marked the course of that church during nearly fifty years; and the effrontery which all Presbyterian slave-holders display, who deceitfully profess to be Christians, not only in direct contradiction to the gospel of Jesus, but also in profound contempt and defiance of their own *pretended* and solemnly avowed creed of faith!

METHODISM AND SLAVERY.

THE volume entitled "*the Doctrine and Discipline of the* Methodist Episcopal Church" is always referred to as the standard book which contains "the form of discipline, the articles of religion, and canons of" the Methodist Societies in the United States. In the ensuing review, we have compared two editions published by themselves, and regularly attested by their bishops; that of the year 1804, and of the year 1832. We mention this fact, because the disagreement between them probably is not known to one Methodist out of a thousand, the preachers themselves included; and because it will prove that slavery contains "*the vilest iniquity, the worst of vices and wickedness, and a grand imposture; for it is one great lie, one grand cheat.*"

Both editions contain this unequivocal statement. "There is only one condition previously required of those who desire admission into these societies, a desire to flee from the wrath to come, and to be saved from their sins. But wherever this is really fixed in the soul, it will be shown by its fruits. It is therefore expected of all who continue therein, that they should continue to evidence their desire of salvation, by doing no harm, by avoiding evil of every kind, especially that which is most generally practised, such as—"*the buying and selling of men, women or children, with an intention to enslave them.*"

From this doctrine it follows; that the Methodist Episcopal church do formally avow, that no slaveholders ever did evangelically desire to "flee from the wrath to come, and to be saved from their sins." Thus the Presbyterian Assemblies and the Methodist Conferences exactly agree *in the abstract.* The former declare, that all slaveholders are "sinners of the first rank, and guilty of the highest kind of theft"—and the latter affirm, that from his sins he never had a desire to be saved. Now, no anti-slavery man ever uttered truth in stronger language than these ecclesiastical denouncers of the slave-holding confederacy.

The last article in both editions is entitled, OF SLAVERY; and the question is the same in both books.

"*Question.*—What shall be done for the extirpation of the evil of slavery?

Answer 1.—We declare that we are as much as ever convinced of the great evil of slavery; therefore no slaveholder shall be eligible to any official station in our church hereafter; where the laws of the state in which he lives will admit of emancipation, and permit the liberated slave to enjoy freedom."

This clause is from the edition of 1832; and is much more concisely expressed than in the edition of 1804; where they tell us for the *twelfth* time, as it is the *twelfth* edition of their articles and discipline, that they "*are as much as ever convinced of the great evil of slavery.*" But it may properly be asked, how much are they convinced? for the number of slaveholders has been continually multiplying in the Methodist churches from their first Conference, about fifty years ago, to the present day. They are convinced of the evil of slavery, declare every slaveholder an impenitent, unredeemed sinner; and nevertheless they sanction the evil which he commits, by acknowledging him to be a Christian. What mockery can transcend this insulting delusion?

The second clause is alike in both editions. "*Answer* 2.—When any travelling preacher becomes an owner of a slave or slaves, by any means, he shall forfeit his ministerial character in our church, unless he execute, if it be practicable, a legal emancipation of such slaves, conformably to the laws of the state in which he lives." This regulation reads very well upon paper, but no man ever seriously believed that the requisition would be carried into execution. In the edition of 1804, the third clause thus reads. "*Answer* 3.—No slave-holder shall be received into full membership in our society, till the preacher who has the oversight of the circuit has spoken to him freely and faithfully on the subject of slavery."

Examine this point! If the preacher spoke to the slave-driver "freely and faithfully," he must talk in this edifying manner: "*Brother!* you are a great sinner: you have caught in your man-trap men, women, and children with an intention to enslave them. You are yet in your sins, from which you never desired to be saved, and you are going to the wrath to come, from which you have never desired to flee. We have no fault to allege against you, except that you are a man-stealer, a sinner of the first rank, and guilty of the highest kind of theft ; the great evil of which we are convinced of as much as ever. Therefore we shall receive you as a good and acceptable member !" Had any remark been made at the admission of a candidate, it must have been in this exemplary and consistent style : but nothing was ever said upon the subject. The Methodist Conferences do not bar out those who wish to join their church, merely because they enslave coloured citizens. That third clause, as it was a dead letter in practice, afterward was expunged, as useless and impracticable. *In the edition of* 1832 *it is not inserted.* This is wondrous ecclesiastical infallibility ! which asserts truth for the *twelfth* time in 1804 ; and in 1832 obliterates it, because the preaching gospel doctrine is inexpedient, and costs too much ! Thus, after their way, they serve God and mammon.

The third clause in the edition of 1832 is not inserted in that of 1804. " *Answer* 3.—All our preachers shall prudently enforce upon our members the necessity of teaching their slaves to read the word of God ; and to allow them time to attend upon the public worship of God on our regular days of divine service." Slave-drivers teach slaves to read the word of God ; and to attend public worship ! and preachers enforce these things prudently ! Yes ; they do it *very prudently ;* that is, they are as earnest and clamorous for the melioration of the wretched condition of the coloured citizens, as the watchmen and shepherds who are described by the prophet, Isaiah lvi. 10, 11.

In the edition of 1832—the fourth and fifth clauses contain regulations concerning the coloured preachers, which are of no importance in this summary. They are not found in the edition of 1804. But in the volume issued thirty years ago, the fourth and fifth clauses combine some important illustrations of slavery in its connexion with the Christian church. Inefficient as they were in practice, yet they had a show of conscience remaining in the Methodist Conferences; but they have been erased. The rules could not be enforced ; and the absurdity of adopting different principles of religious legislation, bounded by geographical lines, is so glaring, that as they would not execute the law of the Lord in reference to slavery, they thought it most advisable to remove every barrier, and admit the slave-drivers into their church, without either scruple or obstruction.

These are the two clauses which have been obliterated : " *Answer* 4.—Every member of the society who sells a slave, except at the request of the slave, in cases of necessity and humanity, agreeably to the judgment of a committee of the male members of the society, shall immediately be expelled the society. And if any member purchase a slave, the ensuing quarterly Conference shall determine on the number of years which the slave shall serve, to work out the price of his purchase. And the person so purchasing, shall execute a legal instrument for the manumission of such slave, at the expiration of the term determined by the quarterly meeting conference ; and in default, such member shall be excluded the society." To these rules were added two items— that " in the case of a female slave, all her children also should be free, the girls at 21, and the boys at 25 ; and that all terms of emancipation should be subject to the decision of the quarterly Conference." The answer closed in these memorable words. "Nevertheless, the *members of our societies in the states of North Carolina, South Carolina, Georgia, and Tennessee, shall be exempted from the operation of the above rules.*" According to this ecclesiastical oracle, what is heinous sin in Maryland is paradisaical innocence in Georgia ; and an excommunicated man-stealer in the Shenandoah valley of Virginia, as soon as he can cross the Allegany mountain to the South West, becomes " a good and acceptable member of the Methodist Episcopal church." This last vestige, however, of decorum, for consistency's sake, after the example of their Presbyterian accomplices in the slave-trade, the Methodist preachers very properly blotted out of their discipline.

The following was the fifth clause in the edition of 1804, but by what process so exquisite a specimen of *carnal policy* was omitted, is unaccountable ; unless the northern preachers in the General Conference resolved, that if that part which bore some resemblance of partial rectitude was effaced, the rule which carried the broad brand of knavery and anti-christianity upon its face should accompany it to the sepulchre of oblivion.

The Southern Methodists must have exulted, when they contrived to procure this exquisitely *edifying* specimen of evangelical instruction to be enacted as obligatory upon all their travelling preachers. It is a marvellous perversion of the ministerial office, and of gospel reciprocity !

"*Answer* 5. Let our preachers from time to time, as occasion serves, admonish and exhort all slaves to render due respect and obedience to the commands and interests of their respective masters." To the influence of this direction, may doubtless be imputed a large proportion of that ungodliness which debases and curses the whole mass of society where slavery develops its demoralizing and withering power. The female slaves are exhorted to obey the commands of their masters!

These extracts are cited from their book of doctrines and discipline ; and yet where can you find a parallel to such duplicity and abandonment of truth, rectitude, and religion, as in these facts? unless among their counterparts in similar deceitfulness upon the subject of slavery, the General Assemblies of the Presbyterian church.

This remarkable inconsistency and dereliction of principle and duty are aggravated by other collateral circumstances in the history of American Methodism. *John Wesley, of whom they boast as their Head and Founder, was a most decided anti-slavery man.* He opposed slaveholding in all its forms, degrees, and exhibitions. His testimony against it remains in all their books, and

has been issued in the recent editions of his works, and formerly
also as a tract; and yet through the artifices of the slave drivers,
the opinions of John Wesley are not more known or believed
among the Methodists, than if he had never lifted up his voice
like a trumpet. There is little doubt that had John Wesley's life
been prolonged, slavery would have been altogether proscribed by
the American Methodists: and even that auspicious fact for the
church and the republic might have occurred, had not another
obstruction been interposed.

Thomas Coke, who was John Wesley's successor in authority
and influence, especially in America, was a most inveterate op-
ponent of slavery—and in consequence, he received, especially on
his last visit to the United States, such marked contempt and
scornful insults from the slave-driving Methodists, who he perceived were encouraged by that spirit of Diotrephes, which in all
things will have the pre-eminence, that he tacitly resolved no
more to interfere with American Methodism. He bade farewell
to his intimate friends, with the full conviction that they should
meet no more in America. Coke's opposition to man-stealing,
with his caustic denunciations of the hypocritical slavites who
pretended to be Christians, were strongly contrasted with the two-
tongued compromisers who faced both ways, condemned slavery
"*prudently*" at the North, and pleading expediency, approved of
it in the South. Coke disappeared, and man-stealing was embo-
died with the Methodist church, where it has "grown with its
growth, and strengthened with its strength," until the official
organs of their Conferences either conceal the horrors of slavery,
or defend its corruption by perverting the scriptures, or revile all
those sincere Christian philanthropists who are striving for its
abolition.

The ensuing extracts clearly unfold the glaring inconsistency
of the Methodists; who, while they profess to bow down to John
Wesley as their earthly oracle, on the most important topic in
our civil and ecclesiastical polity, have ever acted in direct and
flagrant contradiction to the irrefutable truths which he promulged. John Wesley always denounced the existing slavery in
America as equally criminal with the maritime slave-trade, or
the kidnapping and the transportation of Africans from Congo
across the Atlantic for interminable bondage and misery.

John Wesley was also an eye-witness of slavery as it existed in
Carolina and Georgia, at a very early period after the settlement
of those colonies. Consequently, the decisions of the Founder of
Methodism may be received as of great weight and importance
in this exciting controversy, between the sons of God and the servants of mammon.

In the third volume of his works, page 341, Harper's edition, is
the following pungent delineation. John Wesley had been reading a pamphlet against slavery and the slave-trade; and after
expressing his opinion of the work, he thus proceeds—"That
execrable sum of all villanies, commonly called the slave-
trade. I read of nothing like it in the heathen world, whether

ancient or modern. It infinitely exceeds in every instance of barbarity, whatever Christian slaves suffer in Mohammedan countries."

The same sentiments were promulged by John Wesley in reference to domestic slavery, as to the piratical traffic between Africa and America; but whenever the opinions and directions of that Methodist Leader are advanced on behalf of the abolition of that ungodliness among the slave-holders; the pretended respect for him is instantly diminished almost to a nonentity, and he is pronounced to have been but a man, fallible, and in this matter so ignorant of the true circumstances relative to American slavery, that his judgment is of no value, and therefore must be rejected.

Another of John Wesley's incidental illustrations of slavery is found in his Journal for April, 1777. "At Liverpool, many large ships are now laid up in the docks, which had been employed for many years in buying or stealing Africans, and selling them in America for slaves. The *men-butchers* have now nothing to do at this *laudable* occupation. Since the American war broke out, there is no demand for *human cattle;* so the men of Africa, as well as Europe, may enjoy their native liberty." These cursory expressions fully unfold John Wesley's indignation against slavery and slave-holders. When the public mind began to be excited upon the atrocity of man-stealing, Wesley issued the following comprehensive tract, which greatly influenced the English Methodists at that period, and which has more recently contributed to effect the abolition of slavery in the British islands in the West Indies. By its republication, with some unimportant omissions, and by the substitution of a few words to adapt the paragraphs to existing slaveholders, it is proposed to convince American Methodists, and other citizens, who are guilty of the enormous sin of "buying, selling, and enslaving men, women, and children."

THOUGHTS ON SLAVERY, BY JOHN WESLEY.

"I. Slavery imports an obligation of perpetual service; an obligation which only the consent of the master can dissolve. It generally gives the master an arbitrary power of any correction not affecting life or limb. Sometimes even those are exposed to his will, or protected only by a fine or some slight punishment, too inconsiderable to restrain a master of harsh temper. It creates an incapacity of acquiring any thing, except for the master's benefit. It allows the master to alienate the slave in the same manner as his cows and horses. Lastly, it descends in its full extent, from parent to child, even to the last generation.

"2. *The slave-trade* began in the year 1508, when *the Portuguese* imported the first negroes into Hispaniola. In 1540, Charles V., then king of Spain, gave positive orders, "THAT ALL THE SLAVES IN THE SPANISH DOMINIONS SHOULD BE SET FREE." This was accordingly done by Lagascar, whom he sent and empowered to free them all. But soon after Lagascar returned to Spain slavery flourished as before. Afterward other nations, as they acquired possessions in America, followed the example of the Spaniards; and slavery has taken deep root in most of the American colonies.

"II. In what manner are they generally procured and treated in America?

"1. Part of them by fraud. Captains of ships invited negroes on board, and then carried them away More have been procured by force. The Christians, *so called*, landing upon their coasts, seized as many as they found and transported them to America.

"2. It was some time before the Europeans found a more compendious way of procuring African slaves, by prevailing upon them to make war upon each other, and to sell their prisoners. Till then, they seldom had any wars. But the white men taught them drunkenness and avarice, and then hired them to sell one another. Others are stolen. Abundance of little ones of both sexes are stolen away by their neighbours. That their own parents sell them, is utterly false. WHITES, NOT BLACKS, ARE WITHOUT NATURAL AFFECTION.

"3. Extract from the journal of a surgeon who went from New-York in the slave-trade. 'The commander of the vessel sent to acquaint the king that he wanted a cargo of slaves. Some time after, the king sent him word he had not yet met with the desired success. A battle was fought which lasted three days. Four thousand five hundred men were slain upon the spot" Such is the manner wherein the slaves are procured! THUS THE CHRISTIANS PREACH THE GOSPEL TO THE HEATHEN!

"4. England supplies her American colonies with slaves, amounting to about a hundred thousand every year. So many are taken aboard the ships; but ten thousand die on the voyage; about a fourth part more die in the seasoning. So that thirty thousand die, that is, are murdered. O earth! O sea! cover not their blood!

"5. The negroes are exposed naked to the examination of their purchasers: then they are separated to see each other no more. They are reduced to a state, scarce any way preferable to beasts of burden. A few yams or potatoes are their food; and two rags their covering. Their sleep is very short, their labour continual and above their strength, so that death sets many of them at liberty before they have lived out half their days. They are attended by overseers, who, if they think them dilatory, or anything not so well done as it should be, whip them unmercifully; so that you may see their bodies long after waled and scarred from the shoulder to the waist. Did the Creator intend that the noblest creatures in the visible world should live such a life as this?

"6. As to the punishment inflicted on them, 'they frequently geld them, or chop off half a foot! after they are whipped till they are raw all over, some put pepper and salt upon them; some drop melted wax upon their skin, others cut off their ears, and constrain them to broil and eat them. For rebellion, that is, asserting their native liberty, which they have as much right to as the air they breathe, they fasten them down to the ground with crooked sticks on every limb, and then applying fire to the feet and hands, they burn them gradually to the head!

"7. But will not the laws made in the colonies prevent or re- dress all cruelty and oppression? Take a few of those laws for a specimen, and judge.

"In order to rivet the chain of slavery, *the law of Virginia* or- dains—' No slave shall be set free, upon any pretence what- ever, except for some meritorious services, to be adjudged and allowed by the *Governor and Council ;* and where any slave shall be set free by his owner, otherwise than is herein directed, the church-wardens of the parish wherein such negro shall reside for the space of one month, are hereby authorized and required, to *take up and sell the said negro, by public outcry.*'

" Will not these lawgivers take effectual care to prevent cruelty and oppression?

" The law of Jamaica ordains—' Every slave that shall run away, and continue absent from his. master twelve months, shall be *deemed rebellious :*' and by another law, *fifty pounds* are al- lowed to those ' who kill or bring in alive, a *rebellious slave.*' So their law treats these poor men with as little ceremony and con- sideration, as if they were merely brute beasts! But the innocent blood which is shed in consequence of such a detestable law, must call for vengeance on the murderous abettors and actors of such deliberate wickedness.

" But the law of *Barbadoes* exceeds even this—' If any negro under punishment by his master, or his order, for running away, or any other crime or misdemeanor, shall suffer *in life or member, no person whatsoever shall be liable to any fine therefor.* But if any man of wantonness, or only of bloodmindedness or cruel in tention, *wilfully kill* a negro of his own'—now observe the severe punishment!—' he shall pay into the public treasury, fifteen pounds sterling : and not be liable to any other punishment or forfeiture for the same.'

" Nearly allied to this, is that law of *Virginia*—' After procla- mation is issued against slaves that run away, it is lawful for any person whatsoever to kill and destroy such slaves by such ways and means as he shall think fit.'

" We have seen already some of the ways and means which have been *thought fit* on such occasions : and many more might be mentioned. One man, when I was abroad, thought fit *to roast his slave alive!* But if the most natural act of running away from intolerable tyranny deserves such relentless severity, what punishment have those *law-makers* to expect hereafter, on ac- count of their own enormous offences?

" III. This is the plain, unaggravated matter of fact. Such is the manner wherein our slaves are procured : such the manner wherein they were removed from their native land, and wherein they are treated in our colonies. Can these things be defended on the principles of even heathen honesty? Can they be reconciled, setting the Bible out of the question, with any degree of either justice or mercy?

"2. The grand plea is, 'They are authorized by law.' But can law, human law change the nature of things? Can it turn darkness into light, or evil into good? By no means. Notwithstanding ten thousand laws, right is right, and wrong is wrong. There must still remain an essential difference between justice and injustice, cruelty and mercy. So that I ask; Who can reconcile this treatment of the slaves, first and last, with either mercy or justice? where is the justice of inflicting the severest evils on those who have done us no wrong? Of depriving those who never injured us in word or deed, of every comfort of life? Of tearing them from their native country, and depriving them of liberty itself; to which an Angolan has the same natural right as an American, and on which he sets as high a value? Where is the justice of taking away the lives of innocent, inoffensive men? Murdering thousands of them in their own land by the hands of their own countrymen; and tens of thousands in that cruel slavery, to which they are so unjustly reduced?

"3. But *I strike at the root of this complicated villany. I absolutely deny all slave-holding to be consistent with any degree of natural justice.* Judge Blackstone has placed this in the clearest light, as follows:

"'The three origins of the right of slavery assigned by Justinian are all built upon false foundations. 1. Slavery is said to arise from captivity in war. The conqueror having a right to the life of his captive, if he spares that, has a right to deal with them as he pleases. But this is untrue, that by the laws of nations a man has a right to kill his enemy. He has only a right to kill him in cases of absolute necessity, for self defence. And it is plain this absolute necessity did not subsist, since he did not kill him, but made him prisoner. War itself is justifiable only on principles of self-preservation. Therefore it gives us no right over prisoners, but to hinder their hurting us by confining them. Much less can it give a right to torture, or kill, or even enslave an enemy, when the war is over. Since therefore the right of making our prisoners slaves, depends on a supposed right of slaughter, that foundation failing, the consequence which is drawn from it must fail likewise. 2. It is said, slavery may begin by one man's selling himself to another. It is true, a man may sell himself to work for another; but he cannot sell himself to be a slave, as above defined. Every sale implies an equivalent given to the seller, in lieu of what he transfers to the buyer. But what equivalent can be given for life or liberty? His property likewise, with the very price which he seems to receive, devolves to his master the moment he becomes his slave: in this case therefore, the buyer gives nothing. Of what validity then can a sale be. which destroys the very principle upon which all sales are founded. 3. We are told that men may be *born slaves,* by being the children of slaves. But this, being built upon the two former false claims, must fall

with them. If neither captivity nor contract, by the plain law of nature and reason, can reduce the parent to a state of slavery, much
less can they reduce the offspring.' It clearly follows, that all
slavery is as irreconcilable to justice, as to mercy.

"4. That slave-holding is utterly inconsistent with mercy is
almost too plain to need a proof. It is said: 'These negroes,
being prisoners of war, our captains and factors buy them, merely
to save them from being put to death. Is not this mercy?' I answer; 1. Did Hawkins, and many others, seize upon men, women,
and children, who were at peace in their own fields and houses,
merely to save them from death? 2. Was it to save them from
death, that they knocked out the brains of those they could not
bring away? 3. Who occasioned and fomented those wars,
wherein these poor creatures were taken prisoners? Who excited
them by money, by drink, by every possible means to fall upon
one another? Was it not themselves? They know in their own
consciences it was, if they have any consciences left. 4. To bring
the matter to a short issue: Can they say before God, that they
ever took a single voyage, or bought a single African from this
motive? They cannot. *To get money, not to save* lives, was the
whole and sole spring of their motives.

"5. But if this manner of procuring and treating slaves is not
consistent with mercy or justice, yet there is a plea for it which
every man of business will acknowledge to be quite sufficient.
One meeting an eminent statesman in the lobby of the House of
Commons said—'You have been long talking about justice and
equity; pray, which is this bill? Equity or justice?' He answered very short and plain—'Damn justice; it is necessity.'
Here also the slaveholder fixes his foot; here he rests the strength
of his cause. 'If it is not quite right, yet it *must* be so: there is
an absolute *necessity for it*. It is necessary we should procure
slaves; and when we have procured them, it is necessary to use
them with severity, considering their stupidity, stubbornness, and
wickedness.' You stumble at the threshhold; I deny that villany is ever necessary. It is impossible that it should ever be necessary for any reasonable creature to violate all the laws of justice, mercy, and truth. No circumstances can make it necessary
for a man to burst in sunder all the ties of humanity. *It can never
be necessary for a rational being to sink himself below a brute. A
man can be under no necessity of degrading himself into a wolf.*
"The absurdity of the supposition is so glaring, that one would
wonder any one could help seeing it.

"6. What is necessary? and to what end? It may be answered;
'The whole method now used by the original purchasers of Africans is necessary to the furnishing our colonies yearly with a
hundred thousand slaves.' I grant *this* is necessary to *that end.*
But how is that end necessary? How will you prove it necessary
that one hundred, that *one* of those slaves should be procured?
'It is necessary to my gaining a hundred thousand pounds.' Perhaps so: but how is *this* necessary? It is very possible you might
be both a better and a happier man, if you had not a quarter of

it. I deny that your gaining one thousand is necessary, either to your present or eternal happiness. 'But you must allow these slaves are necessary for the cultivation of our islands : inasmuch as white men are not able to labour in hot climates.' I answer ; 1. It were better that all those islands should remain uncultivated for ever ; yea, it were more desirable that they were altogether sunk in the depth of the sea, than that they should be cultivated at so high a price, as the violation of justice, mercy, and truth. 2. But the supposition on which you ground your argument is false. White men are able to labour in hot climates, provided they are temperate both in meat and drink, and that they inure themselves to it by degrees. *I speak no more than I know by experience.* The summer heat in Georgia is frequently equal to that in Barbadoes, and to that under the line : yet I and my family, eight in number, employed all our spare time there, in felling of trees and clearing of ground, as hard labour as any slave need be employed in. The German family likewise, forty in number, were employed in all manner of labour. This was so far from impairing our health, that we all continued perfectly well, while the idle ones round about us were swept away as with a pestilence. It is not true therefore, that white men are not able to labour, even in hot climates, full as well as black. If they were not, it would be better that none should labour there, that the work should be left undone, than that myriads of innocent men should be murdered, and myriads more dragged into the basest slavery. 'But the furnishing us with slaves is necessary for the trade, wealth, and glory of the nation.' Better no trade, than trade procured by villany. It is far better to have no wealth, than to gain wealth at the expense of virtue. Better is honest poverty, than all the riches bought by the tears, and sweat, and blood of our fellow-creatures.

"7. 'When we have slaves, it is necessary to use them with severity.' What, *to whip them for every petty offence till they are in a gore of blood? To take that opportunity of rubbing pepper and salt into their raw flesh? To drop burning sealing-wax upon their skins? To castrate them? To cut off half their foot with an axe? To hang them on gibbets, that they may die by inches with heat, and hunger, and thirst? To pin them down to the ground, and then burn them by degrees from the feet to the head? To roast them alive?* When did a Turk or a heathen find it necessary to use a fellow-creature thus? To what end is this usage necessary? 'To prevent their running away, and to keep them constantly to their labour, that they may not idle away their time. So miserably stupid is this race of men, so stubborn and so wicked!' Allowing this, to whom is that stupidity owing? It lies altogether at the door of their inhuman masters, who gave them no means, no opportunity of improving their understanding ; and indeed leave them no motive, either from hope or fear to attempt any such thing. They were no way remarkable for stupidity while they remained in Africa. To some of the inhabitants of Europe they are greatly superior. Survey the natives of

18

Benin, and of Lapland. Compare the Samoeids and the Angolans. The African is in no respect inferior to the European. Their stupidity in our colonies is not natural; otherwise than it is the natural effect of their condition. Consequently it is not *their* fault, but yours: and you must answer for it before God and man. 'But their stupidity is not the only reason of our treating them with severity: for it is hard to say which is the greatest, this, or their stubbornness and wickedness. But do not these, as well as the other, lie at *your* door? Are not stubbornness, cunning, pilfering, and divers other vices the natural necessary fruits of slavery, in every age and nation? What means have you used to remove this stubbornness? Have you tried what mildness and gentleness would do? What pains have you taken, what method have you used to reclaim them from their wickedness? Have you carefully taught them, 'that there is a God, a wise, powerful, merciful Being, the Creator and Governor of heaven and earth; that he has appointed a day wherein he will judge the world, will take an account of all our thoughts, words, and actions; that in that day he will reward every child of man according to his works: that then the righteous shall inherit the·kingdom prepared for them from the foundation of the world; and the wicked shall be cast into everlasting fire, prepared for the devil and his angels?' If you have not done this, if you have taken no pains nor thought about this matter, can you wonder at their wickedness? What wonder if they should cut your throat? and if they did, whom could you thank for it but yourself? You first *acted the villain in making them slaves*, whether you stole them or bought them. You kept them stupid and wicked, by cutting them off from all opportunities of improving either in knowledge or virtue; and now you assign their want of wisdom or goodness as the reason for using them worse than brute beasts!

" V. I add a few words to those who are more immediately concerned.

" 1. To *Traders*. You have torn away children from their parents, and parents from their children; husbands from their wives; wives from their beloved husbands; brethren and sisters from each other. You have dragged them who have never done you any wrong, in chains, and forced them into the vilest slavery, never to end but with life; such slavery as is not found among the Turks in Algiers, nor among the heathens in America. You induce the villain to steal, rob, murder men, women, and children, without number, by paying him for his execrable labour. It is all your act and deed. Is your conscience quite reconciled to this? does it never reproach you at all? Has gold entirely blinded your eyes, and stupified your heart? Can you see, can you *feel* no harm therein? Is it doing as you would be done to? Make the case your own. 'Master,' said a slave at Liverpool, to the merchant that owned him, 'what if some of my countrymen were to come here, and take away Mistress, and Tommy, and Billy, and carry them into our country, and make them slaves, how would you like it?' His answer was worthy of a man—'I will never buy a slave more while I live.' Let his resolution be yours. Have no more any part in this detestable business. Instantly leave it to those unfeeling wretches, ' who laugh at human nature and compassion.' Be you a man; not a wolf, a devourer of the human species! Be merciful, that you may obtain mercy.

"Is there a God? You know there is. Is he a just God? Then there must be a state of retribution; a state wherein the just God will reward every man according to his works. Then what reward will he render to *you?* O think betimes! before you drop into eternity! Think now. 'He shall have judgment without mercy that hath showed no mercy.' Are you a *man?* Then you should have a *human* heart. But have you indeed? what is your heart made of? Is there no such principle as compassion there? Do you never *feel* another's pain? Have you no sympathy? no sense of human wo? no pity for the miserable? When you saw the streaming eyes, the heaving breasts, the bleeding sides, and the tortured limbs of your fellow-creatures, were you a stone or a brute? Did you look upon them with the eyes of a tiger? Had you no relenting? Did not one tear drop from your eye, one sigh escape from your breast? Do you feel no relenting *now?* If you do not, you must go on till the measure of your iniquities is full. Then will the great God deal with *you,* as you have dealt with *them,* and require all their blood at your hands. At that day it shall be more tolerable for Sodom and Gomorrah than for you. But if your heart does relent; resolve, God being your helper, to escape for your life. Regard not money! All that a man hath, will he give for his life. Whatever you lose, lose not your soul; nothing can countervail that loss. Immediately quit the horrid trade; at all events be an honest man.

"2. To *Slaveholders.* This equally concerns all slaveholders, of whatever rank and degree; seeing *men-buyers are exactly on a level with men-stealers!* Indeed you say, 'I pay honestly for my goods; and I am not concerned to know how they are come by.' Nay, but you are: you are deeply concerned to know they are honestly come by: otherwise you are partaker with a thief, and are not a jot honester than he. But you know they are not honestly come by: you know they are procured by means *nothing near so innocent as picking pockets, house-breaking, or robbery upon the highway.* You know they are procured by a deliberate species of more complicated villany, of fraud, robbery, and murder, than was ever practised by Mohammedans or Pagans; in par ticular, by murders of all kinds; by the blood of the innocent poured upon the ground like water. Now it is *your* money that pays the African butcher. *You* therefore are principally guilty of all these frauds, robberies, and murders. *You* are the spring that puts all the rest in motion. They would not stir a step without *you:* therefore the blood of all these wretches who die before their time lies upon *your* head. 'The blood of thy brother crieth against thee from the earth.' O whatever it costs, put a stop to its cry before it be too late; instantly, at any price, were it the half of your goods, deliver thyself from blood-guiltiness! *Thy hands, thy bed, thy furniture, thy house, and thy lands at present are stained with blood.* Surely it is enough; accumulate no more guilt: spill no more the blood of the innocent. Do not hire another to shed blood; do not pay him for doing it. Whether you are a Christian or not, show yourself a man! Be not more savage than a lion or a bear!

"Perhaps you will say; 'I do not buy any slaves; I only use those left by my father.' But is that enough to satisfy your conscience? Had your father, have *you,* has any man living a right to use another as a slave? It cannot be, even setting revelation aside. Neither war nor contract can give any man such a property in another as he has in his sheep and oxen. Much less is it possible, that any child of man should ever be born a slave. Liberty is the right of every human creature, as soon as he breathes the vital air: and no human law can deprive him of that right which he derives from the law of nature. If therefore you have any regard to justice, to say nothing of mercy, or of the revealed law of God, render unto all their due. Give liberty to whom liberty is due, to every child of man, to every partaker of human nature. Let none serve you but by his own act and deed, by his own voluntary choice. Away with all whips, all chains, all compulsion! Be gentle toward all men, and see that you invariably do unto every one, as you would he should do unto you.

"O thou God of love, thou who art loving to every man, and whose mercy is over all thy works; thou who art the Father of the spirits of all flesh, and who art rich in mercy unto all; thou who hast formed of one blood, all the nations upon the earth; have compassion upon these outcasts of men, who are trodden down as dung upon the earth! Arise, and help these that have no helper, whose blood is spilled upon the ground like water! Are not these also the work of thine own hands, the purchase of thy Son's blood? Stir them up to cry unto thee in the land of their captivity; and let their complaint come up before thee; let it enter into thine ears! Make even those that lead them captive to pity them and turn their captivity. O burst thou all their chains in sunder; more especially the chains of their sins: thou Saviour of all, make them free, that they may be free indeed!"

> "The servile progeny of Ham,
> Seize as the purchase of thy blood;
> Let all the heathens know thy name.
> From idols to the living God
> The dark Americans convert,
> And shine in every Pagan heart!"

———

THE preceding official documents which have been issued by the most imposing and powerful ecclesiastical Assemblies in our republic are strenuously recommended to all American citizens, and especially to those who profess to be Christians, of every denomination. Upon the members of the various churches, the awful responsibility rests, whether the curse of man-stealing shall longer be protracted, and whether the tremendous punishment of this heinous and "complicated villany" shall longer impend over our guilty country. A grosser delusion cannot be indulged, than the anticipation that the evil will be redressed and the crime be abolished by the Southern Legislators. To Christians the work peculiarly appertains. It is their *duty*, to brand slavery with *the mark of Cain ;* and it is their *privilege*, to cleanse the temple of those *"chief Priests and Scribes, who have made the house of prayer a den of thieves."* This can be accomplished only by recurring to the gospel in its authority and holiness; by admitting, in all their legitimate sway, the principles inculcated by the testimonies which have been cited ; and by a prompt and unfeigned compliance with the just and evangelical requisitions which the Presbyterian and Methodist churches promulge.

Presbyterians and Methodists! This subject is urgently addressed to you. Here are your own doctrines, and your own discipline. You solemnly and constantly proclaim before the world as the creed of your respective churches, that every slaveholder is "in the gall of bitterness and in the bond of iniquity." You have publicly declared your conviction of the evil of slavery during nearly fifty years. You have pretended to record rules for its extirpation from among you ; and yet man-stealing is daily extending in your communions, and the number of "sinners of the first rank, who are guilty of the highest kind of theft," augments in the most crying and fearful manner. How long will you tolerate this appalling criminality? How long will you exhibit this marvellous and destructive hypocrisy? How long will you "speak smooth things, prophesy deceits, say peace, peace, when there is no peace?" for "there is no peace," saith the Lord, "unto the wicked ;" and if men-stealers, the most atrocious of all criminals before God and man, who never sincerely desired "to flee from the wrath to come, and to be saved from their sins," are not the wicked ; to what beings in the universe can the epithet be applied?

Preachers! Remember, as John Wesley remarked ; *"the hands, the bed, the furniture, the house, and the lands of every slaveholder at present are stained with blood !"* You are commanded not to be partakers of other men's sins ; instead of which, when you see the men-thieves, you consent with them ; and are involved in all their guilt, as accessories both before and after the fact; for you not only encourage the robbery, but you also receive the donations of those felons into your church treasuries ; and thereby you *"devour the prey, and divide the spoil !"*

We congratulate those Baptist and Presbyterian churches, who have adopted the system which excludes all slaveholders from their communion ; and rejoice in your advancement in pure truth and Christian practice. But we would also affectionately urge upon you an additional measure which will render your principles and

18*

your discipline uniform. Eject all slave-driving preachers from
your pulpits. The refusal of the slaveholder to the Lord's table, and
the reception of the slaveholder into the pulpit, are utterly incon-
gruous; and the latter most antichristian measure, notonly nullifies the former, but absolutely obscures it from sight, and leaves
the public to suppose that the crime of man-stealing is innocence
in a preacher, while it is guilt in a common member. We therefore implore you to be always and decidedly consistent, and renounce altogether "the unfruitful works of darkness."

The appeal is likewise made to all those "Christian people," to
adopt the language of the Presbyterian General Assembly of 1818,
who have "most inconsistently fallen into the practice of enslaving their brethren of mankind;" and your attentive perusal
of the previous extracts from the standards of the Presbyterian and
Methodist churches is earnestly desired. Do you sincerely believe
that the religion which you profess in the smallest degree justifies
American slavery? Did you ever seriously and impartially examine the word of God, and compare its oracular dictates with the
spirit, practice, and effects of slaveholding? Did you at any time
apply the benevolent injunctions of the Mosaic law, and the merciful demands of the Lord Jesus Christ to the system of retaining
your fellow-citizens in a state of bondage unparalleled for cruelty,
baseness, and anguish in the annals of savage man? Have you
ever attempted to review, as far as your imagination could soar,
the stupendous events of that morning of retribution, when all
actions and the motives whence they flowed, will be decided, not
by the horrible codes of human legislation, but by the standard
of unerring rectitude, and will be approved or condemned, as God
the righteous Judge shall announce? Are you fully convinced
that the dreadful debasement, the corroding toil, the constant privations, the agonizing fears, the lawless exactions, the brutal
violations, and the hopeless ignorance to which you doom your
fellow-citizens will be acknowledged by the Judge of the quick
and the dead, as a consistent following of him "who went about
doing good?" "When the Son of man shall come in his glory, and
all the holy angels with him," do you truly anticipate that the
King will admit a slave-driver's treatment of his coloured fellow-
citizens and disciples of Jesus, to be that giving of meat to the
hungry, and of drink to the thirsty; that hospitality to a stranger, that clothing of the naked, that visiting of the sick, and that
consolation to the prisoner; which he will announce as proof of
supreme attachment to the gracious Redeemer? Your consciences
cannot reply to these questions in the affirmative.

How much longer then will you endanger your eternal salvation? How dare you to assert the groundless plea of necessity;
and hypocritically to make it a cover for the love and practice of
man-stealing, and a cozening pretence for your "shameful and
unrighteous conduct?" Therefore, "thus saith the Lord my God—
feed the flock of the slaughter; whose possessors slay them, and
hold themselves not guilty, and they who sell them say, blessed
be the Lord, for I am rich, and their own shepherds pity them

not. My soul loathed them, and their soul abhorred me." Zechariah xi. 4, 5, 8. "Loose the bands of wickedness; undo the heavy burdens, let the oppressed go free, and break every yoke." Isaiah lviii. 4—7. "Wo unto him that buildeth his house by unrighteousness, that useth his neighbour's service without wages, and giveth him not for his work." Jeremiah xxii. 12, 17. "Weep and howl for your miseries that shall come upon you." James v. 1—6.

APPENDIX II.

THE DUTY OF EXCLUDING ALL SLAVE-HOLDERS FROM THE "COMMUNION OF SAINTS."

In April 1833, the following chapter, with the exception of a few verbal generalizing alterations, was addressed to the Presbyterian church in pamphlet form; and subsequently was transmitted to ministers of all denominations throughout the United States. One of them, it appears, travelled to a slave-driver in Georgia. Some time after, a letter was received by the publisher, signed, S. J. C. dated and post marked, *"Washington, Ga."* His long communication was full of chicanery, Jesuitism, and falsifications. Among other specimens of the Christianity which it contained, are these words: *"The minister that should preach emancipation from the pulpit would be tarred and feathered, and I should conceive justly."* In other words, S. J. C. declares that a sincere preacher of the gospel, who discourses like Jesus of Nazareth, Luke iv. 16—22; ought to be "TARRED AND FEATHERED!" The writer of that letter from Washington, Ga. may "conceive" and avow what he pleases; but if he professes to be a Christian, *he is either devil deceived, or a hypocrite!*

ADDRESS TO ALL THE CHURCHES.

THE signs of the times plainly indicate that a change, in reference to slavery, must speedily take place in our republic. Loud lamentations over the *evil* of human bondage have been resounded, until the voice of wailing and anguish makes no more impression than the mock sorrows of an Irish wake. Promises of amendment, and *gradual* emancipation have been repeated until the most credulous infatuation can no longer be deceived by their emptiness and vanity. During this period, the sin of slavery has incalculably been multiplied, and the groans of the tortured, and the barbarity of their task-masters, have been infinitely extended.

The most melancholy portion of all this wickedness and misery, is, that it has been clothed with a mask, and honoured by a Christian name. It is indubitable, that the present existence of slavery in the United States, may chiefly be imputed to the professed disciples of Jesus, the Prince of Philanthropists, one part of whose divine mission it was to "preach deliverance to the captives." All the denominations of Christians, with one or two exceptions, are culpable in this respect, in a higher or less degree; and the censure is not less generally applicable, than those churches are peculiarly condemnable. With the exception of the Episcopal Methodists, and the Friends, with some of the minor divisions of the Christian family, whose influence is comparatively unimportant, I know not any one of the large compacted churches, which has formally recorded in their standard of faith and discipline, an indignant denunciation of slavery, except the Presbyterian church.

When it was resolved to adopt their present ecclesiastical organization, the Confession of Faith, Catechism, and Book of Discipline were ordered to be published, that all persons might know the doctrines and forms of the church, in the most authentic manner. The question of slavery was discussed, and alas! against their consciences, the northern brethren entered into a compromise with the slave-holders, something like the federal compact, and agreed to tolerate the highest possible iniquity, rather than dissolve the Presbyterian confederacy. Yet, the understandings, sensibilities, and consciences of many revolted against that perfidious departure from godliness; and, to pacify the clamour of their minds against this abandonment of truth, they inserted the following illustration of slavery,—which the slave-holders permitted to stand in the book, being convinced that in practice, it would be only a dead letter.

It is found in nearly all the editions of "the Constitution of the Presbyterian Church," printed before the year 1818; and constitutes the note appended to the hundred and forty-second question of the larger Catechism;—"What are the sins forbidden in the eighth commandment?" The answer states, among other sins, *man-stealing!* This they write : 1 Tim. i. 10. "The law is made—for men-stealers. This crime, among the Jews, exposed the perpetrators of it to capital punishment; Exodus **xxi**. 16 ; *he that stealeth a man and selleth him, or if he be found in his hand, he shall surely be put to death :* and the apostle here classes them with sinners of the first rank. The word he uses, in its original import comprehends *all who are concerned in bringing any of the human race into slavery, or detaining them in it.* Hominum fures, qui servos vel liberos abducunt, retinent, vendunt, vel emunt. STEALERS OF MEN ARE ALL THOSE WHO BRING OFF SLAVES OR FREEMEN, AND KEEP, SELL, OR BUY THEM. To steal a freeman, says Grotius, is the highest kind of theft. In other Instances we only steal human property, but when we *steal or retain men in slavery, we steal those, who, in common with ourselves,* are constituted by the original grant, lords of the earth. Genesis i. 28. God blessed them, and God said unto them, be fruitful and multiply, and replenish the earth, and subdue it; and have dominion over the fish of the sea, and over the fowl of the air, and over every living thing that moveth upon the earth. Vide Poli synopsin in loco."

This was the authorized doctrine of the Presbyterian church, on the subject of slavery, until the General Assembly of 1816, when that body determined that the note above quoted was no part of the belief and doctrine of the Presbyterian church. In reply to this fallacy, it must be observed, that every minister ordained prior to that meeting, solemnly declared his assent to the constitution of the church as it then existed, not as it was altered by that deceiving body. The question is not so much, however, whether that doctrine be obligatory upon all Presbyterians, merely because it is found in the constitution of their church; but whether it is the decision of the oracles of God? and I maintain that it is infallibly correct.

It has been stated, and the heinous allegation cannot be disproved, that the Presbyterian church is mainly chargeable with the guilt of slavery in the United States. The proposition is thus declared: On the fourth of July, 1776, every person then in the United States, or who should afterward be born in them, was pronounced free, and in the undisputed possession of certain inalienable rights. After a contest of seven years, the truth was recognized by all the European nations; and the country was entirely delivered from foreign control. Notwithstanding the national declaration, all the coloured people were inhibited by force, from asserting or obtaining their "*inalienable* rights."

During the revolutionary contest, most of the religious denominations had become so scattered and disorganized, that there was no union, and scarcely any intercourse among the members. The Presbyterians alone maintained, in some measure, their compactness of organization, and immediately after the peace, resumed their usual meetings, with an imposing influence. The question of slavery was early agitated; but "the fear of man, which bringeth a snare," swayed the Synod. All the southern states combined, at that period, probably did not contain one tenth part of the Presbyterian church. Nothing, therefore, could have been more easy, than to have fulfilled the claims of Christian equity, and to have told the slave-holders—We cannot conscientiously, we dare not scripturally acknowledge you to be Christians and Presbyterians. You must quit man-stealing, or we cannot hold gospel fellowship with you. Instead of this plain, honest dealing, the people of that day entered upon a course of expediency, prudence, and carnal policy. They first denied their own principles, by acknowledging that a person is *not* born free; and then, by holding out in practice the atrocious error, that a slave-holder is an acceptable follower of the Lord Jesus Christ, they opened the floodgates of all possible iniquity: because this topic is now decided, not by the standard of truth revealed in the scriptures, but according to the ever-shifting principles of "men of corrupt minds, and destitute of the truth, who suppose that gain is godliness."

Will slave-holding professors of religion, and preachers hear with any degree of patience and candour, a just application of the principles of natural justice, and of the great law of love, to the crime of slave-holding? Like all other persevering sinners, they hate the light, neither come to the light, lest their deeds should be reproved. And can Christian charity receive men who are thus persisting in the highest kind of theft, as true disciples of Jesus the Son of God?

All persons acquainted with the southern states, well know that slavery is there the grand source of infidelity; that slave-holding professors of religion are an insuperable stumbling-block to men of reflection and conscience, who are opposed to slavery; and that slavery constitutes an almost impassable barrier to the progress of the light and the truth as it is in Jesus. It is in vain any longer to palliate or conceal the enormity of this sin,—a sin which renders callous the hearts of all who apologize for it, and sears as with a hot iron, the consciences of those who are guilty of this impious practice.

From the Presbyterian Confession of Faith, we deduce these principles :—

1. Slave-holding, under every possible modification, is man-stealing.

2. Man-stealing, as combining impiety in principle, falsehood in claim, injustice and cruelty without intermission and without end, is the most flagrant iniquity which a sinner can perpetrate.

3. All profession of religion, by a man who thus acts, is a gross deception.

4. The tolerance of such men as preachers and Christian professors is a direct insult to Him who searcheth the hearts and trieth the reins of the children of men.

5. All the pleas of expediency which are offered for this perversion of God's truth are not less criminal than they are destructive.

6. Slavery in the United States can never be abolished as long as it is sanctioned and approved by the various denominations of Christians.

7. Therefore it is the incumbent duty of every church to excommunicate, without delay, all those persons who will not cease to "steal, buy, sell, and enslave their fellow-citizens."

The Presbyterian church, as a body of people, stands convicted before the world of rank and constant hypocrisy. On several occasions, the questions connected with slavery have been introduced into the General Assembly ; and uniformly the heart-rending subject has been evaded ; or a cold, unmeaning, or Jesuistical minute has been recorded, instead of an efficient testimony and pungent resolution against sin. Conscientious men have asked for a fish, and the temporizers have given them a serpent—we ave begged gospel bread, and they have given us the stone of mammon,—we have solicited the egg of truth for our nourishment, and they have given us the slave-holder's scorpion to poison our morals and benumb our consciences. Forty-seven years have passed away ; men have pretended to lament the evil, to deplore the national guilt, to reprehend the inconsistency of professing gospel honesty, and constantly performing the villany of kidnappers; and nevertheless, the crime increases, the hypocrisy extends, and the men-stealers augment in the most fearful manner.

It is one of the remarkable characters of our age, that the principle of liberality extends itself to the greater, while it denounces the lesser obliquity. No design is formed to institute a comparison between the degrees of particular sins : but surely in ecclesiastical discipline, it is evidently unjust to permit the grosser offence to escape with impunity, much less to be honoured, while the inferior transgression receives the pouring out of the full vial of indignant censure.

The Temperance cause is justly eulogized as one of the noblest efforts of modern times to redeem the character of mankind from debasement; but it will not be asserted that there is any justice in excluding from the church a sober man, otherwise irreproachable, because he has not adopted the principle of total abstinence from spirituous liquors, and at the same time to recognise the Christian profession of a man-stealer. It is presumed that no Christian community would admit the profession of religion by an avowed gambler, or a person habitually profane—why then, it may be asked, are slave-holders tolerated in the Christian church, who are constantly manifesting an irreconcilable contradiction against all that is righteous, true, and merciful ?

We are told that all the practitioners of slavery are enemies to slave-holding, *in the abstract!* This assertion is not true; as is manifest from two undeniable facts. The first is this; that the slave-drivers make no effort to extirpate slavery, and pertinaciously resist every attempt to meliorate not only the condition of the slave, but also to elevate the character and capacities of the free people of colour. The second proof that all professions of dislike to slavery, in the abstract, are deceptive, is derived from an everyday occurrence;—when a slave has providentially been enabled to escape from the house of bondage, the slave-holder, who, contrary to the word of God, the natural conscience of man, and the laws of Christianity, claims the human being as his property, instead of permitting the slave thus to liberate himself, in person, and by his hired kidnappers, will ransack every portion of our country, from Eastport to New Orleans, and from Boston to the Missouri, expressly to recover possession of the slave, that the victim may be tortured to satiate his revenge. To talk, therefore, of such persons being opponents of slavery, is most insulting prevarication : and yet this abhorent violation of the divine precept is committed in open day, and boasted of and defended by preachers of the gospel, as if it was the very cap-stone of Christian phi-

lanthropy and righteousness. Therefore, hear the word of the
Lord. Mark the solemn prohibition! Deut. xxiii. 15, 16: "Thou
shalt not deliver unto his master the servant who is escaped from
his master unto thee: he shall dwell with thee, even among you, in
that place which he shall choose, where it liketh him best: thou
shalt not oppress him." Remember the illustration: 1 Samuel xxx.
11—15. "They found an Egyptian in the field.—And David said unto
him, whence art thou? And he said, I am a young man of Egypt,
servant to an Amalekite, and my master left me, because three days
ago I fell sick. And David said, canst thou bring me down to this
company? And he said, swear unto me by God, that thou wilt neither kill me, nor deliver me into the hands of my master." Well
may all these enemies of slavery in the abstract, but who are
practical kidnappers, tremble at the divine denunciation! Obadiah
14, 15. "Neither shouldst thou have stood in the crossway, to
cut off those who did escape; neither shouldst thou have delivered up those that did remain in the day of distress; as thou
hast done, it shall be done unto thee; thy reward shall return
upon thine own head."

The Presbyterian church is unequivocally to be numbered
among those friends of truth, and enemies of ungodliness, in the
abstract. At the period of their organization, they were theoretical
opponents of man-stealing, but they recognised the men-stealers
as their Christian brethren. The pungent truth followed? The pungent truth
remained in the confession a dead letter; and like the book of the
law in Josiah's time, when it was discovered in 1815, it excited
universal consternation among the slave-holders, who never
would rest until by their clamours and menaces they intimidated
the northern brethren to consent that it should be expunged. On
several intermediate occasions, when the subject was presented to
the General Assembly, and some minute was obliged to be made
of the reference, to pacify them who desired to "do justly and to
love mercy"—the Assembly recorded a condemnation of slavery
in the abstract, and *coldly* urged the necessity of adopting the
means to effect a gradual abolition of slavery. The consequence
was this; that the slave-holders professed to admit the theory,
but the time was not come for a simultaneous movement—and
the hardships, the fetters, the degradation, the irreligion, the ignorance, and the anguish of the slaves have increased, "grown
with their growth, and strengthened with their strength:" till
now, at the end of forty-seven years, there are undoubtedly forty-
seven times the number of slave-holding preachers and elders and
members in the Presbyterian church, more than those who could
have been enumerated in the month of May, 1787. This is the
result of hating slavery in the abstract, and loving it in the practice. According to the present system, did not the divine procla-
mation, as proved by the signs of the times, plainly declare to that
grim man-stealing monster, Thou shalt die; thy days are nearly
ended—it might be safely affirmed, that before the lapse of another forty-seven years, the coloured people, from their vast dispro-
portionate increase, will have possession of the whole southern

section of the Republic; and this will be the effect principally of the sanction given to slavery by those temporizing Christians, who, when they see a man-thief, consent with him, because they hate instruction and cast the words of the Lord behind them. Psalm 50, 16—21.

There is yet a much more alarming view of this subject in its Christian reference. Many coloured persons are acknowledged and believed to be subjects of converting grace; and yet they are property, debased as slaves, and even bought and sold as beasts by their nominal fellow-Christians, members even of the same society of professed believers. This is the climax of all the atrocities connected with the system of slavery. A man or woman whose principles are settled by the oracles of God, and whose consciences are directed by the gospel, will command a much larger sum of money on account of the spiritual gifts with which they are endowed; and the owner of this property, as he is scandalously termed, can safely calculate upon a large additional bonus for the faithfulness and integrity of a slave actuated by the heaven-born feelings of a genuine disciple of the Friend of sinners. These Christians are tortured and trafficked, and deprived of all comfort, religious instruction, and earthly hope, by their professed fellow-Christians, with equal indifference as if they were worn out horses, and as if no human sensibility, and no gospel emotion had ever quickened their souls; and thus these slave-holding professors exhibit their hatred of slavery in the abstract.

This deceivableness is rendered more repulsive, and the iniquity more flagrant, by the continuous implied or actual promises which are made by all the parties, to desist from their ungodly course. The last minute of the General Assembly was made in the year 1818. It professses to be a full exposition of the. sentiments of that ecclesiastical body, upon the subject of slavery; and was promulged expressly to conceal the erasure of the note appended to the hundred and forty-second question of the larger Catechism, already quoted. In their address to the churches, the General Assembly declare that, "*the voluntary enslaving of one part of the human race, by another, is utterly inconsistent with the law of God, and totally irreconcilable with the spirit of the gospel of Christ. The evils to which the slave is always exposed, often take place in fact, in their very worst degree and form. It is manifestly the duty of all Christians to use their honest, earnest, and unwearied endeavours, as speedily as possible, to efface this blot of our holy religion, and to obtain the complete abolition of slavery.*"

The General Assembly then exhort all Presbyterians "to increase their exertions to effect a total abolition of slavery, and to suffer no greater delay than the public welfare *truly* and indispensably demands." They also warn the churches "against unduly pretending the plea of necessity, as a cover for the love and practice of slavery, or a pretence for not using all efforts that are lawful and practicable, to extinguish the evil." They recommend religious instruction and Sabbath schools for the slaves; and prohibit cruelty to the slaves,—the forcible separation of families, and the selling of slaves to persons who will deprive them of religious blessings. Since that period sixteen years have elapsed; and what has been done? Has "the very worst degree and form" of slavery been amended? To use the language of the General Assembly, has any one of "all the hardships and injuries which inhumanity and avarice may suggest," ceased to be inflicted? Have slaveholding ministers, elders, or members of the Presbyterian church "used their honest, earnest, and unwearied endeavours to obtain the complete abolition of slavery?" Has there been "no delay?" Have they "increased their exertions to effect a total abolition of slavery?" Name the slaveholder who has facilitated and encouraged the instruction of slaves in the principles and duties of the Christian religion, according to the gospel of Christ, without slavery notes and evasive comments? Where is that slaveholder in the church, who iniquitously grasps his fellow-citizens as his property, that will not sell a man or woman, boy or girl, at any time, if his "inhumanity and avarice" can be satisfied? What Church Session, and what Presbytery ever took cognizance of any man for "all cruelty of every kind, in the treatment of slaves, or for selling Christians, the purchase of the gracious Redeemer's agonies, like horses, sheep, and hogs?" No church Session, no Presbytery, no Synod, and no General Assembly dare to call to account the preacher who exchanges a man for a horse, or a woman for a ram; or the elder who scourges a man's wife in the last stage of pregnancy, until her life is endangered; or the member who ties up a youth, and whips him till he expires almost immediately after his release from the barbarity of his inhuman task-master? Church Sessions, Presbyteries, and Synods of slaveholders take no notice of these acts, performed as the General Assembly say, by "*the most virtuous part of the community, who abhor slavery.*" All their "harsh censures, uncharitable reflections, and discountenancing by discipline and suspension from the church," are directed and enforced against the preacher or member who has the hardihood to delineate, in his own genuine character, "the Christian broker in his trade of blood." This state of things cannot much longer continue. France, with all her infidel levity, is now arranging a project for the universal and immediate emancipation of every slave in her colonies. British colonial slavery has already received its death blow. Ere seven years have revolved, no free-born American citizen will be held as property. The flood has set in, and nothing can stem the force of the current. Now, then, is the time for the church to "arise and shine; to awake and put on strength; to put on her beautiful garments, like the holy city, that the uncircumcised and unclean may no more come into her." The command of God is not less imperative to us, and the implied promise no less suitable, than to Jerusalem. "Shake thyself from the dust; arise and sit down; loose thyself from the bands of thy neck, O captive daughter of Zion." The American churches wear the collar of the slaveholders, and are led captive by those who are constantly *violating* "*the most precious and sacred rights of human nature,*"—all whose life is "*utterly inconsistent with the law of God,*"—and all whose opinions and actions are "totally irreconcilable with the spirit and principles of the gospel of Christ."

This is the doctrine of the Presbyterian church. Now then for the application of the subject. I appeal to your consciences. How can you longer tolerate the wicked inconsistency of acknowledging as followers of the meek and lowly Jesus, who came to seek and save the lost, men who are wilfully, obdurately, and constantly guilty of "a gross violation of the most precious and sacred rights of human nature?" This is the authorized description of slavery. Is it not just as rational, and as fraught with good sense, to say that a sleepless pirate is an exemplary just man and philanthropist? How can you sanction before the world the astounding and mischievous anomaly, that men and women, whose lives are obstinately and "utterly inconsistent with the law of God," are faithful servants of Him who came to do the will of God, whose meat it was to do the will of Him that sent Him ; who was sent to heal the broken-hearted, to preach deliverance to the captives, to set at liberty them that are bruised ; and who left us an example, that we should follow his steps ?" How can a resolute and hardened disobedience to the law of God be palmed upon the world as the offspring of "pure religion and undefiled," and as exemplifying the attributes of "the most virtuous part of the community," who, we are assured by the General Assembly, "abhor slavery, and wish its extermination as sincerely as any others"—which abhorrence of slavery they constantly prove by their calumny and persecution of all who strive for its extinction, and which wish "to extinguish the evil" they develop, by increasing the number of their slaves as fast as they can possibly be multiplied. Grosser theoretical and practical contradictions cannot be found in the annals of hypocrisy.

How can you continue to recognise as acceptable members of the church and disciples of Jesus, the supreme liberator, men all whose feelings, acts, and determinations, are inveterately and "totally irreconcilable with the spirit and principles of the gospel of Christ?" How can you justify yourselves before the Judge of all for this consummate duplicity ? How can you possibly lull your consciences while guilty of this tremendous "all deceivableness of unrighteousness?" You say, "the slave is *always* exposed to evils in their very worst degree and form, from the hands of a master who may inflict upon him all the hardships and injuries which inhumanity and avarice may suggest"—you *know*, that all these evils are perpetually realized by coloured Christians, and from the hands of the officers and members of the church ; and yet the taskmaster meets with no censure, no interruption, no discipline, and no suspension, but is caressed, flattered, dignified with imposing titles, and not only journeys on to eternity with a palpable lie in his right hand, but blindfold leads his willingly deceived flock also to the judgment of God, there too late to learn that human expediency and carnal policy only receive the accursed doom which the Son of God will denounce against "the fearful, the unbelieving, and whosoever loveth and maketh a lie." Revelation xxi. 8, 27; and xxii. 14, 15.

The Synod of New-York and Philadelphia, in the year 1787, promulged similar doctrines and injunctions; they were occasionally repeated, until the year 1818—then in an elaborate form the subject was concocted; and we have already seen, slavery was denounced as unchristian; speedy abolition urged; all delay branded as hypocrisy, and a cloak for sin; the immediate melioration of the degraded state of the people of colour recommended; and church Sessions and Presbyteries were enjoined to exercise discipline, censure and suspend all transgressions of justice and benevolence, so far as equity and kindness can be exhibited by a slaveholder. Sixteen years have revolved, and what has been achieved? Not one single object so pompously enumerated by the General Assembly.

What preacher resounds the duty to abolish slavery, what minister of the gospel puts away the stumbling block of his iniquity? The American churches, so far as slavery is concerned, have neither "ceased to do evil, nor learnt to do well. They have neither washed nor made themselves clean, nor put away the evil of their doings from before the eyes of the Lord. The oppressed are not relieved; the fatherless are not judged; they smite with the fist of wickedness. The bands of wickedness are not loosed; the heavy burdens are not undone; the oppressed go not free; the yoke is not broken; they deal not their bread to the hungry; the cast out poor they bring not to their house; they cover not the naked; and they hide themselves from their own flesh." Isaiah i. 16, 17; and lvii. 4—7. Well, therefore, may they dread lest the Lord should speedily say of them as he did of the Jews; "When ye spread forth your hands, I will hide mine eyes from you; when ye make many prayers, I will not hear; your hands are full of blood. Bring no more vain oblations;—the calling of assemblies I cannot away with; it is iniquity, even the solemn meeting. They are a trouble unto me; I am weary to bear them. If ye be willing and obedient, ye shall eat the good of the land; but if ye refuse and rebel, ye shall be devoured with the sword; for the mouth of the Lord hath spoken it." Isaiah i. 10—20. The long suffering of God, and the patience of man, in reference to slavery, are nearly exhausted. Slavery *must*, and slavery *will* soon be abolished in this union. "The wild and guilty fantasy, that one man is the property of another" cannot longer be defended, except by men who have abandoned all moral sensibilities and conscience, and who have become incorrigible in transgression. There is not an intelligent reflecting person upon earth, who does not instantly perceive that slaveholding and Christianity, as the General Assembly truly maintain, are "utterly inconsistent and totally irreconcilable." No alternative exists; either the sanctuary must be cleansed, prior to the abolition of slavery, or it will be overwhelmed in the overthrow of the system. If slaveholders are solicitous to verify their title to Christianity, and to demonstrate that they are sincere in their abhorrence of slavery and their wish for its extermination; let them come forward now, and by their voluntary act, obey God rather than man, and abolish slavery, every one for himself. Let others do as they please; it is their duty, without delay, to effect the abolition of slavery. Every man must proclaim liberty to his own captives; then we will hail him as a penitent sinner who has brought forth "the fruits of righteousness;" but if he gripes the descendants of the kidnapped Africans, until the mandate of Omnipotence has crumbled the shackles of slavery into impalpable dust—we shall hold his Christianity, even then, as of no more sterling value than it is now. He will be exactly in the situation of a felon, who, having robbed the bank, upon his discovery, is forcibly divested of his plunder, and so situated, that he can steal no more. Just such will be the coerced honesty of every slaveholding professor of religion, who pertinaciously refuses to emancipate his slaves, until resistless authority, in some mode, hinders him from longer grasping the produce of their toil, and "their most precious and sacred rights."

Now then, to your duty. Every thing claims that you immediately "efface that blot of our holy religion," slavery, from the church. Banish all the pleas of expediency, and substitute gospel honesty. Cast away "the fear of man, which bringeth a snare," and put your trust in the Lord; then shall you be safe. Enjoin upon the slaveholders, within a short definite period, to emancipate their slaves; or, if they refuse, assure them that they shall be excluded from the church. Put not off to the uncertain future, your present obligations. Half a generation have passed away since the General Assembly met in 1818; hundreds of thousands of slaves have accused us before the throne of God; and tens of thousands of Christian men-stealers have already answered for the "hardships, injuries, and evils, in their worst degree and form, which their inhumanity and avarice suggested and inflicted!" Remember Lot's wife! She lingered, and loved Sodom in preference to the word of God, and yet remains an awful monument of that procrastination which cries, "*To-morrow!*"—while God thunders in our hearing, "To-day!"

APPENDIX III.

DECLARATION

OF THE

ANTI SLAVERY CONVENTION,

Assembled in Philadelphia, December 4, 1833.

THE Convention, assembled in the city of Philadelphia to organize a National Anti-Slavery Society, promptly seize the opportunity to promulgate the following DECLARATION OF SENTIMENTS, as cherished by them in relation to the enslavement of one-sixth portion of the American people.

More than fifty-seven years have elapsed since a band of patriots convened in this place, to devise measures for the deliverance of this country from a foreign yoke. The corner-stone upon which they founded the TEMPLE OF FREEDOM was broadly this—"that all men are created equal; that they are endowed by their Creator with certain inalienable rights; that among these are life, LIBERTY, and the pursuit of happiness." At the sound of their trumpet-call, three millions of people rose up as from the sleep of death, and rushed to the strife of blood; deeming it more glorious to die instantly as freemen, than desirable to live one hour as slaves. They were few in number—poor in resources; but the honest conviction that TRUTH, JUSTICE, and RIGHT were on their side, made them invincible.

We have met together for the achievement of an enterprise, without which, that of our fathers is incomplete; and which, for its magnitude, solemnity, and probable results upon the destiny of the world, as far transcends theirs, as moral truth does physical force.

In purity of motive, in earnestness of zeal, in decision of purpose, in intrepidity of action, in steadfastness of faith, and in sincerity of spirit, we would not be inferior to them.

Their principles led them to wage war against their oppressors, and to spill human blood like water, in order to be free. *Ours* forbid the doing of evil that good may come, and lead us to reject, and to entreat the oppressed to reject the use of all carnal weapons for deliverance from bondage; relying solely upon those which are spiritual, and mighty through God to the pulling down of strong holds.

Their measures were physical resistance—the marshalling in arms—the hostile array—and the mortal encounter. *Ours* shall be such only as the opposition of moral purity to moral corruption—the destruction of error by the potency of truth—the overthrow of prejudice by the power of love—and the abolition of slavery by the spirit of repentance.

Their grievances, great as they were, were trifling in comparison with the wrongs and sufferings of those for whom we plead. Our fathers were never slaves—never bought and sold like cattle—never shut out from the light of knowledge and religion—and never subjected to the lash of brutal task masters.

But those, for whose emancipation we are striving,—constituting at the present time at least one-sixth part of our countrymen,—are recognised by the law, and treated by their fellow-beings, as marketable commodities—as goods and chattels—as brute beasts; are plundered daily of the fruits of their toil without redress; really enjoying no constitutional nor legal protection from licentious and murderous outrages upon their persons; are ruthlessly torn asunder—the tender babe from the arms of its frantic mother—the heart-broken wife from her weeping husband—at the caprice or pleasure of irresponsible tyrants. For the crime of having a dark complexion, they suffer the pangs of hunger, the infliction of stripes, and the ignominy of brutal servitude. They are kept in heathenish darkness by laws expressly enacted to make their instruction a criminal offence.

These are the prominent circumstances in the condition of more than two millions of our people, the proof of which may be found in thousands of indisputable facts, and in the laws of the slaveholding States.

Hence we maintain—That in view of the civil and religious privileges of this nation, the guilt of its oppression is unequalled by any other on the face of the earth; and, therefore;

That it is bound to repent instantly, to undo the heavy burden, to break every yoke, and to let the oppressed go free.

We further maintain—That no man has a right to enslave or imbrute his brother—to hold or acknowledge him, for one moment, as a piece of merchandise—to keep back his hire by fraud—or to brutalize his mind by denying him the means of intellectual, social, and moral improvement.

The right to enjoy liberty is inalienable. To invade it, is to usurp the prerogative of Jehovah. Every man has a right to his own body—to the products of his own labour—to the protection of law—and to the common advantages of society. It is piracy to buy or steal a native African, and subject him to servitude. Surely the sin is as great to enslave an AMERICAN as an AFRICAN.

Therefore we believe and affirm—That there is no difference, *in principle*, between the African slave trade and American slavery;

That every American citizen, who retains a human being in involuntary bondage as his property, is, according to Scripture, Exodus xxi. 16; Deut. xxiv. 7., a MAN-STEALER;

That the slaves ought instantly to be set free, and brought under the protection of law:

That if they had lived from the time of Pharaoh down to the present period, and had been entailed through successive generations, their right to be free could never have been alienated, but their claims would have constantly risen in solemnity;

That all those laws which are now in force, admitting the right of slavery, are therefore before God utterly null and void; being an audacious usurpation of the Divine prerogative, a daring infringement of the law of Nature, a base overthrow of the very foundations of the social compact, a complete extinction of all the relations, endearments, and obligations of mankind, and a presumptuous transgression of all the holy commandments—and that therefore they ought to be instantly abrogated.

We further believe and affirm—That all persons of colour, who possess the qualifications which are demanded of others, ought to be admitted forthwith to the enjoyment of the same privileges, and the exercise of the same prerogatives as others; and that the paths of preferment, of wealth, and of intelligence, should be opened as widely to them as to persons of a white complexion.

We maintain that no compensation should be given to the planters, for emancipating their slaves—

Because it would be a surrender of the great fundamental principle, that man cannot hold property in man;

Because SLAVERY IS A CRIME, AND THEREFORE IT IS NOT AN ARTICLE TO BE SOLD;

Because the holders of slaves are not the just proprietors of what they claim; freeing the slaves is not depriving them of property, but restoring it to its right owners; it is not wronging the master, but righting the slave—restoring him to himself;

Because immediate and general emancipation would only destroy nominal, not real property: it would not amputate a limb or break a bone of the slaves, but by infusing motives into their breasts would make them doubly valuable to the masters as free labourers:

And, Because if compensation is to be given at all, it should be given to the outraged and guiltless slaves, and not to those who have plundered and abused them.

We regard, as delusive, cruel, and dangerous, any scheme of expatriation which pretends to aid, either directly or indirectly, in the emancipation of the slaves, or to be a substitute for the immediate and total abolition of slavery.

We fully and unanimously recognise the sovereignty of each State, to legislate exclusively on the subject of slavery, which is tolerated within its limits; we concede that Congress, *under the present national compact*, has no right to interfere with any of the slave States, in relation to this momentous subject:

But we maintain that Congress has a right, and is solemnly

bound, to suppress the domestic slave trade between the several
States, and to abolish slavery in those portions of our territory
which the Constitution has placed under its exclusive jurisdiction.

We also maintain, that there are, at the present time, the highest obligations resting upon the people of the free States, to remove
slavery by moral and political action, as prescribed in the Constitution of the United States. They are now living under a pledge
of their tremendous physical force to fasten the galling fetters of
tyranny upon the limbs of millions in the Southern States; they
are liable to be called at any moment to suppress a general insurrection of the slaves: they authorize the slave owner to vote for
three fifths of his slaves as property, and thus enable him to perpetuate his oppression; they support a standing army at the south
for its protection; and they seize the slave who has escaped into
their territories, and send him back to be tortured by an enraged
master, or a brutal driver. This relation to slavery is criminal,
and full of danger : IT MUST BE BROKEN UP.

These are our views and principles—these, our designs and
measures. With entire confidence in the over-ruling justice of God,
we plant ourselves upon the Declaration of our Independence, and
the truths of Divine Revelation, as upon the EVERLASTING ROCK.

We shall organize Anti-Slavery Societies, if possible, in every
city, town, and village in our land.

We shall send forth Agents to lift up the voice of remonstrance,
of warning, of entreaty, and rebuke.

We shall circulate, unsparingly and extensively, anti-slavery
tracts and periodicals.

We shall enlist the pulpit and the press in the cause of the
suffering and the dumb.

We shall aim at a purification of the churches from all participation in the guilt of slavery.

We shall encourage the labour of freemen rather than that of
the slaves, by giving a preference to their productions :

And, We shall spare no exertions nor means to bring the whole
nation to speedy repentance.

Our trust for victory is solely in GOD. *We* may be personally
defeated, but our principles never. TRUTH, JUSTICE, REASON, and
HUMANITY, must and will gloriously triumph. Already a host is
coming up to the help of the Lord against the mighty, and the
prospect before us is full of encouragement.

Submitting this DECLARATION to the candid examination of
the people of this country, and of the friends of liberty throughout
the world, we hereby affix our signatures to it; pledging ourselves
that, under the guidance, and by the help of Almighty God, we
will do all that in us lies, consistently with this Declaration of
our principles, to overthrow the most execrable system of slavery,
that has ever been witnessed upon earth—to deliver our land
from its deadliest curse—to wipe out the foulest stain which rests
upon our national escutcheon—and to secure to the coloured
population of the United States, all the rights and privileges which
belong to them as men, and as Americans—come what may to

our persons, our interests, or our reputations—whether we live to witness the triumph of LIBERTY, JUSTICE, and HUMANITY, or perish untimely, as martyrs in this great, benevolent, and holy cause.

Done in Philadelphia, this sixth of December, A. D. 1833.

MAINE.

DAVID THURSTON,
NATHAN WINSLOW,
JOSEPH SOUTHWICK,
JAMES FREDERIC OTIS,
ISAAC WINSLOW.

NEW HAMPSHIRE.

DAVID CAMBELL.

VERMONT.

ORSON S. MURRAY.

MASSACHUSETTS.

DANIEL S. SOUTHMAYD,
EFFINGHAM L. CAPRON,
JOSHUA COFFIN,
AMOS A. PHELPS,
JOHN G. WHITTIER,
HORACE P. WAKEFIELD,
JAMES G. BARBADOES,
DAVID T. KIMBALL, JR.
DANIEL E. JEWETT,
JOHN R. CAMBELL,
NATHANIEL SOUTHARD,
ARNOLD BUFFUM,
W. LLOYD GARRISON.

RHODE ISLAND.

JOHN PRENTICE,
GEORGE W. BENSON,
RAY POTTER.

CONNECTICUT.

SAMUEL J. MAY,
ALPHEUS KINGSLEY,
EDWIN A. STILLMAN,
SIMEON S. JOCELYN,
ROBERT B. HALL.

NEW-YORK.

BERIAH GREEN,
LEWIS TAPPAN,
JOHN RANKIN,
WILLIAM GREEN, JR.
ABRAHAM L. COX,
WILLIAM GOODELL,
ELIZUR WRIGHT, JR.
CHARLES W. DENISON,
JOHN FROST,
GEORGE BOURNE.

NEW-JERSEY.

JONATHAN PARKHURST,
CHALKLEY GILLINGHAM,
JOHN McCULLOUGH,
JAMES WHITE.

PENNSYLVANIA.

EVAN LEWIS,
EDWIN A. ATLEE,
ROBERT PURVIS,
JAMES McC. CRUMMILL,
THOMAS SHIPLEY,
BARTHOLOMEW FUSSELL,
DAVID JONES,
ENOCH MACK,
JAMES M. McKIM,
AARON VICKERS,
JAMES LOUGHHEAD,
EDWIN P. ATLEE,
THOMAS WHITSON,
JOHN R. SLEEPER,
JOHN SHARP, JR.
JAMES MOTT.

OHIO.

JOHN M. STERLING,
MILTON SUTLIFF
LEVI SUTLIFF.

INDEX.